San Francisco Bay Area
FISHING GUIDE

Ray Rychnovsky

Frank Amato
PORTLAND

Table of Contents

When I came to the Bay Area about 35 years ago, I wasn't too excited about fishing here. I thought, "Too many people, fishing can't be very good." I drove for hours to fish in mountain lakes and streams then fished in the Delta catching catfish and striped bass. But I was totally unaware of the great variety of excellent fishing. I visited the Monterey Wharf and was intrigued by the sacks of fish anglers were catching on charter boats. The chance to catch large rockfish and lingcod overcame my apprehension about getting seasick. I found I had good resistance to motion sickness and became a regular on charter boats along the coast and in the bays. I caught rockfish and lingcod and soon started taking trips for salmon. I tried fishing in the bay and caught striped bass first from a charter boat and later from my own boat—great fishing.

A few years later, friends bought large, seaworthy boats and we fished mostly for salmon out of many of the ports. Camping in Westside Campground at Bodega Bay, fishing for salmon and rockfish, the great camaraderie with other anglers and catching salmon up to 42 pounds, are still some of the fondest memories of my life. I caught sturgeon, albacore, more trout from local lakes than I can count, black bass in the lakes and Delta and dozens of other species. WOW! This is an angler's paradise.

The author as a teenager and his brother tie flies.
Left: The author hoists a yelloweye rockfish.

My fishing education took years and much of it came after I started writing for magazines in 1981. I have learned a lot more since I became the San Francisco Bay Area columnist for Fishing & Hunting News in 1992 and I filled in more details doing the research for this book.

The variety and quality of fishing in the Bay Area are almost staggering—it can take a lifetime just to learn about a part of it. I have thought often during these years that a book that described this fishing, its variety and quality would have been priceless.

Recently Tom Stienstra's book, California Fishing, was published giving an overview of fishing throughout the state including fishing in the Bay Area. This is a great overview but I wanted a book with more details specifically for the waters I fished within about a one hour drive from some part of the metropolitan San Francisco Bay Area.

This book—*San Francisco Bay Area Fishing Guide*—is what I wanted. It describes all types of fishing in the area and includes enough detail for anglers to find its best fishing spots and know when, where and how to catch each major game fish at each location.

CHAPTER 1:

Introduction

Most major metropolitan areas have a lot of tall buildings surrounded by concrete and not many fishing opportunities. If you were to choose areas that have the best fishing in our country you probably would immediately dismiss densely populated areas including the San Francisco Bay Area. Like me, you might think, "Too many people and too much fishing pressure—fishing can't be very good." But that would be a big mistake.

The San Francisco Bay Area with its ocean, bays, the Delta and lakes has the best quality and variety of fishing in the continental United States. While our area has very good freshwater fishing, it is the saltwater and anadromous species that make it really special. This area has the finest off-shore salmon fishing in the lower 48 states. Seven of every 10 salmon caught off our West Coast from the Mexican border to the Canadian border are caught in the ocean of the San Francisco Bay Area. That alone makes this a very special place to fish but there is much more.

You can catch halibut in the bay, stripers in the Delta, bays and lakes, huge sturgeon and sharks all in protected bays or the Delta, a dozen different varieties of rockfish and maybe even catch 20 to 30 pound lingcod. Some years we have great albacore fishing and there is no limit on these fish—I've seen one angler catch 16 of these super fast, strong fish in a day and know people have caught 20 or 30 and maybe more in a day. When these fish are here they are the fastest, hardest fighting, most exciting fish in the area. Albacore fishing is only really good about two out of every 10 years so don't miss it when these fish are in the area.

Very large fish are caught in the Bay Area including the world's largest sports fish caught in freshwater, a 468 pound white sturgeon caught by Joey Pallotta in the Carquinez Strait near Benicia. Albacore are pursued in both the Atlantic and the Pacific Ocean by anglers around the world but the largest one ever caught, a 90-pound fish caught by Don Giberson in 1997, came from the Bay Area in the ocean west of Santa Cruz. We also claim a world record for the largest landlocked striped bass ever caught, a 67-pound 8-ounce striped bass caught from O'Neill Forebay east of Gilroy by Hank Ferguson.

The floating tackle shop and boat rental at Lake Del Valle rises and falls with the lake level.

Freshwater fishing is also very good. You may catch trophy sized trout from many lakes and black bass larger than 17 pounds in Lake Chabot and in San Pablo Reservoir. We have perhaps the finest black bass fishing in California in the Delta. Anglers can fish after work or take a few hours on a morning or afternoon to fish from a pier, in a lake or in the bay and catch large, exciting game fish. Anglers catch anything from salmon, halibut and striped bass off the Pacifica Pier to surfperch, mackerel, kingfish and occasionally sturgeon, striped bass and salmon off piers all around the bays.

Coastal rivers from the Russian River that flows to the ocean at the town of Jenner at the northern end of the Greater Bay Area to rivers in Marin County, San Mateo County, Santa Clara and Monterey counties all at one time had steelhead and salmon. Though some still have these fish, they are only a whisper of their historic levels. Efforts to improve their

Three anglers fish in the early morning fog at Lake Berryessa.

in-stream habitats are slowly improving returns but only a few fish migrate to these rivers today and fishing is either prohibited or very restricted. Even in places where you can catch and keep these fish, it is wise to release any steelhead to build up these fish for the future. Better yet, fish in the ocean, the bays, the Delta or the Sacramento River for the more plentiful Sacramento River run salmon that are doing well and can be kept without threatening their survival.

Fish may be caught from lakes and piers managed by several public agencies. County parks or marinas often have fishing and may have camping. The State Parks Department and the Recreational Park Districts manage many parks in the Bay Area that have fishing. The East Bay Municipal Utilities District and utility districts that supply water to many of the cities in the area also provide excellent fishing lakes such as San Pablo Reservoir in Contra Costa County and Laganitas Lake in Marin County. Santa Clara County manages about two dozen lakes that have fish. The list goes on and on.

The agency that has the most diverse and some of the best fishing locations is the East Bay Regional Park District (EBRPD) encompassing much of Contra Costa and Alameda counties. An extensive stocking program for trout and catfish gives anglers a chance to catch limits of fish including some very large fish. From some of the best fishing lakes in the area to piers into the bay and Delta, EBRPD has more than 30 fishing areas that have fishing ranging from fair to excellent. One of the people who makes these parks special places to fish is EBRPD fisheries specialist Pete Alexander who spends most of his time evaluating and analyzing fish and fishing opportunities in these various parks.

A part of Lake Del Valle has been netted off and trout and catfish are stocked in this confined area for a kids fishing seminar.

As anglers we are fortunate to live in the Bay Area. With the great diversity of species, we have a large variety of excellent fishing and can expand our fishing to many new species or new destinations. If you have restricted your fishing to freshwater, you can fish for saltwater fish; if you have concentrated on offshore saltwater species, you may want to try fishing in the saltwater bays. This book is your guide to this great fishing, to help you learn more about your favorite fishing locations and to find and master new fishing areas in freshwater, the open ocean, bays, the Delta or off piers.

Greater Bay Area: This book covers an area that San Francisco Bay Area anglers can easily fish in a day—within an hour's drive from some part of the Metropolitan Bay Area. The region is from Bodega Bay and Jenner to the north (within an hour of Marin), Stockton to the east (an hour from the East Bay) and Monterey to the south (an hour from San Jose). At the northeast corner sits Lake Berryessa and Sacramento; at the southeast corner, San Luis Reservoir and O'Neill Forebay. It includes all or parts of 15 counties—all of Alameda, Contra Costa, Marin, San Francisco, San Mateo, Santa Clara and Santa Cruz and parts of Napa, San Benito, Sacramento, San Joaquin, Sonoma, Solano, Stanislaus and Yolo counties. It is 140 miles north to south and averages about 80 miles wide. In addition, a very rich 20 to 40 mile wide shallow water shelf extends from our shores into the ocean.

Every destination described in this book can be fished in a day but it

It takes two young anglers to hold up this sturgeon caught in San Pablo Bay.

is a treat to take a second day and make a more relaxing trip. You can enjoy local activities (like the Monterey Bay Aquarium) and avoid the rush hour driving after a day of fishing. Campground information when camping is available at a park, lodging and occasionally recommendations for very special attractions and outstanding restaurants are included.

After this introduction, Chapter 2 is a schedule of the best species of fish to catch each month. Best bets for freshwater, saltwater, the Delta and San Pablo and San Francisco Bays are identified. Good alternatives are described. As you plan a fishing trip, look at the month by month schedule to decide what species are your best bets.

Then check Chapter 3, The Best of the Best. This chapter guides you to fishing under different conditions or with different objectives. Often a lake can be great for a species at certain times of the year or under certain conditions and not very good at other times. For example, trolling for trout at San Pablo Reservoir is excellent when the water is clear but, after a storm, it gets a lot of runoff, is muddy and fishing suffers. Other lakes like Shadow Cliffs and Lake Merced don't get much runoff, remain clear and have good fishing after a storm. It tells where to fish for salmon early in the season, where to catch the largest lingcod, the largest bass, etc.

Chapters 4 to 6 describe fishing in lakes and rivers divided into northern, middle and southern areas. Chapter 7 describes fishing in the Delta; Chapter 8 covers saltwater bays (the San Francisco and San Pablo Bays). Chapter 9 describes ocean fishing and Chapter 10 covers piers. After a general description of the fishing in each region, every public body of water with significant fishing in this area is described and rated.

I do not include every pond or body of water that contains fish or give every waterway equal treatment. Waters that have relatively good fishing are described in detail but waters with lesser fishing opportunity are given only short descriptions or are not included if fish are caught only occasionally.

Each fishing section tells what is unique about the body of water, what species dominate, when and how to catch each species. A description of the best fishing methods and a description of the best fishing spots is included for the best fishing lakes.

Tips From an Expert: Tips from an expert are scattered throughout this book. These experts are world record holders like Joey Palotta (468 pound sturgeon) and Don Giberson (90 pound albacore). Acknowledged expert anglers include Abe and Angelo Cuanang, Dan Blanton, Keith Fraser and Tom Stienstra. Other experts are bass pro anglers, guides, the charter boat skippers that are the best at what they do and the best anglers at local lakes who consistently catch the largest bass or trout or catch limits when fish "aren't biting".

They have a wealth of knowledge; and have graciously revealed their secrets to help you catch fish. Their tips can get you started fishing in the best way from the first day you try a new water and help you learn better fishing methods in familiar waters.

Chapters 11 and 12 describe each major freshwater and saltwater sports fish in the Bay Area. These chapters will help you identify your catch but also will teach you more about each species—what they eat, their typical size, where they live and the best bait, lure and fishing techniques.

Fin fish are emphasized but Dungeness Crab and rock crab are caught all along our coast; clams are dug from our beaches at low tide; shrimp may be caught in saltwater (most are used for bait) and crayfish and frogs are taken in freshwater. Abalone are a delicacy that is astronomically priced if you can find them in a store but divers get them with a little effort.

Rating from 1 to 10

Fishing for each major fish is rated on a scale of 1 to 10. Stienstra, in his book California Fishing, rates fishing at each body of water from 1 to 10. But I want to include more specific information for each species so I rate each major game fish at each destination. In one lake, bass might be rated a 9, trout may rate a 7 and catfish a 4. At a saltwater area salmon might be rated 10, lingcod 7 and rockfish 8. Species that are rarely caught and non-gamefish species (i.e., carp and squawfish) may be mentioned in the text but are not rated.

Many lakes in the area have at least one pier with wheelchair access. This one at San Pablo Reservoir has good trout fishing.

A 10 means this is an excellent fishery—one of the best locations to catch that species in the United States. Very few 10s are given. A nine and even a rating of eight denotes very good fishing. A very high rating means top rating for some period during the year—it doesn't mean fishing is always good for that species. For example, some lakes fish really well in spring and fall for trout but these fish are rare in the summer. They can rate a 9 or 10 based on the periods of excellent fishing but fishing may be poor to almost non-existent for that species at other times of year. Resident trout fight harder and are rated higher than put-and-take fish. Lake Berryessa gets a 10 for trout on that basis.

Each fishing destination section describes the facilities for launching a boat, boat rentals, sport fishing boats and bait shops. It tells if gasoline powered motors are allowed or if boats may only have electric motors or no motors at all. It explains whether water skiing and jet skiing (the bane of anglers on small lakes) are permitted, and depicts camping when it is at nearby areas.

Fishing Regulations: California fishing regulations are complex but only a small part of them apply to the Bay Area. Summaries of the 1998 fishing regulations that apply are included in each section. Most of these remain the same or have minor changes but salmon regulations may change dramatically from year to year. Pick up and read a copy of the current California Sport Fishing Regulations published by the California Department of Fish and Game (free copies are available wherever you purchase fishing licenses) to get more details and review any changes paying particularly attention to the salmon regulations.

Everyone 16 years of age or older must have a fishing license displayed on his upper body when fishing except anglers fishing from saltwater piers don't need licenses. One spring and one fall day are designated as free fishing days throughout our state and anglers don't need licenses on those days. Anglers fishing for striped bass must purchase a striped bass stamp. Anglers may purchase a two-rod stamp that allows them to fish with a second rod on lakes. They may still only use one rod on rivers,

in the Delta, in the bays and when fishing for salmon in the ocean. Many lakes have a vigorous stocking program for trout and catfish paid by daily fishing permits—usually about $3.00 per day. Both a state fishing license and a permit are required to fish these lakes. One lake, Parkway Lake, is privately owned and charges a much higher fee but doesn't require a state license.

Health Warnings: Today many of our waterways are contaminated with heavy metals or other toxins and the Department of Fish and Game recommends consumption of fish from these areas should be minimized or in some cases avoided. When eating fish from areas where limitations are suggested, remove and discard all the fat before cooking and do not eat the liver, eggs or other internal parts as these parts accumulate the highest concentrations of toxins. The following are guidelines but read the health warnings at the back of the California Sport Fishing Regulations for details and any changes.

Lake Berryessa and some other lakes have naturally high levels of mercury so consumption of fish including planted trout should be limited. The recommended maximum consumption is 10 pounds of trout per month caught from Lake Berryessa so that isn't very restrictive but no more than one pound of black bass from this lake should be eaten in a month. Several lakes and rivers south of San Jose are particularly high in mercury. People are advised to not consume any fish taken from Guadalupe Reservoir, Calero Reservoir, Almaden Reservoir, Guadalupe River and Creek, Alamitos Creek and ponds along this river and creek.

The Delta has high levels of toxins introduced from industry and agricultural runoff so consumption of resident fish including striped bass and sturgeon should be limited (see the DFG fishing regulations for details). The Richmond Bay Channel is especially toxic and the DFG advises most fish taken from this area should not be eaten. Salmon, rockfish, lingcod and fish like surfperch caught from the open ocean have not been subjected to high levels of toxins and are generally safe for consumption. Salmon migrating through the bays or returning to rivers may be eaten.

Despite these limitations, we have a great variety of excellent quality food fish that are free from toxins. To be safe, I eat ocean caught fish or non-resident fish like planted trout or planted catfish. When in doubt,

John Caulfield holds up a tagged trout he is getting ready to release for a fishing derby.

release the fish and enjoy the sport of fishing.

Fishing is as much about getting out in the fresh air, enjoying the green hills, watching the ducks and maybe even bald eagles or wild turkeys, seeing deer drinking from the edge of a lake, hearing the whoosh as a whale blows and seeing its head, back and finally its huge tail come out of the water then gracefully slip beneath the surface. But catching fish is the primary objective and this guide will help you learn when, where and how to catch more fish throughout this area.

CHAPTER 2:

Best Fishing for Each Month

The Bay Area has so many different fish to catch, you need a schedule to choose the best options when you go fishing. This chapter gives month by month recommendations for the best type of fishing in four categories—(1)freshwater (FW), (2)the Delta, (3)bays and (4)saltwater(SW). Every one of these areas has at least one very good option every month but they are listed in the order I consider the best starting with the best option at the top of the list.

The schedule for fish is very predictable. Different fish migrate to certain areas and are active at certain times. Fish for them at the appropriate time and you maximize your fishing success. This isn't quite like clockwork—different weather conditions can delay the fish a week or two or draw them early. Questions that affect their schedule include, when will the water chill enough for the lakes to turnover bringing trout to the surface? Will albacore show up this year? When will live bait be available so anglers can start taking live bait trips in the bays for halibut and striped bass? But the date when fishing for each species will peak at each location varies no more than a few weeks from year to year so we know when fishing will be best.

Don't overlook species that aren't listed. For example, black bass can be caught every day of the year. It is just much easier to catch them in the spring when they are getting ready to spawn or guarding nests. (If you catch bass from a nest, put them back where you caught them so they can resume their duty of protecting the fish for future generations.) But use the right fishing method and you can catch bass anytime.

Rockfish and lingcod are caught all year. When fishing peaks for our most exciting species like salmon or albacore, most anglers would rather fish for them but some anglers prefer the almost constant action of rockfish and fish for them all year. Use this section as a guide but considered other species if they are more interesting to you.

January:

Bays:	Sturgeon
Freshwater:	Trout
Delta:	Striped Bass
Saltwater:	Rockfish

In January, the hottest fishing ticket is sturgeon in San Pablo Bay, Carquinez Strait and the mothball fleet at Martinez. You don't always catch one but just the chance to catch a 100 pound or larger fish is worth taking several trips. Striped bass may be landed as well. Trout fishing is very good—anglers catch limits trolling or bait fishing at local lakes. In the Delta, striped bass with a chance for sturgeon is the best bet and rockfish and lingcod are number one off charter boats or private boats in saltwater. January is the beginning of the best fishing for surfperch caught off beaches, piers or in the bays.

February:

Freshwater:	Trout
Saltwater:	Rockfish
Bays:	Sturgeon
Delta:	Striped Bass

Trout are shallow in all Bay Area lakes and anglers are catching a lot of these fish. San Pablo Reservoir opens mid-February after a three month shutdown. Trout fishing there is very good unless it has been a wet winter and the lake is dirty from runoff. Then bait will be better than trolling but fishing will not be up to the lake's potential and other lakes with clearer water like Lake Merced and Shadow Cliffs have better fishing. Rockfish and lingcod are still the primary saltwater fish and catches are good when the wind is calm, seas are low and anglers can get to the Farallon Islands, Cordell Bank, Point Sur or the local reefs. Sturgeon and striped bass are the primary catch in the bays and the Delta.

March:

Saltwater:	Salmon
Bays:	Sturgeon
Delta:	Black Bass
Freshwater:	Trout, Bass

Salmon season opens mid-month south of Pigeon Point (between Half Moon Bay and Santa Cruz) and at the end of the month north of this point. Early season salmon catches are particularly good in Monterey Bay with anglers going after them from Santa Cruz, Moss Landing and Monterey. Charter boats from Pillar Point go south to cross into the open region to catch salmon after mid-March. Sturgeon catches remain high in the bays as long as rains produce heavy runoff. Black bass fishing in local lakes and the Delta begins to get good as we go into a prespawn time and trout fishing is excellent in most lakes.

April:

Saltwater:	Salmon
Delta:	Bass
Freshwater:	Bass, trout
Bays:	Halibut

By the first weekend in April, salmon season is open throughout the Bay Area and salmon mooching in Monterey Bay tops the list. Anglers have the best chance to catch a limit of two salmon of the year in April—providing the weather cooperates and you can get out to fish. Black bass fishing is good in the Delta and in lakes but most anglers will still be going for trout that are plentiful in all lakes. Sturgeon is still good in the bays and at the Mothball Fleet inland from Martinez if we have had late rains. Halibut fishing starts in the San Francisco Bay as soon as live bait is available near the end of April.

May:

Saltwater:	Salmon
Bays:	Halibut
Delta:	Bass, catfish
Freshwater:	Bass, Trout

Salmon catches get most of the excitement in May with catches remaining excellent from all Bay Area ports. Halibut off the Berkeley Flats and Alameda is very good and some striped bass are mixed in with the halibut catch. Most anglers go on charter boats out of bay ports or launch boats and buy live bait at Fisherman's Wharf, Berkeley or Sausalito to catch these fish. Black bass fishing is very good in the Delta and in freshwater lakes—it won't get much better. This is the last month to count on trout at all of the local lakes though good fishing will continue in the cooler lakes. Anglers can sit on the shore in the Delta and land a mess of catfish.

June:

Saltwater:	Salmon
Bays:	Halibut, Stripers
Delta:	Bass, Catfish
Freshwater:	Bass, Catfish

Offshore anglers still will be pursuing salmon with boats from all ports finding good catches although the best catches are shifting from Monterey Bay north to the San Francisco Area. Halibut is peaking in the bays and more and more stripers are included in the catch. The catch in freshwater lakes and the Delta is shifting toward catfish and good black bass fishing continues. Only the coolest lakes like San Pablo Reservoir, Lake Merced, Loch Lomond north of Santa Cruz and Lake Chabot still have good trout fishing.

July:

Saltwater:	Salmon, Albacore
Bays:	Stripers, Halibut
Delta:	Catfish
Freshwater:	Catfish

Salmon continues as the top fish in July with good catches from San Francisco harbors. Bodega Bay Area salmon fishing peaks—Monterey Bay salmon fishing typically falls off in June and July. Striped bass replace halibut as the prime catch in the bays. If water is warm off our coast, albacore will be in the area and anglers may begin to make good catches this month. Freshwater catches are limited with catfish planted in local lakes replacing trout and catches of these fish in the Delta can be very good. Bass, panfish, and some striped bass are also caught this time of year.

August:

Saltwater:	Albacore, Salmon
Bays:	Stripers
Delta:	Catfish, Bass
Freshwater:	Catfish

If albacore are going to arrive, they should appear by August and this is the best overall month to catch these fish. Salmon fishing is still good from the northern ports. Monterey Bay boats have largely gone back to rockfish unless they are chasing albacore. Now the emphasis has shifted from halibut to striped bass in the San Francisco and San Pablo Bays. Most salmon are still caught in the open ocean but some salmon are caught inside the San Francisco Bay. Live bait fishing can be very good in the bays. Catfish are the number one catch in most freshwater lakes and the Delta; black bass and striped bass are also landed.

September:

Saltwater:	Salmon, Albacore
Bays:	Striped Bass
Delta:	Catfish, Bass
Freshwater:	Catfish

Salmon are still the most prized game fish in September unless albacore are plentiful as in 1997. Then these tuna become the top prize. Salmon limits are caught infrequently but their large size compensates for reduced

numbers. Striped bass are the premium fish in the bays with the best catch beginning to come from San Pablo Bay. Catfish are still landed in the Delta and anglers began to catch more striped bass though some stripers are caught in the Delta all year. Anglers on freshwater lakes are catching catfish and are thinking about trout. Lakes like San Pablo Reservoir, Lake Merced and Loch Lomond have okay trout fishing all summer and it is now beginning to be good. After the summer doldrums, black bass are caught in the Delta and lakes but not up to the numbers in their spring catch. During the month salmon continue to migrate into the bays and up the Sacramento and San Joaquin Rivers. Anglers who troll off California City northeast of Angel Island often catch a few large salmon without leaving the protection of the bay.

October:

Freshwater:	Trout
Bays:	Striped Bass
Saltwater:	Salmon, Albacore
Delta:	Striped Bass

October is the month when lakes begin to turnover bringing bait fish and trout to the surface. Stocking programs resume in the lakes that were too warm for trout during the hottest months. Trout are caught on bait in relatively shallow water on trolling lures or bait near the surface. San Pablo Bay has its best striped bass catch of the year during this month and November. Stripers are moving into the lower Delta and the catch improves there as well. Albacore catches are falling off as are salmon; the numbers are down but the size is up for both these species. In October, 1997 a state record for salmon caught in the ocean was set when a 52.2 pound salmon was landed near San Francisco. Charter boats like *The New Sea Angler* out of Bodega Bay and the *Cobra* out of Richmond take lingcod special trips where they concentrate on lings and make excellent catches of these fish on calm weather days.

November:

Freshwater:	Trout
Bays:	Striped Bass
Saltwater:	Rockfish
Delta:	Striped Bass

The last of the lakes that have trout turnover in November and catches are from the shallows in all lakes. San Pablo Reservoir closes at mid-month to act as a wildfowl refuge. Striped bass catches in San Pablo Bay are the highest of the season. Salmon season ends and offshore anglers devote their fishing time to rockfish and lingcod. More and more stripers move into the Delta and the Rio Vista Area peaks for striper fishing. Before the water cools too much, trolling or casting lures is a good way to catch these fish but in the next month, it will be time to go to all bait fishing for stripers.

December:

Freshwater:	Trout
Bays:	Stripers, Sturgeon
Delta:	Striped Bass
Saltwater:	Rockfish

Trout continue to dominate the freshwater catch as they will until the spring weather warms the waters but the most dedicated black bass anglers will slow down their retrieve to catch some bass. As rains begin to come, sturgeon fishing picks up in San Pablo Bay and will improve later in the Lower Delta. By mid-month it is time to use bait exclusively for striped bass in the Delta with butterfly cut threadfin shad the number one bait. Rockfish and lingcod are the dominant species in the open ocean. Between winter storms when the wind is calm, the seas low and the drift slow, anglers can work the bottom slowly and effectively and make excellent catches of these bottom dwellers.

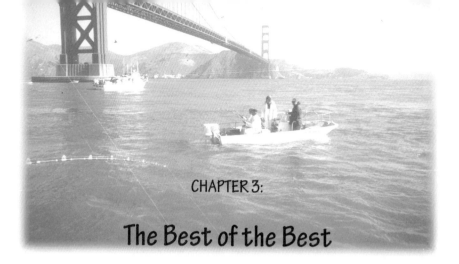

CHAPTER 3:

The Best of the Best

While many waters in the Bay Area have very good fishing much of the time or under certain conditions, they may have rather poor fishing at other times or under other conditions. Some have better facilities like fine campgrounds to compliment excellent fishing; others just plain have large fish like huge bass while others may produce a lot of fish. This chapter is your guide to finding the best fishing locations for the fish you want to pursue under different conditions. It starts with a freshwater section followed by a saltwater section and finally a general section that applies to both freshwater and saltwater.

FRESHWATER

Best trout fishing after a storm: Shadow Cliffs Reservoir and Lake Merced

Most reservoirs and lakes have stream runoff that washes silt into the lakes and makes them muddy after a storm. Some fish go for muddy water

Many of the lakes and the Delta have large catfish. San Pablo Reservoir has some of the largest catfish as this angler with a 23-pound catfish caught from this lake can attest.

but not trout so you need to find a lake or stream with clear water for good trout fishing. Shadow Cliffs Reservoir, a reclaimed gravel pit east of Pleasanton, and Lake Merced, a ground water lake in southwest San Francisco, both have very little runoff. Many lakes take weeks to clear after a storm but these two remain almost clear and have good fishing right after a storm.

Best summer trout fishing: Lake Merced, San Pablo Reservoir, Lake Chabot, and Loch Lomond

Some lakes are cool enough to always be in a good temperature range for trout. Lake Merced near the ocean in southwest San Francisco always holds trout. San Pablo Reservoir receives trout plants all year but they go deep during July, August and September so anglers need to fish 15 to 25 feet deep during part of this time. Lake Chabot in Castro Valley is in a cool area so its water remains cool into the summer and trout fishing is good through June and into July — later than more inland lakes. Loch Lomond is near the ocean north of Santa Cruz, gets cool ocean breezes and stays cool for trout into the summer months.

Best winter trout fishing from shore: Lake Chabot, Lake Del Valle and Parkway Lake

Some lakes fish very well if you have a boat to get to the fish but others have good access and anglers from shore do very well. Three of the best lakes for shore fishing for trout are Lake Chabot, Lake Del Valle and the pay-to-fish lake, Parkway Lake. The narrows section and the launch ramp at Del Valle are easily accessible and have good fishing. The west and north sides of Lake Chabot have easy access to places that seem to always have trout and the peninsula at Parkway Lake consistently produces these fish. Most lakes that have trout have some locations with good shore fishing so the one nearest you or the one you know best may be your best lake.

Best Winter Trout fishing from a boat : Lake Berryessa

Many lakes in the Bay Area have great trout fishing from a boat where anglers troll or anchor and bait fish. Lake Berryessa gets the nod because, not only does this lake have excellent fishing, but the fish have been planted as small fish and have thrived and grown tough—it's almost like they were native fish.

Best Place to fly fish for trout: Putah Creek

Putah Creek below Lake Berryessa, Alameda Creek east of Fremont and the Novato River that runs through the north bay town of Novato all have stocked trout where anglers can fly-fish. Putah Creek has catch and release fishing and is a favorite destination for fly fishers. Local lakes including San Pablo Reservoir, Shadow Cliffs and Lake Del Valle also have good fly fishing opportunities. Use a float tube to get close to fish in reservoirs or troll for trout to find them, then cast a black woolly bugger or damsel fly imitation to catch them with the long rod.

Best waters to catch many bass: The Delta

The Delta is full of black bass. On good days anglers can catch a dozen or more bass. While most will be small, a sprinkling will be really quality bass— five pounds or better. Fish there on one of these days and you will think you have died and gone to bass heaven.

Best place to fly fish for striped bass: O'Neill Forebay and Frank's Tract

O'Neill Forebay has shallow flats that hold striped bass in the spring and fly anglers using large flies catch them. The Delta also produces stripers on flies and Frank's Tract out of Bethel Island is a top fly fishing option for striped bass as well as largemouth bass.

Best lake for large bass: San Pablo Reservoir and Lake Chabot

These lakes have each yielded a number of bass weighing more than 16 pounds with the largest bass heavier than 17 pounds at both lakes. Fishing is tough, particularly at Lake Chabot where anglers don't catch many small bass but if you want big ones these are the two places to fish.

Best place to catch catfish: The Delta, Lake Del Valle and San Pablo Reservoir

The Delta is full of wild catfish ranging from juvenile eight to ten inch fish to mature fish weighing 20 pounds or more. Lake Del Valle and San Pablo Reservoir and several other lakes in the area have excellent catches of planted catfish during the summer months and produce a few really giant resident catfish.

Best place to catch large catfish : San Pablo Reservoir and Lake Chabot

Two Bay Area lakes have a lot of large catfish. Lake Chabot has yielded a catfish weighing more than 35 pounds and San Pablo Reservoir has pro-

An angler holds up a large, prized chinook salmon.

Cathy Lambert caught this largemouth bass while trolling at San Pablo Reservoir.

duced catfish up to 31 pounds. If you are looking for the best, it has to be San Pablo Reservoir where anglers catch many 15 pound class catfish some weighing more than 20 pounds every year.

Where to fish without a license: Parkway Lake

If you have friends from out-of-state coming to fish with you and don't want to have them buy a license or if you are planning a company fishing trip where most of the people don't have licenses, think about taking them to Parkway Lake south of San Jose. Anglers at this private lake pay a daily fishing fee of $12 per person, catch trout in the cool months, catfish in the warm months and a few sturgeon every month. At other lakes a one day fishing license costs about $9 and a daily fishing permit typically costs $3.00—about the same total as the fee at Parkway Lake.

SALTWATER

Best early season salmon: Monterey Bay

The salmon season opens south of Pigeon Point two weeks earlier than opening day out of San Francisco. This gives anglers from Monterey, Moss Landing and Santa Cruz a jump on the season. Pillar Point boats also go south across this line into the open area to catch early season salmon. Monterey Bay has good quantities of large fish in the early season— March though June or July—so is a good place to fish.

Best mid-season salmon: Everyplace

By June, salmon fishing is good throughout the Bay Area from Monterey to Bodega Bay.

Harlan Merryman lands a salmon for an angler
fishing out of Santa Cruz.

Best late season salmon: San Francisco area

As the season winds down, salmon congregate at the entrance to the Golden Gate getting ready to start their spawning run up the Sacramento River and to a lesser degree to the San Joaquin River and its tributaries. Now the best chance to catch salmon is from Pacifica to Duxbury and at this time of year the largest fish are moving in gorging on bait fish for their spawning run. Don't expect limits but the size of fish makes up for any deficiency in the quantity.

Best place to camp and catch salmon: Bodega Bay

With several campgrounds in the area, good launching ramps and salmon close to the harbor, Bodega Bay is the best place to camp and fish for salmon. My favorite camping area is Sonoma County's Westside Campground on the west side of Bodega Harbor. It has a good two lane launch ramp with docks and is the best launching ramp in the area. It is used by many day boaters as well as campers and lines get long. This campground fills up fast but Doran Park on the south side of Bodega Harbor, Bodega Dunes State Beach a half mile north of Bodega Bay and private campgrounds give camping anglers many options.

Best boat launch for salmon day trip: Moss Landing, Santa Cruz or Pillar Point

For day trips for salmon, the best launching sites are at the Santa Cruz small boat harbor, Pillar Point and Moss Landing. When salmon are being caught, parking lots fill at all these launch sites on weekends. Parking at Santa Cruz is particularly limited and you need to get there early on weekends when salmon are in the area to find a parking space. Pillar Point is right on the ocean with short runs to salmon. Santa Cruz is cradled in a cusp of land that protects it from northwesterly seas. Some days you can fish inside this protection and get a few salmon when seas are too rough to motor to unprotected waters. Moss Landing located on the middle coast of Monterey Bay often is very close to schools of salmon so the run to the fish is short.

Best place to catch the largest sturgeon: Carquinez Strait or San Pablo Bay

The largest sports-caught sturgeon ever recorded in the United States is a 468 pound fish caught in the Carquinez Strait that connects San Pablo

Bay to the Delta. This and San Pablo Bay are the places to expect super-sized fish. With the maximum size limit of 72 inches for sturgeon—that's about a 100 pound fish—you will be catching the really big one just to release. Heck, these large fish are many tens of years old, are fantastic producers of little sturgeon and I'd release any large sturgeon I caught even if I could legally keep it.

Best place to catch the largest shark: San Francisco Bay

Deep holes in the San Francisco Bay hold large six gill and seven gill shark. Seek these out on your own or go on the charter boat, Fury, out of San Pablo Yacht Harbor to learn where and how to catch these fish.

Best place to catch striped bass: South Tower or San Pablo Bay

Fishing for striped bass with live bait at the south tower of the Golden Gate Bridge is super effective on an outgoing tide in the summer. Live bait is also very good in many other places in the bay. In the fall, the best action turns to San Pablo Reservoir and now lures are almost as good as live bait. In the winter the Delta is the hot spot for striped bass.

Several lakes have large striped bass. Matt Desimone shows off this
pair of fish he caught from Lake Del Valle.

Best place to fly fish: San Francisco Bay

The flats in the San Francisco Bay have good fly fishing for striped bass. Try the Berkeley Flats or the waters off the San Francisco Airport or the Alameda Beach and use a light colored Lefty Deceiver or Blanton Whistler.

Best place to catch the largest halibut: The open ocean

Most halibut caught inside the San Francisco Bay and along the entrance to the Golden Gate are California Halibut that can't match the size of Pacific Halibut. To get the large Pacific Halibut, fish in the open ocean. The largest one I have seen was a 53 pound fish caught near the Farallon Islands. These halibut are sparse and most are caught accidentally by anglers fishing on the bottom for rockfish and lingcod.

A quiet lake in the Bay Area makes a pretty picture.

Best place to catch the most halibut: Berkeley Flats or off Alameda

When bait boats start getting live bait —usually in late April—halibut catches take off. The Berkeley Flats and the bay off the city of Alameda are the most consistent producers of halibut.

Best place to purchase live bait: Fisherman's Wharf, Berkeley, Sausalito and Pillar Point

The only place to purchase live bait fish in the Bay Area has been Pier 45 at Fisherman's Wharf but other places have recently installed bait receivers and also sell live bait. Pillar Point, Berkeley and Sausalito now have live bait and Monterey and Santa Cruz have live bait sometimes. This seems to change every year so check to be certain the supplier where you plan to purchase your bait does have live bait.

Best place to catch live bait: Richmond Piers

Shiner surfperch make great live bait and I have had my best success catching them around the piers at Richmond. However, they are found

A young angler shows his catfish caught at a kids fishing seminar.

around most piers so arm yourself with a few pile worms; use little bits of these worms on small size 6 hooks and you can catch shiners for bait at many piers.

Best place to catch large lingcod: Farallon Islands or Point Sur

In the fall, the Farallon Islands rank as the best place to catch large lingcod. Take a lingcod special trip on the Cobra charter boat out of Richmond or The New Sea Angler out of Bodega Bay when skipper Rick Powers takes the trip to the northern Farallons. Choose a calm day so the seas are low and the drift is slow and get ready to do battle with lingcod up to 20 or 30-pounds and sometimes larger. At one time Point Sur ranked as high as the Farallons for lings but it has lost a bit in recent years and now ranks a very respectable second place.

Best place to catch large rockfish: Cordell Bank

A number of prepared baits and salmon eggs are excellent bait for trout.

For big reds, bocaccio and large rockfish of a variety of species, Cordell Bank ranks number one. It also has darn good lingcod fishing, not far behind the Farallon Islands and Point Sur.

Best place to catch both crab and fish: Bodega Bay

Sport fishing boats take combination crab and bottom fish or crab and salmon trips out of Bodega Bay. These trips are very popular—think about bringing home a limit of six big delectable Dungeness crab with a rockfish and lingcod or a salmon bonus and you don't have to be a rocket scientist to see the attraction. These trips have become very popular and skippers out of Berkeley, Emeryville and other ports are starting to take these combination trips.

Where to fish without a license: Saltwater Piers

Except for the two free fish days, the only public water where adults can fish without a fishing license is off public saltwater piers. That is about the only thing that isn't licensed, taxed or illegal in California.

FRESH AND SALTWATER

When to fish without a license: Free fishing days in June and in September.

The California Department of Fish & Game offers two free fishing days. You, your family and friends can fish without a license on one Saturday in June and another in September but these are the only times to fish without a license. At all other times anyone 16 years of age or older must display his or her license above the waist—you risk a large fine if you fish without a license and can be fined even if you have but are not displaying your license.

Section II: Freshwater

Introduction: The Greater Bay Area is sprinkled with dozens of lakes. On nice weekends anglers in boats almost cover the most popular lakes; many anglers fish from shore and most of the anglers make good catches of trout in cool months, catfish in the warm months, and some bass and panfish all year. How can so many anglers catch so many fish? The answer is excellent stocking programs of trout when the water is cool and catfish after the water warms. Truckloads of trout are delivered as many as three times a week to several lakes keeping the fish count high in both the water and in the catch. Most loads of planted trout include a few very large fish so anglers always have a chance at a trophy. These are not wild fish; the big fish you catch probably came from the fish delivery truck a few days earlier, but it is big, healthy, and powerful.

If planted trout don't excite you, bass, catfish and panfish in many of the lakes may stir up your adrenaline. Or the Delta has great fishing for bass, striped bass, catfish, sturgeon, and shad.

Lakes: Lakes and reservoirs are the prime freshwater fishing areas outside the Delta (the Delta will be covered in a separate chapter). Each region within the Bay Area seems to have its own character. The northern region is anchored by Lake Berryessa that has trout planted in the spring and caught in the fall after they have grown tough and they fight like wild fish. This lake is also one of the best lakes for largemouth, smallmouth, and spotted bass but several lakes throughout the Bay Area have good bass fishing. Many lakes in the northern and southern areas are planted with trout by the California Department of Fish and Game. While these pan sized trout are fun to catch, for really large trout try one of several lakes in the East Bay, Lake Merced, or Parkway Lake.

The East Bay is the hot spot for large trout. Several East Bay Municipal Utilities District lakes (San Pablo Reservoir and Lafayette Reservoir), and East Bay Regional Parks District lakes (Del Valle, Shadow Cliffs, Lake Chabot, Contra Loma, Lake Temescal, Cull Canyon and Don Castro) purchase and stock larger trout and charge daily fishing fees to fish. All but the last three of these lakes have very large fish—you have a chance to catch a 15-pound or larger trout from them.

Rivers: Fishing in rivers is limited. From mid-November to the end of April, Putah Creek is fly-fishing catch and release only and anglers have good success catching a mix of wild and stocked rainbow and brown trout. When the sandbar that almost blocks entry to the Russian River in the summer is washed away by gushing water from heavy rains, salmon and steelhead swim upriver to spawn. Some are caught but this is tough fishing and anglers won't catch a fish on every trip. Smallmouth bass and some shad in this river in the spring are more reliable options. Many rivers in the Bay Area are tributaries to the Sacramento or San Joaquin Rivers and are part of the Delta. They have striped bass, black bass, catfish, sturgeon, carp, and panfish. (See the section on the Delta for fishing information.)

Several coastal rivers or streams off the bays have a few steelhead and salmon. Most steelhead in the Bay Area are listed as threatened or endangered. Steelhead fishing in the American, Sacramento, and Russian Rivers and some coastal rivers is permitted but runs are at precarious levels. Other creeks and rivers in the area have small runs of steelhead but they can't stand much fishing pressure and I won't identify them in this book. You can search out some streams that have these fish and have some success catching them but check the latest fishing regulations to be sure fish-ing for them is permitted. Even in rivers where you can keep these fish, runs are so fragile I encourage you to release them. Catch the fish you eat from lakes that replenish fish via active stocking programs or from the ocean or saltwater bays. Check the health warning in the DFG fishing reg-ulations to see what fish are safe to eat and what ones should be released.

Fly-fishing: The Bay Area is not a prime fly-fishing area but we have many fly-fishing opportunities. Putah Creek below Lake Berryessa, Alameda Creek out of Fremont and Novato Creek near the town of Novato have good fly-fishing. But we can also catch shad on flies in the American and Russian Rivers and catch trout in many of the lakes that are more traditional bait or trolling waters. Salmon and steelhead are caught fly-fishing in rivers; striped bass are caught fly-fishing in the bays and striped bass, black bass, trout, or panfish can be caught fly-fishing in most rivers, lakes and the Delta.

I've caught trout fly-fishing in San Pablo Reservoir, Lake Chabot, Del Valle Reservoir and Shadow Cliffs Lake and many other lakes have decent fly-fishing for trout. Laganitas Lake in Marin County is mostly catch and release fishing using artificial lures with barbless hooks. Trout in any lake can be caught on flies but when fish are sparse and scattered it may take a lot of casts to catch one and bait or trolling may be a better option.

A separate rating identifies the lakes and rivers that are best for fly-fishing. Most of the time this refers to trout but may mean good fly-fish-ing for black bass, panfish or striped bass.

Three Regions and Delta

Three chapters describe fishing in freshwater lakes and rivers. Chapter 4 covers the northern region including Marin County and north. Its south-ern boundary extends east along the north shoreline of San Pablo Bay, east through Carquinez Strait, along the San Joaquin River and along False River to Franks Tract Lake then east along Eight Mile Road to Interstate Highway 5.

The middle region described in chapter 5 is from this boundary south to a line east and west from northern San Jose. It includes the San Francisco Peninsula, all of the East Bay to Stockton and Tracy. The south-ern region described in chapter 6 is south of this east-west boundary through San Jose. Fishing in the Delta is covered in chapter 7.

Turnover Trout

The lakes in the Bay Area go through a change in the spring and fall. In the spring as the air warms, the surface of lakes heat up. Since warm water is less dense and rises to the surface, the lake stratifies into a warm water section at the top and cool water remains deep in the lake. Where these two meet is called the thermocline and makes an abrupt change in temperature.

The warm area above the thermocline goes through a mixing process and oxygen that is whipped into the water at the surface by the wind is mixed through the warm water to the thermocline. The cool water has no new oxygen so this life-giving gas is gradually depleted. Fish must have oxygen and trout thrive in cool water. The only place they have both is at the thermocline and this is where trout live throughout the summer. They can move out of this comfort region but must soon return.

You can find the thermocline by observing the fish's depth on a fish finder, measuring the water temperature with a remote device or asking at the bait shop. By trolling at that depth, you have good success catching trout throughout the warmer months. The thermocline can be 20 to 60 feet deep so you may need to troll deep to catch trout.

As the air cools in October or November, the surface of the lake cools at most Bay Area lakes. Warm water rises so this sets up a mixing between the cool and warm water. Soon the entire lake is cool and then the best place for trout is in the oxygen rich, cool water near the surface. Now you find the trout in the shallow water near shore and catch them with bait or casting lures. You may catch them trolling with shallow running lures or flashers and bait. I find flashers effective but they interfere with playing a hooked fish. Lures used alone are equally successful and I fight the fish, not the flasher— I troll for trout with lures and haven't used flashers in several years.

The largest black bass are caught from San Pablo Reservoir and Lake Chabot. EBRPD fisheries specialist Pete Alexander shows off a large Lake Chabot bass that was electroshocked.

Basic Fishing

No matter where you fish, some really basic fishing techniques will usually catch fish. If you are fishing for trout, you want your bait at the right depth. For trout cruising the bottom, fish with Power Bait or night crawlers but float them off the bottom. Use a sliding egg sinker on your main line, a snap swivel then an 18-inch to 2-foot long leader to the hook and bait. The Power Bait floats so the bait will be the leader length above the bottom. To float a night crawler at the same depth, inflate it with air (a squeeze bottle with a hollow needle you purchase at a tackle shop will do this) or thread a miniature marshmallow on the hook in front of the night crawler. A spinning outfit makes this easy to cast.

If you have a boat, trolling with monofilament line and a weight, lead-core line, or a downrigger is a great way to catch trout particularly during the cool months when trout are shallow in the lake. While many anglers use flashers, I have caught more fish using lures without flashers like small Needlefish, Triple Teazers, Cripplures, Dick Nites or on minnow imitations like a Rapalas or Rat-L-Traps. The author's book, *The Troller's Handbook,* will show you how to troll at the right depth.

Far more bass are caught on soft plastic artificial baits than on any other lure. Worms in a dozen different styles and hundreds of colors, tube

baits, lizards, and crayfish imitations all catch fish. Top water lures are great fun in the morning and evening when fish are feeding in the shallows; spinner baits or buzz baits fished through tulles or along docks are great bass producers and many different crankbaits will catch them. Minnows, crawfish and worms are good natural baits. Whether you are fishing in the Delta, a lake or a river, one or more of these will be good fish attractors.

For striped bass, start with threadfin shad, sculpin or mudsuckers for bait; for catfish use clams, mackerel, anchovies, chicken liver or prepared bait. In both cases fish the bait on the bottom. Learn the basic fishing methods and you can catch fish anytime, any place.

Tips From Experts

Tips from an expert scattered throughout this book give you special insight on how the most knowledgeable anglers catch fish and how some use special techniques to catch large fish. Use their tips to quickly start catching fish from the first time you fish a new waterway.

Each section includes a summary of facilities at the lakes, fees for the services, records of the largest fish taken from the lake (when records have been kept), any special programs like awards for large fish, fishing derbys or special fishing clinics and directions to the lake. Cost information is current as this book goes to press but inflation drives up prices so don't be surprised to pay a bit more.

Outboard Motor Restrictions

A trend in drinking water reservoirs (most lakes in the Bay Area are drinking water reservoirs) is to prohibit two cycle outboard engines. This type of engine has a lot of unburned gas in its exhaust that is dumped into lakes. The gasoline contains a number of potential carcinogens, including MTBE that was recently added to gasoline to reduce air pollution. Chemical tests of water from lakes with heavy outboard motor use have shown significant levels of MTBE and the exhaust from two cycle engines is a leading culprit. Managers of lakes and the state legislators are considering restrictions to outboard motor use to reduce gasoline derived pollutants in our drinking water.

The first step typically is to prohibit two cycle engines and the second step in some lakes is to prohibit all motors except electric motors. Some water districts like the Marin Municipal Water District have prohibited all body contact (including boats and float tubes) on their drinking water reservoirs for years. Many of the Santa Clara lakes permit only non-powered boats while others allow only electric-powered boats. Boaters on San Pablo Reservoir are to be restricted to four cycle or fuel injected two cycle engines (these exhaust about one-fifth the pollutants of standard two cycle engines) in January 2000 and then are restricted to only electric motors after January 2002. Several other lakes will probably impose similar restrictions.

Legislation has been considered that would prohibit the sale of two cycle engines unless they have fuel injection. At least one bill being considered would restrict or prohibit gasoline powered engines on all lakes that are used for drinking water. So far that legislation has been rejected but either a state wide standard or lake-by-lake regulations will probably restrict outboard motors on drinking water reservoirs.

If you are buying a boat primarily for fishing in freshwater lakes in the Bay Area, consider purchasing an aluminum fishing boat with a four cycle engine or even consider buying only electric motors. An electric motor with one or two batteries and a battery charger will meet all of your needs on most Bay Area lakes and is a lot cheaper than an outboard engine. If you need more power, buy a second electric motor and another battery. If you are buying a conventional outboard motor, buy a four cycle engine.

Regulations: Anyone 16 years of age or older fishing in public waters must have a valid state fishing license visible above his or her waist. To fish for striped bass, you must have a striper stamp affixed to your license. You may purchase two rod stamps that authorize you to fish with two rods in most lakes but only one rod is permitted while fishing in rivers, the Delta or in the bays. Some lakes require you to purchase a daily fishing permit in addition to a state license.

Freshwater Map

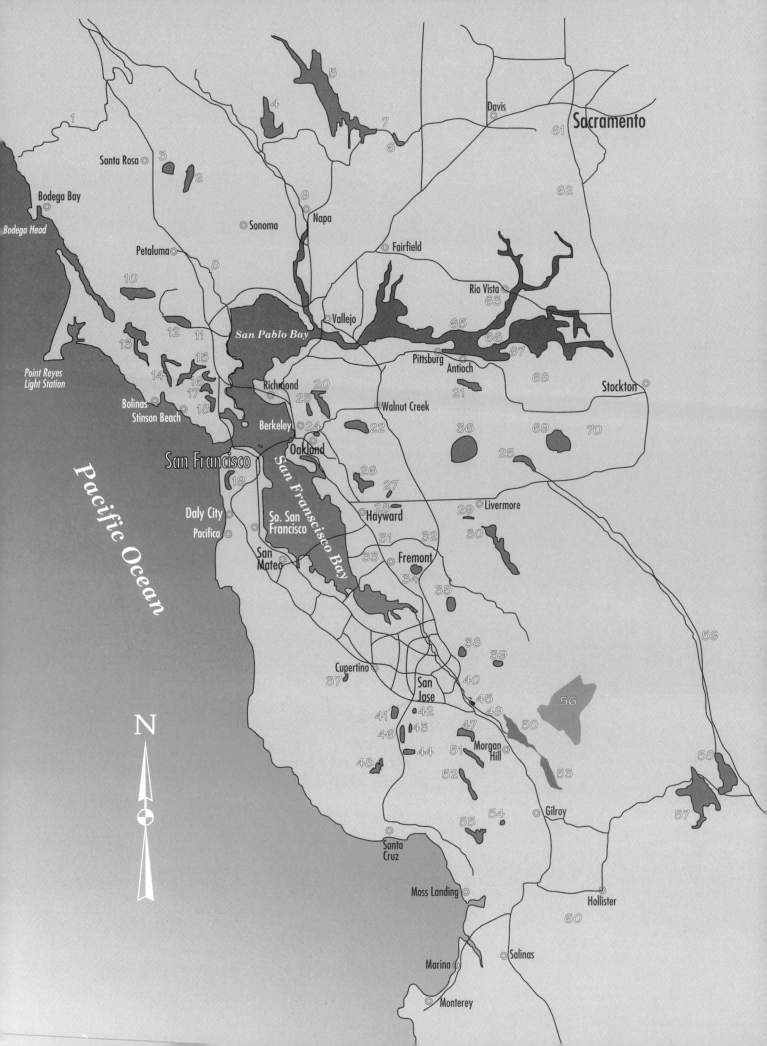

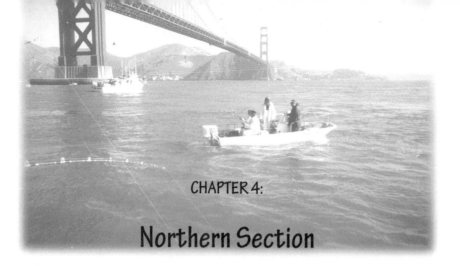

CHAPTER 4:

Northern Section

The northern part of the Bay Area has a lot of fair to good freshwater fishing lakes but lacks the large fish that are planted in the San Francisco and East Bay lakes to bring it up to really high ratings for trout. One exception is Lake Berryessa. The DFG plants small trout in the spring; they go deep in the lake and grow rapidly throughout the summer when fishing pressure is low. By fall they are acclimated to the lake, feed on natural food and fight like wild trout. During their first winter at the lake they have grown to 12 to 15-inches and are already quality fish. A few survive another year. These are 16 to 18-inch fish and are very worthy fighters. While they aren't as large as the trophy sized fish planted in other lakes, catching these almost wild trout is a special treat—don't overlook this lake.

Guide Jim Munk launches his boat at
Markley Cove in Lake Berryessa.

Trout are the most popular freshwater fish but warm water fish thrive in this area and some lakes have very good bass fishing. The ones that come to mind are Lake Berryessa, Lake Hennesey near Napa, and Spring Lake in Santa Rosa. A reported 24-pound bass was caught and released from Spring Lake. It was weighed on a bathroom scale (not an accurate way to weigh fish) and examination of photos of the fish suggest it was smaller than record size. Several bass fishing lakes in Northern California have produced bass weighing 17 to 18 pounds. The largest bass ever caught and weighed on certified scales in Northern California tipped the scale to 18 pounds. While anything is possible, a bass six pounds larger than the largest ever caught in the area is very unlikely. Still, Spring Lake produces large bass. Scott Green caught a 12-pound 5 ounce bass there and verified reports of bass up to about 15-pounds have been made.

The lakes in Marin County are drinking water reservoirs operated by the Marin Municipal Water District. They do not permit boats on their lakes but anglers may fish from shore. Several of these lakes are stocked by the DFG and fishing is good for a few days after the stocking truck has made its delivery. Some have good bass fishing.

Rivers in the area have had steelhead and salmon runs and some are coming back. One of the great conservation stories comes out of Petaluma where students under advisor Tom Furrer at Casa Grande High School have restored Petaluma Creek. They have developed a small state-of-the-art hatchery and rearing facility to bring back salmon and steelhead to this creek. The good news is they have been very successful and now get regular returns of these salmonidae.

A creek in Muir Woods, the San Lorenzo River in Santa Cruz, and many other small coastal rivers also have returning salmon and steelhead. The number of returning steelhead and salmon are so low in most rivers they are not sufficient to support fishing and, with the fishing pressure they would receive, some probably never will allow fishing. Just knowing they can come back is a great victory for conservationists and the students at Casa Grande High School.

1. Russian River:

Bass	8
Steelhead	6
Catfish	6
Panfish	7
Shad	6
After a storm	0
Fly-fishing	7

About Russian River: The Russian River is most noted for flooding. Heavy winter rains north of San Francisco seem to mean flooding of this river driving Guerneville residents along the river from their homes, sometimes twice or three times in a year. But the river goes down quickly and it has good fishing for smallmouth bass and shad in season and has some steelhead, salmon, catfish, and panfish.

During the summer, a sand bar forms across the mouth of the river and little water flows to the ocean. When winter rains come, flow down the river increases; the bar is washed away and steelhead and salmon migrate up the river. In the spring shad join the possession and all these species provide good fishing.

Bass: Floating sections of this river for smallmouth bass produces good catches. Fly anglers cast popper flies to the shoreline and spin casters use floating or diving lures. Spring is the best time to catch these fish.

Catfish: Anglers fishing from shore at night using mackerel, anchovies, chicken or turkey liver or prepared bait catch catfish.

Steelhead: This river, the American and Sacramento Rivers are the only rivers in the greater Bay Area that have sufficient steelhead to recommend fishing. Recent changes listing most steelhead runs in our area as endangered or threatened have created a lot of changes in regulations from year to year. You may fish with only barbless hooks and even if catch-and-keep is permitted, I highly recommend that you release all steelhead. Check the latest regulations specific to each river before fishing.

Shad: Anglers catch shad during their spring run from the end of May through June. Shad swim along the bottom so heavy lures that tick along the bottom catch these fish. Shad darts, teeny rounders or weighted beadhead flies fished on a fast sinking fly line will all catch these fish.

Other Fish: Salmon and striped bass are caught occasionally.

Records: Records have not been kept.

Facilities and Contact: Call King's Sport & Tackle in Guerneville at 707-869-2156 for fishing information, canoe rental and guided trips. Private campgrounds include the Cassini Ranch near Ducan Mills at 707-865-2255. For general information contact the Russian River Visitor's Bureau at 800-253-8800.

Cost: Canoe Rental   About $30.00 per day
       Camping: $15 - $20 per day

Directions to Russian River: Take Highway 101 north from Santa Rosa to Highway 116. Take this exit and turn west to Guerneville. Highway 116 follows the Russian River all the way to Jenner.

Regulations: Below the confluence of the east branch of this river, fishing is open all year except it is subject to temporary closure to trout and salmon fishing when the flow is below 500 cubic feet per minute at Guerneville. Call 707-944-5533 for closure information. When fishing for salmon or steelhead, only barbless hooks may be used. The limit is two salmon or steelhead and the minimum size limit is 8-inches but due to the reduced populations, all steelhead should be released. The limit for bass is five (12-inches minimum length) and there is no limit on sunfish. The river above the east branch and all tributaries of this river are spawning areas for salmon and steelhead and are closed to fishing all year.

2. Spring Lake:

Bass   8
Trout   6
Panfish   5
Catfish   4
After a storm   4
Fly-fishing   5

About Spring Lake: Spring Lake is a 72 acre lake on the outskirts of the city of Santa Rosa and is managed by the Sonoma County Regional Parks Department. Electric motors are permitted and it has a launching ramp. It even has 30 campsites but campers don't get extra fishing time—fishing is permitted only during the day. It has planted trout and panfish but its claim to fame is large bass.

The most exciting catch are large bass with verified fish up to about 15 pounds. Larger ones have been reported but their weights have not been verified.

Bass: Florida largemouth bass have been stocked in this lake and confirmed reports of fish up to about 15 pounds have been made. Scott Green recently caught, weighed and released a 12-pound 5 ounce bass and he tells you how to catch these fish.

Tips from an Expert: "I caught my 12-pound 5 ounce bass on a

Anglers of all ages catch trout at
Bay Area Lakes. The author's father, Ernest, caught this one.

Crappie like this one are an important catch from several warm water lakes in the North Bay Area.

February morning on a one ounce citrus chartreuse Fat-Free Shad lure," says outdoor writer and expert fisherman Scott Green. "The lake was muddy from heavy rains and the fish was in deep water off a shallow point with a deep drop-off. I fished the lure over the deep drop-off with a really slow retrieve, pausing between cranks."

"This lake warms early and bass spawn in March or April. I leave them alone during spawning but fish large trout imitations like a Castaic Lure in deep water drops-offs or over humps before or after the spawn. You have to fish during low light hours, morning or evening to catch these bass."

"If you fish for big bass you may go all day without a bite," Green says. "To catch a number of three to five-pound fish, pitch pig and jigs to heavy cover. Later in the year, weed beds form and a weedless lure like a snag proof frog in white, black or chartreuse will pull bass out of cover. Big fish go down deep as the water warms and then a Carolina rig or jig and pig in deep water or over humps will catch large fish."

Trout: The primary fish is planted trout. Half-pound trout are planted by the DFG once a month from October through May. Power Bait, night crawlers, Kastmasters, Roostertails, and Needlefish are favorite baits and lures.

Other Fish: Small catfish (bullheads), and panfish are also caught from this lake.

Lake Records: Records have not been kept but bass to 15 pounds or larger have been caught.

Facilities and Contact: Spring Lake has a launching ramp, camping, and rental row boats in the summer. For information call Spring Lake 707-539-8092. For county park information, call 707-527-2041.

Cost: Entry and Parking $4.00 per car
       Boat launch   No extra fee
       Boat Rental $10.00 per hour
       Camping $15.00 per day

Directions to Spring Lake: This lake is at the east side of the city of

A young angler shows off a trout caught at Lake Berryessa.

Santa Rosa. Take Highway 12 east from Highway 1 in Santa Rosa and turn right onto Mission Boulevard. Turn right on Mongomery Drive then left on Summerfield Road. Turn right onto Channel Drive, right again onto Violette Road and another right into the park.

Regulations: Fishing is permitted during normal day use times from 7:00 AM to sunset. Limits are five trout, five bass (12-inches minimum length), and no limit on sunfish and bullheads. Only rowboats and electric powered boats are permitted.

3. Lake Ralphine:

Trout	7
Bass	5
After a storm	6
Fly-fishing	3

About Lake Ralphine: Lake Ralphine on the east side of the city of Santa Rosa in Howard Park is an urban lake primarily for general recreation. Its narrow gauge train, carousel, and demonstration farm with petting animals get most of the attention—fishing is secondary. Trout are stocked by DFG and bass, panfish, and catfish are caught. This lake is a small version of Spring Lake and plays second fiddle to this nearby lake when it comes to fishing.

Trout: The DFG stocks this lake with trout in the winter and early spring. For best catches, use Power Bait or night crawlers. Anglers fishing for trout from shore here generally have better success than trout anglers in nearby Spring Lake.

Bass: Bass may be caught here but the serious bass anglers go to Spring Lake where they have a chance for larger bass.

Other Fish: Panfish may be caught on worms or other bait.

Lake Records: Records have not been kept.

Facilities and Contact: This is a day use lake with children's attractions. Fishing is not emphasized. Call Howarth Park 707-543-3282 for information or 707-543-3424 for boat rental.

Cost	Entry and Parking	No Fee
	Boat launch	$2.00
	Boat rental	$6.00 per hour

Directions to Lake Ralphine: This lake is at the east side of the city of Santa Rosa about a mile west of Spring Lake. Take Highway 12 east from Santa Rosa and turn right on Mission Boulevard. Turn right on Montgomery Drive then left on Summerfield Road. Watch for the signs to parking at Lake Ralphine. It is a left turn.

Regulations: Fishing is permitted during normal day use hours from 7:00 AM to sunset. Limits are five trout, five bass (12-inches minimum

length), and no limit on sunfish and bullheads. Only non-powered boats are permitted.

4. Lake Hennessey:

Bass	7
Trout	6
Catfish	6
Panfish	4
After a storm	4
Fly-fishing	5

About Lake Hennessey: This 800 acre lake is a drinking water reservoir for the city of Napa and is managed by that city's water department. DFG plants trout in this lake and it has a good population of largemouth bass with some smallmouth bass, catfish, crappie, and bluegill. Many anglers go right past this lake to get to Lake Berryessa without even knowing this is a good lake for bass and planted trout.

Bass: The number one fish in this lake is largemouth bass. "Fish plastic worms and crank baits in tulles and brush and off points to catch them," suggests Water District Supervisor Rich Bagley. "March and April are the best months to catch these fish."

Trout: Plants of trout by DFG from October through May provide the most reliable fishing. Trolling with needlefish, triple teazers or Rapalas is the most productive; shore anglers catch trout on Power Bait or night crawlers and marshmallows. Plants are made at the boat launch and this is a good area to start fishing.

Other Fish: Some very large catfish inhabit this lake. Bagley knows of a 32-pound cat that was caught there. Catches of catfish peak when runoff stains the water; crappie, and bluegill are also caught in this lake.

Lake Records: Lake records have not been kept but catfish to 32 pounds and bass to about 10 pounds have been caught.

Facilities and Contact: Lake Hennessey has minimal facilities but it does have a boat launch and restrooms. Call the Napa Department of Parks and Recreation at 707-257-9520 for information. Call Sweeney's Sports Store in Napa at 707-255-5544 for fishing information.

Cost	Entry and Parking	No fee
	Daily fishing permit	$1.00 per person
	Boat launch	$4.00 per day

Directions to Lake Hennessey: Take Highway 29 north from Napa through Yountville and on to Rutherford. Turn right (east) on Highway 128 (Rutherford Cross Road) and continue on Highway 128 to the lake. The lake is just north of this highway and the boat launch and public areas are east of the dam.

Regulations: The park is open from one hour before sunrise to one hour after sunset. State DFG regulations apply including limits of five trout, five bass (a minimum of 12-inches in length), 25 crappie, and no limit on sunfish and catfish. This is a drinking water reservoir; boating, and fishing are permitted but all water contact is prohibited and some areas are closed to fishing. Currently outboard motors up to 10 hp are permitted but the trend is to restrict outboards on drinking water reservoirs so check the latest regulations before you launch a boat.

5. Lake Berryessa:

Trout	10
Bass	9
Panfish	8
Catfish	6
After a storm	7
Fly-fishing	5

About Lake Berryessa: Lake Berryessa northeast of Napa and north of Fairfield is a premiere trout and bass lake. This 22 mile long by five mile wide lake has excellent trout fishing from October through May and into June. Bass fishing peaks in the spring from April through June.

Some coves have speed limits but most of the lake has no speed restriction—I've zoomed across this lake at 70 mph when the water was flat calm. That means water skiers and jet skiers are permitted. During the cool months when trout and bass fishing are best, the water is too cold for water skiers, and I have not been bothered by them. Besides, this is a big lake and a few water skiers coexist with anglers fine. In the summer when skiers come out in droves, it is a different story. Early morning fishing is good but then it is time to find a quiet cove or turn the lake over to the high speed users.

All the resorts are on the south and west shore of this lake—the eastern shoreline is private property and is off limits to boaters and anglers.

Trout: Trout are planted in the spring as small six to eight-inch fish. This lake is full of food and trout grow quickly. Deep trollers catch them in the summer but most anglers wait until fall when the lake turns over, sometime during the last half of October. Then these fish are shallow, easy to catch and average 12 to 14-inches long. They have been feeding on natural food for some time, have grown strong, fight hard and jump frequently—almost like wild trout. In another year they will be 14 to 17-inches long and a real prize.

Trout in this lake get their high rating because they are hard fighting, almost wild fish—you will find larger fish in put-and-take lakes.

In the fall through spring, trolling lures shallow is an excellent way to catch trout. Needlefish, Triple Teazers, Cripplures, Rapalas or similar lures trolled in the top 10 or 15-feet of water produce good catches of fish. During the summer, you must troll deep with downriggers, heavy weights or a lot of leadcore line.

Tips from an Expert: I've fished with Joe Ambrulevich many times at Lake Berryessa and I know to follow his lead to catch trout. He fishes here about twice a week in the fall, winter and spring when trout are shallow and fishing is good. "I troll with one to three colors of leadcore line, a 30-foot long leader and a small lure like a Needlefish, Cripplure, or Triple Teazer, Rapala or Rat-L-Trap," Ambrulevich says. "You can catch fish on live minnows under a float or with flashers but troll one of these lures, without flashers, near shore, and you will land more fish most days."

Bass: Bass are ranked high in this lake because it may produce 50 fish or more for a couple of anglers in a day of fishing. While a few very large Florida bass are landed including the 17-pound 8 ounce lake record, most anglers catch a mix of small largemouth and smallmouth bass. Plastic worms, crank baits and plastic jerk baits are very good lures. Minnows are good bait for bass, trout and crappie. April, May and June are the best bass and crappie months.

Tips from an Expert: Jim Munk grew up in Napa and Lake Berryessa was his home lake. He has learned bass fishing here like no one else. "Change your approach as the water temperature changes and you can catch bass here all year," Munk advises. "As water begins to warm early in the spring, look for shallow, stained water in the sun. The darker water absorbs the sun's rays and it will be warmer than nearby water and bass will find that water. Just a degree or two makes a difference and you will

Hal Wilson fishes for bass off a point of Lake Berryessa.

catch fish in that warm water."

"One of the most exciting ways to catch bass here is sight fishing meaning wearing good Polaroid sun glasses and looking for bass on beds. Drop a plastic lure in the middle of its bed and the bass may pick it up in its mouth to move it out of the bed. Set the hook and you will probably have a big fish." It is maddening to see a large fish on a bed only to have it move away and avoid your lure time after time. That's what they do most of the time but when a fish takes your lure and you have a large fish, you know it was worth the frustration.

Catfish: Fish with liver, anchovies or mackerel on a warm summer night to catch catfish.

Crappie: Lake Berryessa has a good population of crappie. Find a partly submerged brush for cover or fish from a dock and you will surely find crappie.

Tips from an Expert: Expert crappie fisherman, retired guide and long time fishing guru of Lake Berryessa Claude Davis has probably caught more crappie from this lake than any other angler. He is in poor health now but when he fished regularly, he used small crappie jigs around docks or brush and could catch a mess of crappie in a few minutes.

"Crappie are my favorite fish," says Claude Davis. "Center the crappie jig before each cast," What he means is to rotate the line on the eye of the hook toward the back of the eye and pull the knot tight. "Let the line hang in mid air and the jig should hang horizontal, not with its tail lower than its head. You will catch twice as many crappie by making this simple adjustment."

When I fished with him for bass and crappie, he caught two, maybe three crappie to every one I caught—he just had the touch. We fished jigs under bobbers above brush piles. "Keep the jig moving slowly," he said as he demonstrated. He moved the float just a few inches and waited a moment for the jig to swing under the float, saw the float move and set the hook—bang he had another one. How does he do that so quickly and consistently?

Lake Records: Bass   17 pounds 8 ounces
Records have not been kept on other species

Facilities and Contact: Seven private resorts and one public launching ramp, at Capell Cove, provide access and services at Lake Berryessa. Most resorts have a bait shop, boat launch, camping, and boat rentals. Steele Park and Putah Creek have lodging. The resorts starting from the north are Putah Creek Resort 707-966-2116; Rancho Monticello Resort 707-966-2188; Berryessa Marina Resort 707-966-2161; Spanish Flat 707-966-2101; Steele Park 707-966-2123; Pleasure Cove Resort 707-966-2172, and Markley Cove 707-966-2134.

Guides: Jim Munk 707-995-0438 guides for bass; Jack Short 707-252-0210 guides and teaches trolling techniques for trout.

Lake Berryessa is 22 miles long and up to 7 miles wide and is the largest lake in the Bay Area.

This boat dock and fishing dock are on Lake Solano.

Cost:	Entry and Parking	Free at Capell Cove
	Daily fishing permit	None required
	Boat launch	Free at Capell Cove
	Boat and motor	About $35 per half day
	Boat only	About $20 per half day
	Camping	About $15 per day

Fees at the private resorts are about $12 per day for entry and boat launching. Some like Spanish Flats waive the entry fee if you rent a boat. Camping adds about $15 per night.

Directions to Lake Berryessa: Take Highway 121 northeast from Napa until it intersects Highway 128. Continue straight to Steel Park Marina or turn right to Markley Cove Marina or Pleasure Cove Resort. Turn left then right on Knoxville Road and follow the signs to the free Capell Cove launching ramp and to the other marinas.

Health Warning: The DFG advises people to limit their consumption of fish caught from Lake Berryessa. Adults are advised to eat no more than 1 to 2 pounds of bass (depending on its size) per month, no more than 3 pounds of catfish and no more than 10 pounds of trout. Children and pregnant women should further reduce consumption of fish from this lake. See the California Sport Fishing Regulations for details.

Regulations: Anglers can fish for all types of fish all day and all night at this lake. The limit is five trout, five bass 12-inches or larger, and 25 crappie. There is no limit on catfish and sunfish.

6. Lake Solano:

Trout	7
Panfish	4
Catfish	3
After a storm	4

About Lake Solano: Five mile long Lake Solano on Putah Creek downriver from the Lake Berryessa Dam is narrow and tree lined looking more like a river than a lake. It receives Department of Fish and Game trout plants all year. It is a water supply and irrigation reservoir and is still-water unless heavy rains make it necessary to release water from Berryessa. Then the Lake Solano Dam overflows and fish and fishing is washed away with the muddy water. Located west of Winters and north of Fairfield this is a multi-use recreational lake and fishing for trout is one of its prime recreational uses.

Trout: Both rainbow and brown trout are planted by the DFG all year and trout fishing is permitted all year. Trout are stocked every week from April through September then plants are made every couple of months through the winter.

One couple I talked with preferred salmon eggs but most anglers use Power Bait or night crawlers. Small lures like Kastmasters cast and retrieved or Needlefish, Cripplures, Triple Teazers, Panther Martins

trolled slowly via rowing are also good. Fishing is permitted from the bridge on Pleasant Valley Road. Anglers bring lawn chairs and sit on the walkway on both sides of this bridge for a day of relaxation and a few trout.

Other Fish: Catfish, panfish, and carp are washed into Lake Solano when water overflows Lake Berryessa. More are caught accidentally when fishing for trout than by anglers going after these fish.

Records: Records have not been kept.

Facilities and Contact: The lake has camping, canoe rentals (summer weekends only) and a launching ramp but motors are prohibited. Small rowboats or canoes are most appropriate here. Contact Lake Solano Park 530-795-2990 or Solano Parks Department 707-447-0707 for information.

Cost:	Day Use	$4 per vehicle
	Canoe rental	$8 per hour
	Camping	$15
	Camping with hook ups	$18

Directions to Lake Solano: Take Interstate 80 northeast from Fairfield to the Cherry Glen Road Exit. Turn north on this road and continue on Pleasant Valley Road. Turn right just before you get to the bridge at Solano Lake for day use parking and picnics. Turn left off Pleasant Valley Road into the campground. Pleasant Valley Road is crooked and slow and has been plagued with delay-causing road repair. An alternate route that is longer but generally quicker is Interstate 80 east to Vacaville then Interstate 505 north to the Winters turnoff (Highway 128), west on this road then left (south) on Pleasant Valley Road.

Regulations: Fishing is permitted all year and the limit is five trout but see Putah Creek regulations for special restrictions on this lake.

7. Putah Creek

Trout	8
Fly-fishing	8

About Putah Creek: Putah Creek northeast of Fairfield is an excellent trout river for fly anglers. Most of the fish are planted rainbow with some brown trout but many have taken up residence and fight like wild trout when hooked. Water flowing into this river comes from the bottom of Lake Berryessa and remains cool and ideal for trout all year.

This creek flows from Monticello Dam that holds back waters to form Lake Berryessa to Lake Solano and is only a few miles long. When the lake overflows Lake Berryessa or sometimes during the heavy flows during the spring irrigation season, water may come through here in torrents and wash out all fishing. But in the winter it has a gentle flow and is the premier catch and release fly-fishing river in the Greater Bay Area. From mid-November through April only catch and release fishing is permitted but five trout may be kept during other times of the year.

Trout: This is primarily fly-fishing for trout during the winter and spring

Lake Solano is just a wide spot on Putah Creek.

A young angler shows off a trout he landed from
the Lake Solano Bridge.

months. Use black or brown woolly buggers, prince nymphs, pheasant tail nymphs, or green damsels. Mike Maloney found a number size 12 or 14 Caddis Pupa fly tied with sparkle yarn was so effective, he fished it all year at Putah Creek. He fished the rapids casting upstream using a split shot when he needed it to get the fly down to the bottom, added an indicator and caught fish up to about 22-inches.

Casts can be short and some sections are best fished using a high stick method where the length of line is about equal to the length of the fly rod. Weighted flies are washed down the river, around rocks and anglers must be very alert to set the hook as soon as the fly stops. The take is subtle and a trout's take may be mistaken for a snag or natural line movement in swirling water. Anglers who have perfected this method seem to pull a trout out from behind every rock in the creek.

Records: Records have not been kept.
Facilities and Contact: Camp at Solano Lake County Park off Pleasant Valley Road. Motels and services are in Winters four miles east or in Vacaville and Fairfield south on Highway 80. For information call Lake Solano Park at 707-795-2990. A Thousand Trails Campground on this creek is open only to members of that organization.

Cost: Entry and Parking $5 in prepared parking area, no fee to park along the road
           Camping fees $15 to $18 at Solano Park

Directions to Putah Creek: Take Interstate 80 northeast from Fairfield to the Cherry Glen Road Exit. Turn north on this road and continue on Pleasant Valley Road. Cross Solano Lake and turn left on Highway 128 (Pleasant Valley Road ends at this road) to find parking and fishing access. An alternate route is Interstate 80 east to Vacaville then Interstate 505 north to the Winters turn off (Highway 128) and west on this road beyond Solano Lake.

Regulations: Putah Creek is open to catch and keep fishing from the last Saturday in April through November 15. The limit is five trout. From November 16 through the Friday preceding the last Saturday in April, only fishing with artificial lures with barbless hooks is permitted and you must release all trout you catch. Fishing is allowed from one hour before sunup to one hour after sunset.

8. Petaluma River:

Catfish	6
Sturgeon	2
After a storm	3

About Petaluma River: The best fishing on the Petaluma River is near its mouth where it enters the San Pablo Bay. Sturgeon fishing there can be very good but that is a saltwater story and is covered in the North San Pablo Bay section of this book. Upriver fishing is primarily catfish and panfish.

Fishing: Angers have a chance at a variety of fish including catfish, black bass, striped bass, sturgeon and panfish. Fishing at night with mackerel, anchovies, clams or chicken liver are the best ways to catch catfish.
Records: Records have not been kept.
Facilities and Contact: Launching on this river is at Petaluma Marina at 781 Baywood Drive in Petaluma (707) 778-4489. Motels and restaurants are found throughout Petaluma.

Cost: Boat launch $10
Directions to Petaluma River Launch: Take Highway 116 east from Highway 101 in Petaluma. Turn right on Marina Avenue to the Petaluma Marina.
Regulations: Limits are one sturgeon between 46 and 72-inches total length, five bass 12-inches minimum length, two striped bass at least 18-inches long and no limit on catfish or panfish.

9. Napa River:

Catfish	3
Sturgeon	2
After a storm	2

About Napa River: The best fishing on the Napa River is near its mouth in Vallejo where sturgeon, striped bass, flounder and other saltwater and brackish water fish may be landed. But that is a saltwater story and is covered in the Bays section of this book. Upriver fishing has deteriorated from poor water quality. Neglect of the water quality and the resulting loss of fish makes this a poor fishing choice. Efforts to cleanup this river have begun so fishing should improve if this clean up is successful.
Fishing: Fishing in the upper river is poor but sturgeon and striped bass may be caught at the mouth of the river including the pier in the city of

Plastic baits take the majority of bass landed
in this area but crank baits like these also produce fish.

Kids of all ages catch bluegill like this one or other panfish in most lakes in the Bay Area.

Vallejo.

Records: Records have not been kept.

Facilities and Contact: This river has several launching ramps from Vallejo (see the Bay section for directions to this ramp) and upriver south of the city of Napa. One launch is the Cutting Wharf Launch southwest of Napa.

Directions to Napa River: The Cutting Wharf Ramp is west of Napa on Highway 12 then south on Cuttings Wharf Road.

Regulations: Limits are one sturgeon between 46 and 72-inches total length, five bass 12-inches minimum length, two striped bass at least 18-inches long and no limit on catfish or panfish.

10. Soulajule Reservoir:

Bass	6
Crappie	6
Catfish	5
Trout	4

About Soulajule Reservoir: This lake has good bass fishing as well as catfish and panfish. Large, wild, hard fighting resident trout are in the lake but few are caught. What Soulajule Reservoir lacks is facilities—it doesn't even have parking but anglers can park by the dam and hike a short distance to fish the lake. Its water clears slowly after a rain so inquire locally before making a trip to fish here—you may be wasting your time.

This is one of eight reservoirs managed by the Marin Municipal Water District (MMWD). All prohibit water contact sports including boats and float tubes though management is considering allowing float tubes. Angling is from shore and is very limited. Some lakes have good bass fishing but restricting anglers to shore fishing makes catching them difficult. They also have a few resident trout that are great fighting fish but are rarely caught. A couple of these lakes (not Soulajule) are stocked by the DFG with typical pan sized trout and that produces reliable fishing for small fish. One, Laganitas Lake, is a catch and release fishery where

anglers have decent fishing for larger trout using artificial lures with barbless hooks. If you are a fly-fisher, this is the place to fish.

Bass: Bass at Soulajule are mostly small but several can be caught when the water is clear. Try crank baits that imitate crawfish or plastic worms or red colored lizards (another crayfish imitation) fished on a Texas style rig. A sliding-bullet-sinker on the line provides weight and the plastic lure is rigged weedless by imbedding the point of the hook into the body of the bait.

Crappie: This is the best crappie fishing lake in Marin County but it is not up to the best crappie lakes like Berryessa. You can catch them spring and fall using white, yellow or black crappie jigs but fishing with minnows under a bobber is the best way to catch crappie.

Other Fish: Catfish are also caught on mackerel, anchovies, clams, chicken liver, or prepared bait. Other panfish go for small bits of worm on a small hook fished under a bobber.

Lake Records: Records have not been kept at this lake.

Facilities and Contact: This lake has no facilities, not even parking. Contact the North Marin Municipal Water District at 415-897-4133 for information.

Cost: Entry is Free

Directions to Soulajule Reservoir: Go north on Highway 1 to the San Marin exit in Novato. Turn left (west) to Novato Boulevard and follow this street west (right) to its end; turn right on Petaluma Road then left on Wilson Hill Road. Turn left onto Marshall Petaluma Road then turn left onto Arroyo Sausal Road to the lake. Park at the base of the dam then hike to the lake.

Regulations: Fishing is permitted all year. The limit is five bass a minimum of 12-inches long, five trout and no limit on catfish and panfish. Boats, float tubes and any body contact with the water in this lake is prohibited.

11. Novato Creek:

Trout	6
Fly-fishing	4

About Novato Creek: If your idea of trout fishing is a cool brook, reading the water, looking for pockets or riffles where you will find trout, this kind of fishing is very limited in the Bay Area. But this creek west of the town of Novato stocked with trout by DFG during the summer gives you an opportunity for this type fishing. Plants are made in public parks so access is easy—you can park and fish in the park.

Trout: The DFG stocks this stream with trout during the spring and early summer. Fish from Miwok Park or Ohair Park. Trout can be caught by fly anglers but most are caught on Power Bait, salmon eggs or worms.

"Novato Creek is a favorite fishing area of many of my students," reports outdoor writer and school teacher at Hill Middle School in

A deep diving crank bait like this
will catch bass as they begin to move deeper in a lake.

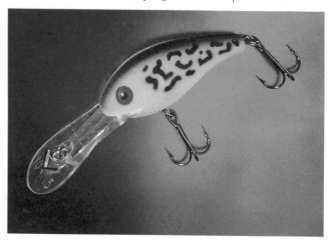

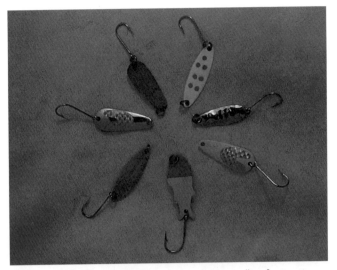
Several small lures are effective attractors trolling for trout.

Novato, Don Vachini. "It isn't a wild trout stream but offers students and local anglers a good chance to catch trout." Plants start with a kids' fishing derby in the spring when the creek conditions are right and continues with plants every couple of weeks as long as the water remains cool. Vachini says the creek is well shaded where the plants are made so the water remains cool; plants continue through most of July, and trout are caught into August.

Records: Records have not been kept—all of the fish are small.

Facilities and Contact: Call the City of Novato Chamber of Commerce at 415-897-1164 for information.

Cost: There is no entry or fishing fee.

Directions to Novato Creek: Follow Highway 1 north to the San Marin exit in Novato. Go west to Novato Boulevard. Miwok Park is left on Novato Boulevard and undeveloped Ohair Park is across Novato Boulevard on Sutro Avenue.

Regulations: The limit is two trout and fishing is permitted the last Saturday in April through November 15.

12. Stafford Lake:

Bass	6
Panfish	4

About Stafford Lake: This MMWD drinking water reservoir west of Novato is a developed lake with a county park on its shores. Fishing is just one of many uses with playgrounds at the park and even a private golf course. It has easy fishing access to part, but not all of the lake. "This lake is a good largemouth bass lake but the best structure in the lake is on private property," says outdoor writer Don Vachini who lives nearby and fishes this lake. "Anglers fish from shore but water contact including boats and float tubes are not allowed— anglers have no way of getting to the best fishing spots."

Bass: Florida strain bass are being emphasized with the goal of developing a trophy bass fishery. So far, bass weighing up to about eight pounds have been landed and new lake record bass are caught almost every year. Use plastic grubs, plastic baitfish imitations or crank baits to catch them during the day or fish top water lures like Zara Spooks or poppers like Pop-Rs in the morning and evening. To avoid introduction of undesirable species, live bait is prohibited. Bass can be caught all year but the best fishing dates are when they spawn in March and April.

Other Fish: Redear sunfish are the other notable fish. They have been stocked as food for the bass but make a good catch on worms.

Lake Records: Records have not been kept.

Facilities and Contact: This lake is part of a county park with parking, picnic sites and restrooms. Contact the Stafford Lake Park at 415-897-

0618 or the North Marin Municipal Water District at 415-897-4133 for information.

Cost: Entry and Parking $5.00 per car

Directions to Stafford Lake: Drive north on Highway 1 to the San Marin exit in Novato. Go west to Novato Boulevard, make a right turn and continue on this road to Lake Stafford on the south side of the road.

Regulations: Fishing is permitted all year from one hour before sunrise to one hour after sunset. The park is open from 7:00 AM to 8:00 PM in the summer and from 8:00 AM to 5:00 PM in the winter. Early anglers can park near the gate and make a short hike to the lake. The limit is five bass a minimum of 12-inches long, twenty-five crappie and no limit on catfish and panfish. Boats, float tubes and any body contact with the water in this lake is prohibited.

13. Nicasio Reservoir:

Bass	6
Catfish	6
Crappie	5
Fly-fishing	4

About Nicasio Reservoir: A number of lakes managed by the MMWD collect rainwater running off the hills and are the source of water for most of Marin County. Nicasio Reservoir at the north edge of this county is the largest of the Marin County lakes with a surface area of 825 acres. It has minimal facilities and boats and water contact sports are not permitted.

Bass: This is one of the best bass lakes in the area for small bass. Boats and float tubes are prohibited so anglers may only fish from shore. Fish with top water lures like Pop-R's in the morning and evenings and with plastic worms or crank baits during the day.

Other Fish: This is one of the best catfish lakes (arguably the best) in Marin County. Crappie are also caught in the spring and fall.

Lake Records: Records have not been kept.

Facilities and Contact: Call the Marin Municipal Water District 415-924-4600 for information. For a recorded detailed planting and fishing report, call 415-459-0888. For camping reservations at nearby Samuel P. Taylor State Park call 800-444-7275.

Cost: Entry and Parking   No Fee
        Camping $16 at Samuel P. Taylor State Park

Directions to Nicasio Reservoir: From the San Francisco area go north on Highway 101 through Corte Madera and take the Sir Francis Drake Boulevard west. Go through the town of Woodacre and turn right (north) on Nicasio Valley Road to the lake. From the East Bay, cross the Richmond San Rafael Bridge and take the Sir Francis Drake Boulevard exit (which is also the Highway 101 south exit). Follow the above directions turning right on Nicasio Valley Road to the lake.

Regulations: Fishing is permitted all year from one hour before sunrise to one hour after sunset. The limit is five bass a minimum of 12-inches long, five trout and no limit on catfish and panfish. Boats, float tubes and any body contact with the water in this lake is prohibited.

14. Kent Lake:

Bass	6
Trout	4

About Kent Lake: This long, narrow, deep, MMWD lake should be a great fishing lake. It is a pretty destination but the hassle getting to the lake rules it out as a fishing lake for most anglers. Access to many of the lakes in Marin County is limited but getting to Kent Lake is really a challenge. You must hike about a half mile from the nearest parking to get to the rim of lake then scramble down into a canyon through thick chaparral to get to the lake. What's more, after you fight your way through to a fishing spot on the lake, you may not be able to move along the shoreline because brush right at the water's edge blocks your path.

Bass: This lake has big largemouth bass. Fishing access is difficult but it is worth the effort for the hearty angler. Anglers who make the trek have a decent chance at a four to five pound bass and could catch a larger one.

Many lakes in Marin County prohibit boating and float tubes. Anglers fishing from shore catch trout.

Fall is a good time to fish this lake because the water level is below the trees surrounding the lake and you can move around the lake on exposed dirt banks. Crank baits like Rebels, Rapalas, Rat-L-Traps and Wiggle Warts along with plastic baits are good choices here.

Trout: Large Coleman Strain trout and some steelhead trapped when the dam was built are caught. They are great wild trout but are caught only occasionally. Even a catch of one trout in a day is not to be taken lightly. Minnows or night crawlers are top baits for these wild trout.

Lake Records: Records have not been kept.

Facilities and Contact: Call the Marin Municipal Water District 415-924-4600 for information. For recorded details of recent plantings and fishing report, call 415-459-0888. For general fishing information, call the Western Sport Shop at 415-456-5454. For camping reservations at Samuel P. Taylor State Park call 800-444-7275.

Cost: Entry and Parking   No Charge
          Camping $16 at Samuel P. Taylor State Park

Directions to Kent Lake: From the south go north on Highway 101 through Corte Madera and take the Sir Francis Drake Boulevard west. Just beyond the town of Laganitas turn left to Kent Lake. From the East Bay, cross the Richmond San Rafael Bridge and take the Sir Francis Drake Boulevard exit (which is also the Highway 101 south exit). Stay on this boulevard to the turn off to Kent Lake. After parking at the trailhead, a hike to the lake followed by a difficult hike through trees and underbrush make this suitable only for the healthy and hardy angler.

Regulations: Fishing is permitted all year from one hour before sunrise to one hour after sunset. The limit is five bass a minimum of 12-inches long, five trout, and no limit on catfish and panfish. Boats, float tubes and any body contact with the water in this lake is prohibited.

15. Alpine Lake:

Bass	6
Trout	5
Fly-fishing	4

About Alpine Lake: A number of lakes clustered around Mt. Tamalpais collect rainwater running off the hills and are the primary source of water for most of Marin County. Alpine Lake, downstream from Bon Tempe and Laganitas Lake has more than 200 surface acres when it is full. Bass fishing particularly just below the dam of Bon Tempe Reservoir is the most accessible and the best fishing on this lake.

This is one of the most picturesque areas in the Bay Area. You may want to take a morning from fishing to climb to the top of Mt. Tam (as locals call it). You are rewarded with a 360 degree view including the Golden Gate and Oakland Bay Bridges, San Francisco, the East Bay and its cities, and Point Reyes. On a clear day you can see the Farallon Islands looming up in the ocean about 30 miles distant.

Trout: Fingerling trout are planted by the DFG so trout fishing is dependent on these fish growing to catchable size. Fishing here is slow but you trade off quantity of catch (not many are caught) against quality of catch (these are hard fighting like wild fish).

Tips from an Expert: "I have caught some large trout by hiking to the Swede George and Van Wych Creek coves in January," reports v. "A night crawler fished under a bobber has been my best fishing method here."

Bass: Fish the upper end of this lake just below the Bon Tempe Reservoir Dam for smallmouth bass. Night crawlers or plastic grubs are two good baits for them. A one to two pound fish is typical but a few will be larger.

Lake Records: Records have not been kept.

Facilities and Contact: Call the Marin Municipal Water District 415-924-4600 or the Sky Oaks Ranger Station at 415-459-5267 for information. For a summary of recent plantings and a fishing report, call 415-459-0888. For fishing information, call the Western Sport Shop at 415-456-5454.

Cost: Entry and Parking $5.00 per car

Directions to Alpine Lake: From the south go north on Highway 101 through Corte Madera and take the Sir Francis Drake Boulevard west. At Fairfax turn left onto Bank Road then make a right onto the Fairfax Bolinas Road. Make a left onto Sky Oaks Road. Stop at the Sky Oaks Ranger Station for information and get final directions to this lake. From the East Bay, cross the Richmond San Rafael Bridge and take the Sir Francis Drake Boulevard exit (which is also the Highway 101 south exit). Follow the above directions to this lake.

Regulations: Fishing is permitted all year from one hour before sunrise to one hour after sunset. The limit is five bass a minimum of 12-inches long, five trout and no limit on catfish and panfish. Boats, float tubes, and any body contact with the water in this lake is prohibited.

16. Bon Tempe Lake:

Trout	7
Bass	3
Panfish	4
After a storm	5
Fly-fishing	3

About Bon Tempe Lake: This 144 acre drinking water reservoir is operated by the Marin Municipal Water District as a put-and-take trout lake and is one of the two best trout lakes in the area. Located on the Laganitas Creek, it is downstream from Laganitas Lake and upstream from Alpine Lake. Laganitas Lake controls the flow into Bon Tempe Lake so this lake clears and is suitable for trout soon after a rain.

Trout: Trout are planted by the DFG from the end of October or the first of November to Memorial Day weekend. That means good catchable 10 to 12-inch trout but not many larger fish. Green Power Bait has been the hot bait recently but any bait seems to lose its effectiveness over time—try different colors of Power Bait or night crawlers to find what fish are

Smallmouth bass like this one are caught in many Bay Area Lakes.

currently hitting.

Other Fish: Bass and panfish are caught occasionally but here you should concentrate on trout if you want to catch fish.

Tips from an Expert: "Work Kastmasters or rooster tail lures the first two or three days after a trout plant then switch to bait—PowerBait or worms," suggests Dick Murdock outdoor writer for the Marin Independent Journal.

Lake Records: Records have not been kept.

Facilities and Contact: Call the Marin Municipal Water District 415-924-4600 or the Sky Oaks Ranger Station at 415-459-5267. For a summary of recent plantings and a fishing report, call 415-459-0888. For fishing information, call the Western Sport Shop at 415-456-5454.

Cost: Entry and Parking $5.00 per car

Directions to Bon Tempe Lake: From the south go north on Highway 101 through Corte Madera and take the Sir Francis Drake Boulevard west. At Fairfax turn left onto Bank Road then make a right onto the Fairfax Bolinas Road. Make a left onto Sky Oaks Road. Stop at the Sky Oaks Ranger Station for information and get final directions to this lake. From the East Bay, cross the Richmond San Rafael Bridge and take the Sir Francis Drake Boulevard exit (which is also the Highway 101 south exit). Follow the above directions to this lake.

Regulations: Fishing is permitted in this lake all year during daylight hours. The limit is five trout, five bass (a minimum of 12-inches long), 25 crappie, and no limit on catfish and sunfish. Boats, float tubes, and body contact with the water in this lake is prohibited.

17. Lagunitas Lake:

Trout 7
Fly-fishing 6

About Lagunitas Lake: This 23 acre lake, the smallest of the MMWD lakes, has periodic plants of trout; then they are allowed to grow and become wild fish. Periodic in this case may mean every two or three years. It is a catch and release fishery for trout (actually two trout less than

14-inches in length may be kept but most anglers release their fish); bait is prohibited, and only barbless hooks may be used. This shallow lake has an oxygen generator to provide oxygen deep in the lake where the water is cool to help trout survive through the warm summer months.

"This is the best place to catch large trout in Marin County," reports Dick Murdock, outdoor writer for the Marin Independent Journal newspaper. "But if anglers want to take fish home, they should go to put-and-take lakes like Bon Tempe just downstream from this lake."

Trout: This is an excellent lake for fly-fishing using flies like Prince Nymphs, olive leeches or black or brown woolly buggers. Many of the fish caught have been here for some time and fight like wild fish.

Lake Records: Records have not been kept.

Facilities and Contact: Call the Marin Municipal Water District 415-924-4600 or the Sky Oaks Ranger Station at 415-459-5267. For a summary of recent plantings and a fishing report, call 415-459-0888. For fishing information, call the Western Sport Shop at 415-456-5454.

Cost: Entry and Parking $5.00 per car

Directions to Lagunitas Lake: From the south go north on Highway 101 through Corte Madera and take the Sir Francis Drake Boulevard west. At Fairfax turn left onto Bank Road then make a right onto the Fairfax Bolinas Road. Make a left onto Sky Oaks Road. Stop at the Sky Oaks Ranger Station for information and get final directions to this lake. From the East Bay, cross the Richmond San Rafael Bridge and take the Sir Francis Drake Boulevard exit (which is also the Highway 101 south exit). Follow the above directions to this lake.

Regulations: Fishing is permitted all year from about sunup to sundown. Anglers may use only artificial lures with barbless hooks; the limit is two trout and any trout more than 14-inches long must released. Fishing is not permitted in Lagunitas Creek or its tributaries. Boats, float tubes, and body contact with the water in this lake is prohibited.

18. Phoenix Lake

Trout 6
Bass 7

About Phoenix Lake: This MMWD reservoir has planted trout and bass. Though most anglers fish for the former, Florida Largemouth Bass planted in 1988 are the most exciting fish. Bass up to about 12 pounds have been landed.

Trout: Trout are planted by the DFG from the end of October to about Memorial Day weekend. That means catchable 10 to 12-inch trout but few larger trout. Use lures like Kastmasters or rooster tail lures right after a plant then switch to Power Bait or worms.

Bass: This lake produces some of the largest Bass in Marin County. Restrictions on body contact—even float tubes makes this a shore fishery only. Try plastic worms rigged Texas Style or crawfish imitation crank baits.

Lake Records: Records have not been kept—trout are small but occasionally a large bass (reports have been made of bass up to about 12 pounds) is landed.

Facilities and Contact: Call the Marin Municipal Water District 415-924-4600 or the Sky Oaks Ranger Station at 415-459-5267. For a summary of recent plantings and a fishing report, call 415-459-0888 and for fishing information call Western Sport Shop at 415-456-5454.

Cost: Entry and Parking $5.00 per car

Directions to Phoenix Lake: From the south go north on Highway 101 through Corte Madera and take the Sir Francis Drake Boulevard west. In Ross turn left onto the Lagunitas Road. Continue straight ahead onto Diblee Road to the lake. From the East Bay, cross the Richmond San Rafael Bridge and take the Sir Francis Drake Boulevard exit (which is also the Highway 101 south exit). Follow the above directions to this lake.

Regulations: Fishing is permitted all year from one hour before sunrise to one hour after sunset. The limit is five trout, five bass (a minimum of 12-inches long), 25 crappie, and no limit on catfish and sunfish. Boats, float tubes, and body contact with the water in this lake are prohibited.

CHAPTER 5:

San Francisco Peninsula and East Bay

Most of the largest trout caught in the Bay Area are taken from East Bay and San Francisco Peninsula lakes. The reason large fish are caught from these lakes is no mystery—stocking trucks bring large trout. I suppose anglers can lament the fact that these are not wild fish. A five-pound stocked trout makes a poor comparison to a five-pound wild trout—but the plants are big, strong, healthy, powerful fish and catching them is no sure thing. Some anglers who have fished these lakes for years have yet to catch their first five-pound or better trout so it is still a challenge and a worthy accomplishment to land one of these large fish.

San Pablo Reservoir, Lake Chabot, Shadow Cliffs Reservoir, Del Valle Reservoir, Contra Loma Reservoir, Lafayette Reservoir in the East Bay Area and Lake Merced in the San Francisco Area account for most of the largest trout.

Trout are the primary fish for most anglers but a number of devotees are on the water for bass and find excellent bass fishing. The largest bass

Anglers tie their boats to tulles and bait fish to catch large trout at Lake Merced.

in the area are in San Pablo Reservoir and Lake Chabot. Frequent plants of trout are key to good bass fishing in both lakes. These stocked fish aren't attuned to predators and aren't able to escape a large bass so bass thrive and grow large eating planted trout.

Lake Chabot seems to produce mostly large fish. East Bay Regional Parks fisheries specialist Pete Alexander suggests the environment is very competitive for small bass but once they reach a size too large to be threatened by most predators such as trout, panfish and larger bass—they flourish and quickly grow very large.

Catfish take over from trout as the prime fish as lakes warm in the spring and summer. Landlocked striped bass in Lake Del Valle and Contra Loma Reservoir offer a real trophy fishery. Occasionally a landlocked sturgeon is caught from San Pablo Reservoir though they haven't been planted for many years. One was caught and released in Lafayette Reservoir even though this lake is not known to have sturgeon and nobody seems to know how it got in the lake.

Not every lake or river that holds fish is included in this book. Lakes that are included are either a place serious anglers go to fish or a children's fishing lake. Some lakes like Lower Crystal Springs Reservoir, San Andreas Lake on the San Francisco Peninsula and Briones Reservoir in the East Bay look like great fishing lakes but are closed to all fishing. A new urban water reservoir, Los Vaqueros, southeast of Walnut Creek has been completed and will soon be full. Fishing piers and a boat launch ramp are to be opened on this lake in the year 2000. This lake is primarily a drinking water reservoir managed by the Contra Costa Municipal Water District. They have decided to permit fishing from shore, from fishing piers and from boats but ban all gasoline powered motors and prohibit water contact sports in the lake.

Regulations: A summary of the regulations in effect as this book goes to press is included with each section but fishing regulations change and these may not be current. Read the California Sport Fishing Regulations (obtained free wherever fishing licenses are sold) for complete information and to learn of recent changes to regulations. Brochures at many of the lakes and parks give fishing regulations and limits.

1. Lake Merced:

Trout	9
Bass	6
Catfish	7
After a storm	8
Fly-fishing	1

About Lake Merced: Lake Merced is actually two lakes at the southwest corner of San Francisco. The northern lake has trophy trout and the southern lake has bass and small trout. Anglers pay a daily fishing fee at each lake but the one for the south lake is cheaper. Both the DFG and the concessionaire plant trout. The latter plants are large trout all greater than two-pounds and include four to five-pound or larger trout. Cormorants are a big problem eating many of the smaller DFG trout but the large concessionaire fish are too large for these birds. These lakes are ground water lakes off Skyline Boulevard just a few hundred yards from the ocean. They are cool all year so get trout plants every month and other fish are strictly secondary to trout. These lakes just get local runoff so stay clear and anglers catch trout right after a storm.

Trout: Trout are large in the north lake—the best fishing of the two lakes. One day you may not catch anything and a few days later you may land limits of three-pound or larger trout. Bait fishing is the way to catch trout here. I've tried trolling and this lake is so full of organic matter, my hook was fouled every time I trolled a few yards. Lures with fouled hooks, even with one small strand of weed, don't catch fish. Fly anglers pick up the dispersed vegetation as well and fly-fishing isn't very successful.

Tips from an Experts: "Use a two hook leader with one hook on a leg about 10-inches long and the other about 24-inches long," says Dave Lyons, a senior citizen angler who is the fishing authority at these lakes. He ties and sells leaders at the concessionaire stand but says anglers can easily tie their own. "Bait both hooks with Power Bait, cast out into the lake and wait for a bite. You are fishing at two levels and catch fish cruising the bottom and the ones that are up a couple of feet." Lyons recommends four-pound test line and six-pound test Maxima leader. His rig is good for bait fishing at all lakes that have trout.

Bass: Bass are not a major species at these lakes but some are caught including some large ones. The largest bass to come from Lake Merced was caught on Power Bait in the south lake. Guess what the angler was after. Some large catfish are also landed.

Lake Records:
Trout	17-pounds 8-ounces
Bass	12-pounds 12-ounces
Catfish	25-pounds 8-ounces

Facilities and Contact: The permanent boathouse burned in 1997 and a temporary facility replaced that structure. Anglers can launch small boats at the boat ramp or rent a boat with an electric motor. Call the concessionaire at 415-753-1101 for information.

Special Programs: One day basic fishing classes are taught frequently. Call the concessionaire for the schedule of classes. Big fish derbies are held a couple of times a year.

Cost:
Entry and Parking	Free
Daily fishing permit	$4.00 North Lake; $0.95 South Lake.
Boat launch	$5.00
Boat	$21.00 per half day
Boat and electric motor	$30.00 per half day
Senior boat and motor	$15.00 per half day (weekdays)

Directions to Lake Merced: Lake Merced is at the southwest boundary of the city of San Francisco south of the zoo and at the entrance to Harding Park. From the south, take Highway 1, turning left onto Skyline Boulevard (Highway 35) south of San Francisco. Make a right turn onto Harding Road to the boathouse on the right. From the west take Interstate 280 south to Daly City and turn right (west) onto Alemany Boulevard. This street deadends into Skyline Boulevard. Turn right onto Skyline Boulevard then turn right on Harding Road to the boathouse.

Regulations: Fishing is permitted during the day year around. The limit is five trout, five bass (12-inch minimum length) and no limit on catfish. A valid state fishing license and daily fishing permit are required. Only electric motors are allowed.

Few lakes have sturgeon but this one was landed from San Pablo Reservoir.

Anglers land a trout from San Pablo Reservoir.

2. San Pablo Reservoir:

Bass	9
Trout	9
Catfish	8
Panfish	7
Sturgeon	2
After a storm	4
Fly-fishing	7

About San Pablo Reservoir: A few years ago San Pablo Reservoir was the place to catch trout in the Bay Area. Now many other lakes have copied their formula for trout fishing success and compete with this reservoir. The formula is to charge a daily fishing fee, spend the money to plant trout like crazy and include lunker trout in every load. Anglers usually catch fish and always know they have a chance for a five to ten-pound trout—even an outside chance at one from 15 to 20-pounds.

This lake also has excellent bass fishing including an occasional very large Florida Bass weighing more than 17-pounds. It has excellent fishing for catfish (thanks to deliveries by the fish farm truck) and very large resident catfish. It produces good crappie, some sunfish and anglers occasionally land a sturgeon from plantings made several years ago.

This lake is a drinking water reservoir and two cycle motors are to be prohibited in January 2000 and all gasoline powered motors are to be banned in 2002. Electric motors will still be permitted. These regulations are just being approved so check before you plan to use your boat to see if these effective dates or policies have changed.

San Pablo Reservoir is a wildfowl refuge during the winter months so is closed to fishing and boating from mid-November to mid-February. This lake clears slowly so it is often muddy from heavy winter rains when it opens in February and doesn't completely clear until the rains subside. Fishing can be excellent when it opens in February, particularly for anglers using bait, or it can be muddy and difficult fishing if it has been a wet winter. Its water remains cool during the summer and it is planted with trout all year. Good trout fishing continues throughout the summer but trout are deep and anglers use downriggers or other means to troll deep to catch them.

Bass fishing is excellent in the spring starting as early as March and continuing into the summer. Catfish are caught whenever the lake is open but they are planted in the summer and most are caught during the warmer months. The best crappie catches are made in May, September and October.

Bass: This lake is one of the best bass fishing lakes in the area and some anglers come here two or three times a week just to fish for large bass. In most years, a few bass weighing more than 15-pounds are caught—in 1995 two bass weighing more than 16-pounds were landed from this lake and the lake record bass weighed more than 17-pounds. These are planted

A boat ramp is suitable to launch small boats at Contra Loma Reservoir.

Florida Bass that have become resident in this lake and planting of these fish continues. Niel Nielsen, retired lake manager, said small Florida Bass were food for other fish and the dollars spent turned out to be very expensive feed—not a good investment. So Nielsen purchased 10-inch Florida Bass for about $40 for each fish. These have a good chance of surviving and some of them grow to the 16 or 17-pound trophy bass.

Plastic baits and pig and jigs are primary attractors for these fish. They are also caught on spinner baits and crank baits. Some are invariably caught by anglers trolling for trout or on worms and even Power Bait. The coves on the northeast side of the lake and Scow Canyon have good bass fishing but one of the best places for bass is the wildlife preserve at the south end of the lake. Only electric motors may be used in the preserve area.

Tips from an Expert: Kevin Bacon who has landed several double digit bass from this lake suggests bass anglers use plastic worms or spinner baits. "The preserve at the south end of the lake is good for large bass but there are spots all around the lake that produce large bass," Bacon said. He advises bass anglers to spend lots of time fishing in the spring. The largest fish are often caught in March, April and May.

Trout: This lake is planted by the concessionaire as often as three times a week with a thousand or more pounds of trout including some whopper-sized fish in every load. The Department of Fish and Game plants smaller half pound size fish every couple of weeks during the fishing season. When the water is clear and fishing is good, San Pablo Reservoir is the equal of any put-and-take lake in the Bay Area for trout.

A great time to catch trout here is after its water has cooled starting sometime in October. The lake is closed to fishing from mid-November to mid-February. Unless we have had a break in the rains when it reopens, the lake is usually muddy and most trout are caught on bait. Cheese is a good bait when the lake is dirty but Power Bait and night crawlers are better as the lake clears. Then anglers trolling begin to score well and may catch as many or more trout than bait fishers. Summer is good but trout are deeper and anglers need a means to get their lure or bait deep to the fish, typically 15 to 30 feet deep. Downrigger, leadcore line, weights, diving planes or heavy lures are required for successful trolling.

Tips from an Expert: Niel Nielsen, the number one catcher of whopper trout from this lake with more than 40 five to 15-pound trout caught in one year, advises trollers to, "Slow down then go slower." He recommends a fire tiger Rapala or similar lure fished on 70 feet of six-pound test line during the cool months. During the summer months when the lake is warm and trout are deep, he fishes a lure off a downrigger. "You will probably catch more fish on small lures like Needlefish, Triple Teazers, Dick Nites and Cripplures," Nielsen advises, "but you catch more large fish on Rapala type lures."

Catfish: Catfish are planted in the spring of the year. They survive well in the lake and are caught all year even though they are only planted during the warm months. For large catfish, this is one of the two or three best lakes in the area.

Other Fish: Crappie are caught spring and fall. April and October are good months but these fish are cyclical and a couple of good years may be followed by two or three years when they almost disappear. We have just had a couple of good years so they are due for a lull. This lake also has an occasional sturgeon, a remnant of a plant several years ago. It also has carp that are large and pull hard. Few people fish for them but they are caught occasionally when fishing for other species.

Special Programs: The lake has a whopper program for trout weighing more than five-pounds, for bass weighing more than eight-pounds and for catfish weighing more than 10-pounds. On a good week, 25 or more whoppers may be landed and the angler who catches each is awarded a hat or a mug with the words San Pablo Reservoir Whopper.

Lake Records:		
	Trout	16-pounds 6-ounces
	Bass	17-pounds 3-ounces
	Catfish	31-pounds 5-ounces
	Sturgeon	62-pounds
	Crappie	2-pounds 4-ounces
	Redear	3-pounds 6-ounces

Facilities and Contact: San Pablo Reservoir has a good eight-lane boat launching ramp with docks at the south end of the lake. The main recreation area at the north end of the lake has a bait shop, boat rentals, a restaurant and a fishing pier with wheelchair access. All the facilities are first rate; the boats are clean and in good condition; the motors on the rental boats usually start on the first pull and the employees are friendly and helpful. The concessionaire is The Dam Company at 510-223-7413.

Cost:		
	Entry and Parking	$5.00 per car
	Daily fishing permit	$3.00 per person
	Boat launch	$5.00 per day
	Boat and motor	$33.00 per half day
	Boat only	$21.00 per half day
	Senior boat and motor	$16.50 per half day (Weekdays)

Directions to San Pablo Reservoir: Take Highway 24 west from Walnut Creek or east from Oakland to Orinda and take the Orinda exit north (this is San Pablo Dam Road). The boat launch is at the southern entrance four miles north of Orinda and the main recreation area is at the northern entry six miles north of Orinda. From Richmond take San Pablo Dam Road south to the lake.

Regulations: Fishing is permitted during the day from mid-February to mid-November. Limits are five trout, 10 catfish, five bass 12-inches minimum length (most anglers release all their bass), 1 sturgeon 46 to 72-inches in length, 25 crappie, and no limit on sunfish. Current plans are to ban two cycle engines after January 2000 and ban all gasoline engines two years later.

3. Contra Loma Lake:

Trout	7
Striped Bass	8
Catfish	6
Panfish	7
After a storm	6
Fly-fishing	7

About Contra Loma Lake: This lake is an 80-acre EBRPD lake south of Antioch and is noted for striped bass—it gets Delta water and that always comes with striped bass. It also has weekly plants of trout during the cool months including both trophy fish planted by the concessionaire and smaller DFG hatchery trout. It has catfish, some black bass, and panfish. It is a popular wind surfing lake as well as a good fishing lake.

This is a fine lake to fish with a small boat or a float tube. You can use electric powered boats or rowboats but both must be less than 17-feet long. The lake is small so, if the afternoon winds blow your float tube across the lake, you can climb out and hike back to your planned fishing area.

Striped Bass: Anglers catch a lot of striped bass at this reservoir. Many weigh 6- to 12-pounds but an occasional lunker is landed. Lures like the Top Water Stud Lure and large Rat-L-Traps are good. Bait like frozen anchovies catch these fish and occasionally a trout fisherman using Power Bait or a night crawler lands a striped bass. Spring and fall are the best times to catch stripers here.

Trout: Anglers fishing for trout from shore at this lake are about as successful as anglers fishing from a boat. The standard baits are Power Bait or night crawlers and sometimes a combination of the two. Anglers trolling with crank baits like Rapalas catch some of the largest fish (a fire tiger pattern has been hot recently but this changes so ask at the bait shop for the best lure). Small Needlefish, Triple Teazers, Dick Nites and similar lures trolled with a light weight or on lead-core line account for many small fish with an occasional trophy fish. The best times to catch trout are October through May but wait for the water to clear after a series of storms.

Catfish: Catfish are planted in the summer when the lake is too hot for good trout survival. Some very large catfish have been landed including a 26-pound fish. Use night crawlers, chicken liver or mackerel to catch catfish. The best catches are made from May through September.

Other Fish: Black bass are caught from this lake occasionally but most people concentrate on striped bass. Bluegill and crappie may also be caught on bits of worm fished under a bobber.

Lake Records:

Trout	13-pounds 10-ounces
Striper	26-pounds
Catfish	also 26-pounds
Bass	no records

Facilities and Contact: This lake has a small bait and tackle shop, a single lane launching ramp with a dock and a fishing dock. Call the concessionaire at 925-757-9606 for information.

Cost:

Entry and Parking	$4.00 per car
Daily fishing permit	$3.00 per person
Boat launch	$3.00
Boat rental	none

Directions to Contra Loma Lake: This lake is south of Antioch. Exit off Highway 4 in Antioch on Lone Tree Way. Go south to Golf Course Road, turn right then right again onto Frederickson Lane to the lake.

Regulations: This is a day use park and fishing is permitted all year. The daily limit is five trout, five catfish, two striped bass (18-inches minimum total length), five black bass (12-inch minimum size), 25 crappie and no limit on sunfish. Visitors may launch rowboats or electric powered boats no larger than 17-feet long.

4. Lafayette Reservoir:

Trout	8
Bass	8
Catfish	8
Panfish	6
After a storm	7
Fly-fishing	7

About Lafayette Reservoir: Lafayette Reservoir with an area of 115 acres is near a busy freeway. From the top of its dam, you can see the road and hear the traffic. Walk down the bank to the lake and the world is transformed to one of solitude and natural beauty tastefully modified with fishing docks and a recreation center. Anglers fish from 12 fishing docks scattered around the lake or from boats but only with electric motors—muffled road noise can be heard from some parts of the lake but the overall effect is quiet and serene. Joggers or walkers exercise on a 2.7-mile paved loop around this lake.

Trout: From October through June, weekly plants of trout keep the fish population and the catch high. One week the concessionaire spends fish-

An angler catches a bass at Lake Del Valle. Largemouth, smallmouth and even striped bass are caught at this lake.

ing fee money to buy and stock large trout; the next the DFG plants half-pound to one-pound trout.

Bass: Tulles around the lake make this a great bass lake. The introduction of Florida Bass several years ago gives anglers a chance at a very large fish. February through October are good bass fishing months.

Tips from an Expert: "I don't throw anything without a rattle; I only fish shallow water and I work fast," says Mike Sutherland who landed the 14-pound 6-ounce record bass from this lake in 1998. "I only use lures I have confidence in and that is usually a jerk bait or a plastic worm with a small rattling bead."

"Bass looking for food are prowling shallow water so I take advantage of this by fishing very shallow water up to about five feet from the bank, retrieve my lure quickly and makes another cast," Sutherland says. "Most anglers work slowly fishing a worm but I work fast. I shake it a couple of times, let it settle to the bottom, shake it a couple more times then retrieve and cast again."

He fishes all around the lake and catches fish at many locations.

Catfish: Catfish are planted occasionally—when fishing fee money is left over, according to concessionaire worker Andie Leandro. Most catfish weigh three to five-pounds. Night crawler, chicken liver, anchovies and mackerel are the favorite baits and May to October are the best times to catch catfish.

Sturgeon: This lake was not known to have sturgeon until Scott Sunkel landed a 45-pound 8-ounce sturgeon in 1997. He was probably thinking about keeping the fish but he almost didn't have a choice. A group of people gathered as the angler was fighting the large fish. Sunkel's wife and children took a poll of the people watching—they voted overwhelmingly to release the large fish. After weighing and measuring the fish Sunkel complied with the group's wishes and released the fish. Isn't democracy great—unless you are the person who caught the fish!

Tips from an Expert: Scott Sunkel suggests that if you want to keep a sturgeon if you catch one, don't take your wife and children fishing with you.

Other Fish: Crappie fishing is good some years and poor others. Spring and fall are the best times to catch these fish.

Lake Records:

Trout	11-pounds 2-ounces
Bass	14-pounds 6-ounces
Catfish	34-pounds
Sturgeon	45-pounds 8-ounces

Facilities and Contact: This reservoir has 12 fishing docks spaced at intervals all around the lake, a bait shop and rental row boats. The lake does not have a boat launching ramp but you can bring your own car-top boat and launch it off the docks. You can also bring an electric motor and batteries for the rental boats or your own boat. For information, call the bait shop at this lake at 510-284-9669.

Cost:

Entry and Parking	$5.00 per car
Daily fishing permit	$3.00 per person
Boat launch	$3.00 per day
Row boat	$18.00 per half day
Senior row boat	$9.00 per half day on weekdays

Directions to Lafayette Lake: Follow Highway 24 east from Oakland toward Lafayette and make a right turn on the first Lafayette exit (Acalanes Road). After exiting the highway, continue straight across Acalanes onto Mt. Diablo Boulevard. Go 1 mile and make a right turn onto the Lafayette Reservoir entrance road. From the east, follow Highway 24 to the last Lafayette exit (Acalanes Road). Go south on this road and immediately after going under the highway make a left turn onto Mt. Diablo Boulevard and continue 1 mile to the lake entrance.

Regulations: The lake is open from 6:00 AM in the summer and 6:30 AM in the winter until about sunset. The limit is five trout, five black bass, 10 catfish, 25 crappie and no limit on bluegill. Bass must be a minimum of 12-inches but I highly recommend releasing your bass. All live bait except worms are prohibited.

5. Lake Anza:

Bass	3
Catfish	3
Panfish	4

About Lake Anza: Charles Tilden park is the East Bay hill's most developed park. It has golf, a train ride for young people of all ages, an antique carousel, pony rides, a botanical garden, swimming and fishing in a 13 acre lake. Fishing almost gets overlooked. This is a beautiful park with lots of activities and is very worth a visit for a variety of reasons but, if your primary objective is fishing, many other lakes are better choices.

Fishing: This is a warm water lake and has bass, catfish, crappie, panfish, carp and squawfish. Worms or night crawlers make a good bait but don't expect a lot of fish. A few bluegill and redear sunfish are the most likely catch.

Lake Records: Records have not been kept. Fish are small.

Facilities and Contact: This EBRPD lake has restrooms nearby but has minimal fishing facilities. Call 510-531-9300 for information.

Cost:

Entry and Parking	$5.00 per car
Daily fishing permit	No fishing fee here

Directions to Lake Anza: From the east take the Fish Ranch Road exit off Highway 24 east of Oakland. Go north and make a right turn onto Grizzly Peak Road. Make a right turn into Tilden Park and follow the signs to Lake Anza. It is just south of the merry-go-round.

Regulations: Fishing is permitted all year; boats are not permitted. This is an EBRPD lake and limits are five bass a minimum of 12 inches long with no limit on sunfish or catfish.

6. Lake Temescal:

Trout	6
Bass	3
Catfish	5
Panfish	4
After a storm	5
Fly-fishing	4

About Lake Temescal: This 13 acre lake is at the junction of the Warren Freeway, Highway 13, and Highway 24 in the foothills east of Oakland. Near a metropolitan area, it is a popular swimming lake in the warm months. During the winter, the swimming area is closed; trout are planted and it becomes a popular fishing lake. Boating is not permitted so anglers fish from shore.

Trout: Trout, the primary fish, are planted by both the DFG and EBRPD from October through June. Anglers catch a few to limits of them on Power Bait, night crawlers or lures like Panther Martins, Mepps Spinners or Kastmasters. This lake is in a cool part of the bay and has decent trout

Bethany Reservoir northwest of Tracy is the beginning of the California Aqueduct. Striped bass and catfish are prime catches here. Electrical generating windmills line its shores.

fishing except in the warmest months of July through early September.

Other Fish: Catfish and panfish are caught in the summer and an occasional largemouth bass is taken.

Lake Records: Records have not been kept.

Facilities and Contact: This is an East Bay Regional Park lake. For information, call 510-531-9300.

Cost:

Entry and Parking	$5.00 per car
Daily fishing permit	$3.00 daily permit

Directions to Lake Temescal: Take Highway 13 north from San Leandro to Oakland. Take the Broadway Terrace exit west and immediately turn right into the park.

Regulations: This is a day use park and fishing is permitted all year. The limits are five trout, five bass (12-inches minimum length), five catfish and no limit on sunfish. Boating is not permitted.

7. Bethany Reservoir:

Striped Bass	7
Bass	5
Catfish	6
Panfish	5
After a storm	7
Fly-fishing	5

About Bethany Reservoir: In the spring, this 162 acre warm water reservoir is set in a grass meadow turned a lush, bright green from spring rains. Hundreds of windmills, part of the Altamont wind power generation system, sit along its banks. It is the origination of the California Aqueduct. Spring is very pleasant but the hills turn brown (the advertising brochures say "golden") in late spring and some summer days are hot. Water is pumped to this lake from the Delta; its level is nearly constant and it doesn't get very muddy. You can catch fish here after storms when other lakes are muddy and unfishable.

Striped Bass: Anglers can troll or bait fish for stripers with good success. Most fish are caught from a boat but shore angling access is good and land-bound anglers have a good chance to catch fish.

Catfish: Anglers catch catfish from shore or from an anchored boat—fishing is best during the spring and summer. Clams, mackerel, anchovies, night crawlers or prepared baits are all good choices.

Other Fish: Black bass and panfish are caught in the spring and early summer.

Lake Records: Records have not been kept.

Facilities and Contact: This lake is a State Recreation lake that is a day-use lake. It has a two-lane boat launching ramp with a dock on one side. Shade trees and covered picnic tables on the other side of the lake provide relief on hot sunny days. For information, call 925-687-1800.

Cost: Entry and Parking $5.00 per car
Boat launch $5.00 per boat

Directions to Bethany Reservoir: Take Highway 580 east from Livermore and take the Grant Line Byron exit. Go east for a short distance on Grant Line then turn left onto Mountain House Road. Turn left onto Kelso Road then turn left onto Burns Road. This road turns and becomes Christensen Road—follow it to the reservoir. From the north take Highway 4 through Brentwood. When Highway 4 turns left, continue straight on the Byron Road through the town of Byron and take Burns Road to the right to the reservoir.

Regulations: Fishing is permitted all year. The limit is two striped bass 18-inches or larger, five bass (12-inch minimum length) and no limit on catfish. The park is a day use park and has pay envelopes at its entrance. The speed limit on the reservoir is 25 mph and water-skiing and jet-skis are not permitted.

8. Lake Chabot:

Trout	9
Bass	8
Catfish	9
Panfish	6
After a storm	7
Fly-fishing	6

About Lake Chabot: Lake Chabot is a 315 acre lake near Castro Valley, a cool part of the Bay Area. It is an excellent fishing lake but has many recreational users including hikers, joggers and bikers. It also has family and group camping in an area away from the lake.

Lake Chabot is a quiet lake and outboard motors are prohibited. It doesn't have a launching ramp but people may hand-launch canoes, kayaks or float tubes or rent boats with or without electric trolling motors. It offers seniors (over 62 years of age) a boat at a bargain rate of $10.50 for a half day on weekdays. Many seniors bring trolling motors and bat-

Hundreds of trout this size are landed at the Bay Area Lakes throughout the winter. Alyce Henry caught this one at Lake Chabot.

Neal Fujita electroshocked this bass from Lake Chabot. Fish are tagged and released. When they are recaptured, lengths and weights of recaptured fish are compared with the original record to study growth rate and health of the fish.

teries on hand carts to take advantage of this offer.

Anglers come to this lake and frequently catch limits of trout including very large trout. The most coveted trophies are trophy Florida Bass—some weigh 17-pounds or more. Anglers don't catch many bass but they sure get some big ones. These fish or their parents or grandparents were planted in this lake but now they are reproducing and provide a great fishery. But the largest fish from the lake are very large catfish—the record is 35-pounds. It also has fair crappie and sunfish catches.

Located in the cool hills above the San Francisco Bay in Castro Valley, it stays cool into early summer and trout are stocked and caught into July. Catfish plants begin after trout stockings end in the summer and continue until the water is cool enough for trout—normally late September.

Lake Chabot is open for fishing all year. The best time to catch trout is October to June—fish are shallow. This lake can get muddy after a heavy rain but clears quickly and then anglers catch trout trolling as well as bait fishing.

Trout: Lake Chabot has excellent trout fishing. Anglers often catch limits—its only shortfall is not having many trophy sized trout. This lake is planted by the concessionaire every week from fall through late spring with a thousand or more pounds of trout including a few whopper-sized fish in every load. The DFG plants smaller half pound size fish every couple of weeks during the fishing season.

Trout fishing is good from the time the water cools in October until the water warms in June or July. Heavy runoff may turn off fishing for a while but the lake clears quickly and both trolling and bait fishing come back strong. Fish are shallow and relatively easy to catch by trolling lures just below the surface to about 15 feet deep. Trout begin to go deeper as the lake warms in May and June; then anglers need to fish deeper water or troll deeper.

Bass: Bass fishing is excellent in the spring starting as early as March. The bass catch is sparse but the fish landed are generally large. Florida Strain bass were stocked about 20 years ago and have become resident in this lake.

A plastic bait from a purple plastic worm to a pig and jig are the primary attractors for these fish. They are also caught on spinner baits and crank baits. Some are invariably caught on night crawlers and even Power Bait.

Tips from an Expert: "I rent a boat at Lake Chabot, mount my own trolling motor, stand in the back of the boat, run the boat backwards and steer with one foot," says Bill Little who has caught 103 bass weighing more than five pounds from this lake since 1984. "I am sight-fishing. I see the bass and make long casts to them." Author's note—I don't recommend standing up in a boat but if you do, wear a life jacket.

Little's favorite lures are pig and jigs. He caught his largest bass at this lake, a 16 pound 8 ounce fish on a black pig and jig. He also likes large crank baits that imitate rainbow trout like Bomber Long A's, as well as spinner baits and 6 to 9 inch long Mann's black and grape jelly worms. "I fish off points, in tulles, and over weed beds—bass hide in weed beds to ambush trout," Little says. When he fishes will probably surprise you. "My favorite time to fish for big bass is from 10 AM to 2 PM on a bright sunny day when the wind is dead calm and it is hot."

Anglers fishing from the shore at Lake Chabot make very good catches of trout.

Catfish: Catfish thrive in the lake. Some are caught all year but they are planted in the summer and most are caught during the warm months.

Other Fish: Panfish are caught spring and fall—April and October are good months. This lake also has carp that are large and strong. Pete Alexander, Fisheries Specialist for the EBRPD, electroshocks these fish and removes them because they wallow on the bottom and foul up the habitat for bass spawning. You can do Alexander and bass anglers a favor by catching and keeping carp.

Special Programs: The lake has a whopper program for any trout weighing more than five-pounds, for a bass weighing more than eight-pounds or for a catfish weighing more than 10-pounds. On a good week, a dozen whoppers may be landed and the angler who catches each is awarded a cap or a cup.

Lake Records: Trout   16-pounds 7-ounces
Bass   17-pounds 2-ounces
(a dead 17.42-pound bass was found floating on the lake)

Carp, though not a favored fish are found in many lakes and the Delta. East Bay Regional Parks District fisheries specialist Pete Alexander electroshocked this one at Lake Chabot.

Catfish   35-pounds
Crappie   2-pound 2-ounces

Facilities and Contact: Lake Chabot has a bait shop, boat rentals, a restaurant, a fishing pier with wheelchair access and campsites away from the lake. All the facilities are clean and first rate; the boats are in good condition; and the employees are friendly and helpful. Call the concessionaire, Lake Chabot Outfitters, at phone 510-582-2198 for information and call the park at 510-562-2267 to reserve a campsite.

Cost:
Entry and Parking	$5.00 per car
Daily fishing permit	$3.00 per person
Boat launch	$2.00 (only canoes, kayaks and float tubes may be launched)
Boat and electric motor	$30.00 per half day
Boat only	$25.00 per half day
Senior boat	$10.50 per half day (weekdays)
Camping	$15.00 per night

Ryan Agamau caught this 7-pound 12-ounce trout from Shadow Cliffs Lake trolling a gold Rapala.

Directions to Lake Chabot: From Highway 580 in Hayward, take Castro Valley Boulevard north to Lake Chabot Road. Turn north and look for the lake to the right. Or go south on Interstate 580 from Oakland, and take the Estudillo Exit. Turn east on Estudillo which becomes Lake Chabot Road and make a left turn to the lake.

Regulations: Fishing is permitted during the day. This is an EBRPD lake and the limits are five trout, five bass (12-inches minimum length), five catfish, 25 crappie and no limit on sunfish.

9. Cull Canyon Reservoir:

Trout 7
Catfish 5
Fly-fishing 4

About Cull Canyon Reservoir: This 25 acre EBRPD lake is open to fishing all year but swimming is the major activity—fishing doesn't have nearly the emphasis. A separate swimming lagoon, kept at a constant level by

An angler casts from shore at Shadow Cliffs Lake. This reclaimed gravel pit is an excellent fishing lake after a storm.

pumping water from the main lake, draws hordes of visitors in the summer. Fishing takes over from swimming after the water has cooled.

Trout: Planted trout by both the EBRPD and the DFG during the winter and spring make up most of the catch at this lake. Use the standard baits like Power Bait or night crawlers floated off the bottom by injecting air into the crawler or by threading a miniature marshmallow on the line in front of the crawler. Lures like Kastmasters or Panther Martins cast from shore also catch fish.

Other Fish: Catfish planted in the summer, an occasional black bass and panfish make up the warm water catch.

Lake Records: Records have not been kept.

Facilities and Contact: Boating is not permitted. This is an East Bay Regional Park. For information, call 510-531-9300.

Cost: Entry and Parking $5.00 per car
        Daily fishing permit $3.00 per person

Directions to Cull Canyon Reservoir: Take Interstate 580 to the east part of Castro Valley and take the Crow Canyon Road exit. Turn north on this road; make a left turn onto Cull Canyon Road and follow the signs to this park.

Regulations: Cull Canyon Reservoir is a day use park and fishing is permitted when the park is open. The limits are five trout, five bass (12-inches minimum length), five catfish, 25 crappie and no limit on sunfish. Boats are not permitted on this lake.

Fishing docks are popular and productive fishing platforms at Shadow Cliffs Lake.

10. Don Castro Reservoir:

Trout 7
Catfish 5
Panfish 6
After a storm 4
Fly-fishing 3

About Don Castro Reservoir: Located in the hills of Hayward, this small EBRPD lake gets plants of trout during late fall, winter and spring. Boats are not allowed on the lake but shore anglers catch stocked trout during the cool months and catfish, bass and panfish during the warm months. Most visitors in the summer come to swim in the swimming lagoon.

Trout: Planted trout in the winter and spring including some large fish planted by EBRPD provide the best fishing at this lake. Shore anglers using Power Bait, night crawlers or lures like Kastmasters, Rooster Tails, Panther Martins and Rapalas catch these fish.

Other Fish: Catfish (planted in the summer), black bass, crappie, bluegill and perch are also caught.

Lake Records: Lake records have not been kept.

Facilities and Contact: This is an East Bay Regional Park. For information, call 510-531-9300.

Cost: Entry and Parking $5.00 per car
        Daily fishing permit $3.00 per person

Directions to Don Castro Reservoir: Take Interstate 580 to Hayward, take the Castro Valley exit and go under the freeway toward Hayward on Center Street. Turn left onto Kelly then turn left again onto Woodroe Avenue to the park entrance.

Regulations: Fishing is permitted during the day. This is an EBRPD lake and limits are five trout, five bass (12-inches minimum length), five catfish, 25 crappie and no limit on sunfish. Boats are not permitted.

11. Shadow Cliffs:

Trout 8
Bass 6
Catfish 5
Panfish 4
After a storm 10
Fly-fishing 7

About Shadow Cliffs Lake: Shadow Cliffs Lake doesn't look like a gem of a fishing lake. It looks good for the 74 acre abandoned gravel pit that it is but for pure natural beauty it isn't special. At least not until you start looking beneath the surface where you will see what attracts anglers to this lake.

A floating shop at Lake Del Valle has bait, tackle and rental boats.

First, the lake is planted with a lot of trout and some very large trout. You never know if your next fish will be an eight-inch fish planted by DFG or one of the 10-pound or larger trophy trout planted by the concessionaire. Secondly, when other lakes are muddy and you would do as well fishing in your hot tub, very little runoff is flowing into Shadow Cliffs Lake; it is almost clear and anglers are catching lots of fish. Third, the main lake has large bass though few people know it and fourth, it has some very large catfish. Finally, three small lakes southwest of the main lake are not stocked but have bass and sunfish.

Shadow Cliffs Lake has a launch ramp with a new dock at the main lake. Only electric motors are permitted. During fall, winter, spring weekends and holidays, it has a catch-out pond for trout. The charge is $5 per fish that average a pound to a pound and a half. This is a great place to take a youngster to catch his first fish or for a preteen to try out a new Christmas or birthday rod—catching is almost guaranteed.

This lake has a swimming area with a sandy beach and the park has waterslides. It is filled to overflowing on summer holidays. Don't go near it on these holidays—it is very crowded with swimmers and picnickers and parking is full early in the morning. But other times it has few people and is a good place to fish from shore or from a boat.

Trout: Shadow Cliffs Lake is a good put-and-take lake for trout. This lake is planted by the concessionaire almost every week from October or November when its waters cool, continuing until June. The Department of Fish and Game plants smaller half pound size fish every couple of weeks during this same period.

Several fishing docks have been installed along the west and northwest side of the lake and anglers catch trout here and from the shoreline. The best trolling is usually across the lake along the east wall and the east half of Stanley Avenue shoreline. This area is off-limits to shore anglers so you don't need to worry about bugging them or catching their lines.

Bass: Most anglers don't know both the main lake and the smaller back ponds have bass. Daryl Bustamante broke the bass record for this lake twice in one week in April, 1998 when he caught a 9-pound bass on a green plastic worm. Six days later he landed a 9-pound 6-ounce bass on a three-inch salt and pepper grub on a lead-head jig. He was fishing the tulle beds in the south end of the lake.

Catfish: Catfish are the primary fish in the summer and Shadow Cliffs is a fair catfish lake. Most notable are some very large resident catfish from before it was made into a park. Derek Ott caught a 30-pound 9-ounce catfish in December 1997 and the lake record is 33-pounds.

Special Programs: The lake has spring and fall trout derbies and a summer catfish derby. Fishing seminars and a special fishing program for the handicapped are conducted here once or twice a year.

Tips from an expert: "Pre-form your Power Bait into bait size balls and roll them in glitter you buy at a craft store," advises Andy Vanderostyne. "Store these in an empty bait jar. When you get ready to fish, grab a bait ball out of the jar; form it onto your hook and cast. The surface sparkle attracts trout and glitter that comes off looks like scales coming off an injured fish. These bait balls with sparkle catch a lot more fish than the commercial sparkle bait."

Lake Records:		
Trout	15-pounds 10-ounces	
Bass	9-pounds 6-ounces	
Catfish	33-pounds	
Crappie	1-pound 5-ounces	

Facilities and Contact: Shadow Cliffs Lake has a single lane launch with a new dock and a bait shop that rents boats and sells bait and fishing tackle. Boats can be launched any day. The bait shop is open all summer but is only open on weekends and holidays including the Christmas/New Years holiday period. A netted part of the lake at the boat docks is stocked heavily with trout and anglers can fish paying a fee for each fish caught. The concessionaire may be reached at 925-846-9263 and the phone number at the main gate is 925-846-3000.

Cost:		
Entry and Parking	$3.00 per car in winter to $5.00 per car in summer	
Daily fishing permit	$3.00 per person	
Boat launch	$3.00	
Boat and motor	$30.00 per half day	
Boat only	$25.00 per half day	
Senior boat rental	$12.50 per half day (weekdays)	

Directions to Shadow Cliffs: From Highway 680 in Pleasanton, take

Lake Del Valle is a good lake for shore fishing. Anglers line the shore when fishing is good.

the Bernal Avenue exit east. Go to Main Street (the third stop light) and turn left. This becomes East Stanley Boulevard—continue on this street to Shadow Cliffs Lake on the right. The lake is a half mile east of the outskirts of Pleasanton. A waterslide is visible on the right as you approach the park and a stop light marks the lake entrance. The number 10 bus that operates between Pleasanton and Livermore stops at the entrance to this lake.

Regulations: This is a day use lake that is open all year. The limit is five trout, five catfish, five bass (12-inches minimum length) and no limit on sunfish. Alcoholic beverages including beer are prohibited in the park. All boats must be no more than 20-feet in length.

12. Lake Del Valle:

Trout	8
Bass	7
Catfish	9
Striped Bass	8
Panfish	6
After a storm	5
Fly-fishing	5

About Lake Del Valle: Lake Del Valle is a 4-mile long, 750 acre water storage reservoir in an inland valley south of Livermore. It is filled by runoff in wet years but takes water from the Delta in dry years. Any lake that gets Delta water also gets striped bass. Stripers in the larvae stage come through the screens and thrive in this lake. It is stocked with many trout including some very large trout and catfish and has black bass and panfish. Trout catches are good in the fall and winter and fishing peaks in the spring. This lake warms early and trout catches subside in June. Then catfish are planted and trout stocks began again in October.

Lake Del Valle has a speed limit of 10 mph so water skiing and jet skis are not permitted. It is a fishing lake and the other primary users, sail boats and windsurfers, are very compatible with anglers. It has a good four-lane boat launch with docks and you rarely find more than a short line to launch a boat. It also has an excellent campground in a secluded valley away from the lake, a resident bald eagle and a flock of wild turkeys—you would never guess you are only a few miles from civilization.

Lake Del Valle is open for fishing all year. The best time to catch trout is November through May. It can get muddy after a rain but fishing near the dam in the deep part of the lake remains good unless the storm is very large. Then the park may flood closing it to visitors. After releasing water for a few days, the lake comes back to a normal level and fishing and other recreation resumes.

Trout: Lake Del Valle is a good "put-and-take" lake for trout. This lake is planted with large trout by the concessionaire almost every week from October through May. On cool years plants may start earlier or continue later. The Department of Fish and Game plants half pound sized fish every couple of weeks during this same period.

This is a particularly good lake for bait fishing from shore. When fishing is good, anglers line the shore of the narrows north of the bait shop and fish around the bait shop to make good catches. Anglers in boats often anchor just beyond the rental boat docks and fish with bait. As the lake warms in May or June, trout are planted by the dam in deep, cool water. Then shore anglers fishing the shallow south end of the lake have limited success but anglers in boats do well fishing the deeper areas near the dam.

Bass: Bass fishing is excellent in the spring starting as early as March. Several bass may be landed but most are small. Plastic worms, pig and jigs, spinner baits and crank baits are top lures.

Striped Bass: Lake Del Valle is one of the best lakes in the area for large striped bass. Anglers catch them in the fall and spring using lures like Stud Lures, Rat-L-Traps and Rebels.

Tips from an Expert: I caught my first striped bass at Lake Del Valle, an 18-pound fish, fishing with Matt Desimone, inventor of the Stud Lure.

Shadow Cliffs Lake is filled with swimmers and picnickers on summer holidays. Choose other days to fish this lake.

Desimone was also one of the best anglers I have ever known and he could always catch stripers with this lure. Tragically Desimone is deceased but here is what he told me about catching stripers in Lake Del Valle.

"Stripers herd planted trout into shallow areas and then attack them. Look for shallow bars near a bank; listen for stripers breaking the surface chasing fish and you can find striped bass." Stripers spook easily so Desimone approached them very quietly. He used only an electric motor—his boat didn't even have a conventional outboard. He kept his distance from his fishing spot and made long casts. He caught stripers on surface lures and shallow diving lures and liked a rainbow trout imitation when fishing in Del Valle or other lakes that have planted trout and striped bass.

Catfish: Catfish are the primary fish in the summer and Del Valle is one of the best catfish lakes in the area. They are caught all year but they are planted in the summer and most are caught during the summer and fall months. Anglers catch eating size catfish fishing where water flows in from the creek at the southern end. Larger, resident catfish are taken from the northern end near the dam. Fish in coves or use your fish finder to locate fish hanging on the bottom—probably catfish.

Tips from an expert: Andy Vanderostyne, a master at catching catfish, saws frozen mackerel in three-eighths inch thick steaks (like you would steak a salmon) and keeps these steaks frozen until he is ready to go fishing.

Using spinning tackle with 12- to 15-pound test line and a size 4/0 live bait hook, he skewers the bait onto the hook and casts. He doesn't use a weight; the mackerel has sufficient weight. "Fish with an open bail and when the catfish picks up the bait, engage the reel," Vanderstyne said. "As soon as the line comes taunt set the hook and reel." He catches good sized catfish—the day I fished with him, he caught five three- to five-pound catfish.

"The bite is definitely an early morning bite so start early and go directly to your best spots," Vanderostyne advises. "Have your tackle rigged and be ready to start fishing immediately. Your first hour of fishing is your best fishing time for catfish and you want to use every minute."

Other Fish: Panfish are caught spring and fall. This lake also has squawfish that are strong but they are not considered gamefish and I have never heard of anyone eating one.

Lake Records:

Trout	17-pounds 7.5-ounces
Largemouth Bass	12-pounds
Smallmouth Bass	5-pounds 12-ounces
Striped Bass	40-pounds
Bluegill	2-pounds 12-ounces

Facilities and Contact: Lake Del Valle has a good, four-lane launch with docks and a floating bait shop that rents boats and sells bait and fishing tackle. All the facilities are clean and first rate; the boats are in good condition, and the employees are friendly and helpful. The concessionaire is at 925-449-5201. Call 925-562-2267 up to 12 weeks in advance to reserve a campsite.

Cost:

	Entry and Parking	$5.00 per car
	Daily fishing permit	$3.00 per person
	Boat launch	$3.00 per day
	Boat motor	$36.00 per half day
	Boat only	$25.00 per half day
	Senior boat and motor	$20.00 per half day (Weekdays)
	Camping	$15 tent sites, $18 RV sites

Directions to Lake Del Valle: From Highway 580 in Livermore, take the Livermore Avenue exit south. Follow this road all the way through town until it turns left and becomes Tesla Road. Go half a mile on Tesla Road then turn right onto Mines Road and follow the signs to Lake Del Valle.

Regulations: Fishing is permitted during the day. This is an EBRPD lake and the limits are five trout, five bass (12-inches minimum length), five catfish, 25 crappie with no limit on sunfish. The speed limit is 10-mph and water skis and jet skis are not permitted.

*John Caulfield gets ready to release
a tagged trout for a trout derby*

13. Jordan Pond at Garin Park:

Catfish   3
Panfish   3

About Jordan Pond: This is a 3 1/2 acre pond in Garin Park in Hayward. The park is primarily an agricultural museum showing some of the ranching equipment and methods of earlier times. It has a blacksmith shop, a barn and an orchard that includes a number of old varieties of fruit trees that are rare today.

Fishing: Fishing at Jordan Pond is in the setting of fishing at an old time farm and better fishing is found at other nearby lakes. Catfish and panfish are caught.

Lake Records: Records have not been kept—fish are small.

Facilities and Contact: This is an East Bay Regional Park. For information, call 510-531-9300.

Cost: Entry and Parking $5.00 per car

Directions to Jordan Pond: From the south take Interstate 680 to Mission San Jose and take the Mission Boulevard off-ramp. Go north on Mission Boulevard to Hayward and turn right onto Garin Avenue into the park. Jordan Pond is to the right. From the north, take Mission Boulevard south from Hayward and turn left on Garin Avenue into the park.

Regulations: This is a day use lake that is open all year. The limit is five catfish and no limit on sunfish.

14. Alameda Creek:

Trout   6
Fly-fishing 6

About Alameda Creek: Alameda Creek flows from Sunol south of Pleasanton to Fremont splashing through a tree-lined Niles Canyon. The only fish of note are trout stocked by DFG when the season opens the first of April. If the water remains cool, plants continue though June. It is one of the few places within minutes of the Metropolitan Bay Area where anglers can fly-fish in a river. It is a great place to sharpen your fly-fishing skills though the catch will be recently stocked fish—not wild fish.

Historically this creek had steelhead and several of these fish returned to a very hostile creek in 1998. Dams blocked their path but environ-

mentalists netted the fish, gently moved them upstream above the dams and released them. Eggs in the lower river were collected, hatched by school children and the fry were released in upper Alameda Creek. Demands to public officials to remove the dams or construct fish ladders and improve the habitat so these fish can return to their creek so far have fallen on deaf ears. Jeff Miller, President of the Alameda Creek Alliance, only sees this as a challenge and is confident changes necessary to restore these steelhead will happen.

Trout: Salmon eggs, worms and power bait produce some fish in the spring. Fly-fishers sharpen their skills and catch a few trout on wet or dry flies.

Records: Records have not been kept—trout here are small.

Facilities and Contact: Trout plants are made by the East Bay Regional Park District. For information, call 510-531-9300. For camping information call Sunol Regional Park at 925-636-1684.

Cost: Entry and Parking Free along Niles Canyon Road.
        Camping $11.00 Walk-in camping at Sunol Regional
                           Park

Directions to Alameda Creek: From Fremont drive north on Mission Boulevard (Highway 238) and take a right on Niles Canyon Road. This road follows Alameda Creek. Or take Interstate 680 south from Pleasanton to Niles Canyon Road exit. Go west (right) on this road.

Regulations: Fishing is permitted the last Saturday in April through November 15. The limit is five trout. If a wild steelhead population can be established, planted trout may compete with these fish and the stocking program will probably be curtailed or eliminated.

15. Shinn Pond at Alameda Creek Trail:

Striped Bass   4
Bass   3
Catfish   4
Panfish   3

About Shinn Pond: This small pond is almost small enough you think you can cast halfway across but stripers boil in its middle and it takes a very long cast to reach them. One of several abandoned quarries in the Niles Canyon region of Fremont, it is only a preview of things to come. The EBRPD has big plans to turn other abandoned gravel quarries into a major recreational area. One lake will be for stocked trophy trout, bass and catfish; another will be a swimming lake and another for recreational non-powered boating. It will be much like Shadow Cliffs Lake where large fish will be planted and fees from daily fishing permits will pay for the stocked fish.

Fishing: Shinn Pond is stocked with striped bass and catfish but plants are irregular. Anglers may catch black bass, catfish, panfish and occasionally a striped bass. Fishing is from shore or from the fishing pier at one end.

Lake Records: Records have not been kept.

Facilities and Contact: Services are minimal. It has a restroom in the park and is near restaurants and stores. For information, call 510-531-9300.

Cost: Entry and Parking   no fee
        Daily fishing permit not required

Directions to Shinn Pond: Take Mission Boulevard north off Interstate 680 from Mission San Jose. Turn left on Niles Boulevard. Make a left onto G street and follow it to its end. Turn right then left into the Niles Community Park. Shinn Pond is beyond the tennis courts.

Regulations: This is an EBRPD day use lake. The limits are five bass (12-inches minimum length), five catfish, two striped bass (18-inch minimum length) and no limit on sunfish. Boats are not permitted.

16. Lake Elizabeth:

Catfish   6
Black Bass   2
Sunfish   3

Andy Vanderostyne is a master at catching catfish.

About Lake Elizabeth: This 63 acre lake in Fremont Central Park is a picturesque lake in the middle of the city of Fremont. It is a shallow, warm lake and holds mostly warm water fish. After several years without any stocked fish, DFG began planting catfish in April 1998.

This is a sailing lake and a general recreation park—fishing hasn't been emphasized. I talked with several people at the marina and they seemed to know very little about fishing except for an occasional kids' derby. I had almost given up on finding out about fishing when I talked with a ranger and he gave me a good update of the new planting program.

Fish: Fishing took a big upswing at this lake when DFG started planting catfish in 1998 and they are the primary catch. Sunfish, bass and a few trout released after a kids' derby are caught occasionally.

Records: Records have not been kept.

Facilities and Contact: A marina at the lake has a launch and rents boats but these are primarily sailboats and paddle boats—not fishing boats. For information, call 510-791-4340.

Special Programs: Kids "fish-in-the-city" days are held here twice a year for children 15 years old or younger. An arm of the lake is netted off and catfish are planted for the May event. Trout are planted for a winter event. The local fish population is high and most participating children catch fish on these days. When the event is over, the net confining the fish is removed and the fish disperse throughout the lake.

Cost: Entry and Parking   no fee
Boat launch $3.00

Directions to Lake Elizabeth: Take Washington Boulevard west from Interstate 280 in Fremont. Turn right onto Dristol Road then left on Paseo Padre. Turn right onto Sailway Drive into Fremont Central Park to Lake Elizabeth.

Regulations: This is a day use lake that is open all year. The limit is five trout, five catfish, five bass (12-inches minimum length) and unlimited sunfish and catfish. Only boats without motors are permitted.

17. Sandy Wool Lake:
Trout   4

About Sandy Wool Lake: This lake is in Ed Levin Park in the foothills east of Milpitas. You probably haven't seen this lake as a prominent fishing lake and it isn't, but it is a good place to take children to do a little fishing from shore. Trout are stocked in the winter and the spring. The more popular recreations including hiking, horseback riding (you can rent horses) and watching people hang-gliding.

Trout: Trout are stocked by the DFG November through May and that is the only time to expect to catch fish. Use Power Bait or night crawlers or cast small lures like Mepps Spinners or Panther Martins.

Lake Records: Records have not been kept—fish are small.

Facilities and Contact: This lake has minimal facilities and offers fishing from shore. For information call 408-262-6980.

Cost: Entry and Parking $4.00 per car

Directions to Sandy Wool Lake: From the East Bay, drive south on Interstate 680 to Calaveras Road. Turn east on Downing Road and turn north to the park. From the South Bay, drive north on Interstate 680 to Calaveras Road; go east on this road and follow the above directions.

Regulations: Fishing is permitted all year. The park is open from 8:00 AM until one-half hour after sunset. The limit is five trout and five catfish.

Bass and catfish compete as the second favorite fish in the Bay Area Lakes. Cathy Lambert landed this bass.

18. Los Vaqueros Reservoir:
A New Reservoir

About Los Vaqueros Reservoir: This new 1400 acre lake is the newest and the largest lake in the Bay Area. It is a freshwater drinking reservoir for Contra Costa County. Policies for this lake are just being formulated so we don't know what fish will be stocked or how it will be managed. Since it gets water from the Delta, it will get fish common to the Delta including catfish, striped bass, black bass and panfish. It is likely that trout will be stocked but that decision has not been confirmed.

Fishing: This large reservoir has a good potential for fish but it is too early to know how it will be managed and to predict the quality of fishing.

Facilities and Contact: This park is to have fishing piers, a boat launch and hiking trails. Contact the Contra Costa Water District at 925-625-6504 for information.

Cost: Costs are not known at this time.

Directions to Los Vaqueros Reservoir: Take Highway 4 east from Walnut Creek to Brentwood. Go south on Vasco Road then make a right turn onto Diablo Road and a left onto Walnut Boulevard. Or take Vasco Road north off Interstate 580 from Livermore. Turn left onto Diablo Road and make another left onto Walnut Boulevard to the lake.

Regulations: Fishing regulations and policies have not been determined.

CHAPTER 6:

South Bay

The most noteworthy fishing in the South Bay Area is good warm water fishing, particularly for bass, crappie and catfish. But there are other choices. Several public lakes have half-pound to one-pound trout stocked by the DFG during the cool months. A few small lakes scattered throughout the city of San Jose provide good opportunity for children to fish for a few days after the stocking truck has made its delivery. Anglers also catch a few panfish in the summer but these lakes aren't noteworthy fishing lakes.

The best fishing lakes are at Henry Coe State Park where anglers catch bass on almost every cast. It is a long, multi-day hike to get to the best lakes so they are only for the hardy angler. More accessible lakes with the best fishing are Calero, Anderson, Chesbro, Uvas, and Lexington for bass and Coyote, Loch Lomond, and Parkway lakes for planted trout.

What South Bay freshwater fishing generally lacks is big trout and big bass. Big bass are coming. The DFG stocked Florida strain bass in some of the lakes like Calero and Anderson and so far anglers have caught bass up to about 13 pounds. In Northern California, these bass have grown to about 18 pounds so we may see similar sized bass coming from these South Bay Lakes.

Most lake managers in the South Bay don't charge fishing fees and don't stock large trout so most trout are the 10 to 12-inch DFG plants. One exception is Parkway Lake, a private lake that charges a substantial fishing fee ($12 for adults as this book goes to publication) and stocks trophy trout, catfish and even sturgeon. If you are after really large fish from the South Bay Area, you may want to pay the fee.

Some larger lakes allow high speed water sports. Anderson Reservoir allows water skiing but prohibits jet skis. Calero Reservoir prohibits water skiing but allowed jet skiers until high levels of MTBE were measured in this drinking water lake in 1998. So now jet skiers are prohibited. Most lakes in this region permit only non-powered boats or electric-powered boats—several small lakes prohibit boating. Brochures by the Santa Clara Valley Water District specify only non-powered boats at some reservoirs but actually permit boats with electric motors. Check the following lake-by-lake descriptions to see what boats and motors are permitted. But policies change so call the lake manager to check their current policy on boats and motors if you aren't certain. Day use fees are collected for vehicles and for launching at some lakes but others, particularly lakes that don't permit boating, often don't charge fees.

A hundred years ago many of the coastal streams and rivers had robust populations of steelhead and salmon but that has all changed. Development has played havoc with the river habitat for fish and to a lesser extent, over-fishing has diminished these runs. The San Lorenzo River has enough steelhead to allow some fishing. In other rivers there are meager remnants of historic runs and they don't have enough fish to support fishing. Even when fishing for steelhead and salmon is permitted, these rivers and streams need tender-loving-care to rebuild populations and I don't advise fishing in any of them at this time. Though I mention them in this book, I don't give any details and would encourage you to concentrate on ocean or lake fishing or on a few inland rivers that are stocked and provide viable fishing. If you really want salmon, catch them in the ocean, the bays or the Sacramento or San Joaquin Rivers or their tributaries. If you have a passion for steelhead, travel to rivers along our North Coast to fish for them.

Health Warning: Several areas in the southern region of the Bay Area have concentrations of mercury that accumulate in fish to unsafe levels.

Three anglers get ready to cast their lures.

The DFG warns that no one should consume fish taken from water of the following lakes and rivers in Santa Clara County—Guadalupe Reservoir, Calero Reservoir, Almaden Reservoir, Guadalupe River, Guadalupe Creek, Alamitos Creek and the percolation ponds along this river and these creeks. Verify that fish are safe to eat before you keep and eat any fish caught from lakes and rivers.

1. Stevens Creek Reservoir:

Trout	5
Bass	4
Catfish	4
Panfish	4

About Stevens Creek Reservoir: This 93 acre reservoir in Stevens Creek County Park south of Sunnyvale has resident bass, bluegill, catfish, crappie and carp and is stocked with trout March through June. This lake has a launch ramp—rowboats and boats with electric motors are permitted.

Trout: Trout fishing is good for a few days after the lake is stocked. Use Power Bait, night crawlers or small spinners like Rooster Tails or Panther Martins.

Bass: Anglers catch a few bass on bait or on plastic worms, spinners or crank baits.

Other Fish: Catfish and panfish may also be caught and are the most prominent catch besides trout. Use worms or prepared baits for these fish.

Lake Records: Records have not been kept.

Facilities and Contact: This reservoir has a boat launch and picnic areas but no camping. Call Stevens Creek Reservoir at 408-857-3654 for information or call Santa Clara County Parks Department at 408-358-3741 for information about a variety of lakes in this county.

Cost: Entry and Parking $4.00 Self Registration Fees
Boat launch $3.00

Directions to Stevens Creek Reservoir: This reservoir is south of Mountain View and Sunnyvale. Take Interstate 280 from San Francisco or San Jose and turn south on Foothill Boulevard. Follow this road that becomes Stevens Canyon Road to the reservoir.

Regulations: Fishing is permitted during park hours from about 8:00 AM in the winter or 7:00 AM in the summer until the park closes at dusk. The limit is five trout, five bass (bass must be 12-inches long or longer), five catfish and 25 crappie. Gasoline powered engines are not permitted but electric trolling motors are okay.

2. Lake Cunningham:

Trout   4
Catfish   3
Panfish   2

About Lake Cunningham: This reservoir is a 50 acre lake on the east side of San Jose in Lake Cunningham Park. It has resident bluegill and catfish and the DFG stocks it with trout November through May. The lake is primarily a quiet water sports lake that also has fishing.

Fishing: Trout fishing with Power Bait or night crawlers is the best bet. The best catches are made a few days after the stocking truck has brought trout. The lake also has catfish and panfish.

Lake Records: Records have not been kept. Most fish are small.

Facilities and Contact: This reservoir has a gravel boat launch without docks. Call Lake Cunningham Park at 408-277-4319 for information.

Cost: Entry and Parking $4.00 per vehicle
Boat launch $2.00

Directions to Lake Cunningham: Take Interstate 280 from San Francisco through San Jose and continue on Interstate 680. Make a right turn on Capital Expressway and follow that to the Tully Avenue exit. Turn east on Tully Avenue. The park and lake are on the north side of this road. From the north, take 680 to Capital Expressway and follow the above directions to the lake.

Regulations: Fishing is permitted during park hours from 8:00 AM until the park closes at dusk. The limit is five trout, five catfish, and no limit on bluegill. Only non-powered boats are permitted.

3. Grant Lakes:

Bass   4
Catfish   2
Panfish   3

About Grant Lakes: These are three small lakes in Joseph P. Grant County Park on the San Jose side of Mount Hamilton. The three lakes, Grant, McCreery and Bass Lakes, are not stocked but have resident bass, bluegill and catfish. The park has family campsites.

Fishing: Night crawlers are a good all-around bait to entice all of these fish. Bass anglers are successful with crank baits or plastic baits.

Lake Records: Records have not been kept.

Facilities and Contact: This park has 22 first-come-first-served family campsites. Call Grant Lakes at 408-274-6121 for information.

Trout can be landed by anglers in float tubes at several Bay Area Lakes.

Cost: Entry and Parking $4.00 per vehicle
Camping $10.00 per site

Directions to Grant Lakes: These lakes are on Mt. Hamilton Road. From the East Bay, go south on Interstate 680. Turn west (left) on Alum Rock Avenue. Before you get to the Alum Rock Park, turn right on Mt. Hamilton Road. It is about eight miles to Joseph D. Grant County Park but the road is windy and slow and will take about a half an hour from Interstate 680. From the peninsula, go south on Interstate 280. Continue east then north on Interstate 680 to Alum Rock Avenue, turn right and follow the above directions.

Regulations: Fishing is permitted during regular park hours from 8:00 AM until sunset. The park is open daily from April though October. It is open on weekends only March through November and is closed December through February. The limit is five bass (bass must be 12-inches long or longer), five catfish, and no limit on panfish. Boats are not permitted on these lakes.

4. Cottonwood Lake:

Trout   4
Catfish   3
Panfish   3

About Cottonwood Lake: This 10 acre lake is in Hellyer Park in the southern part of San Jose off Highway 101. This urban lake emphasizes a variety of water sports and fishing is just one of the activities.

Fishing: This lake has resident bass, catfish, crappie and carp and the DFG stocks it with trout from November through April. Anglers do well on trout for a few days after the lake is stocked. Power Bait is a good bait for trout and night crawlers are a good overall bait for a variety of fish. If you want to catch a large powerful fish, go for the carp.

Lake Records: Records have not been kept.

Facilities and Contact: Call Cottonwood Lake at 408-225-0225 for information.

Cost: Entry and Parking $4.00 per vehicle

Directions to Cottonwood Lake: This lake is along Highway 101 off Hellyer Avenue. Follow Highway 101 south from San Jose onto Hellyer Avenue. Take the off-ramp and turn right (west) onto Hellyer Avenue. Make the first left turn into the park.

Regulations: Fishing is permitted during park hours from 8:00 AM until the park closes at sunset. The limit is five trout, five catfish and no limit on bluegill and sunfish. Boating is not permitted.

Anglers fish from shore at the dam at Lexington Reservoir.

5. Vasona Lake & Los Gatos Creek:

Trout	4
Bass	2
Catfish	3
Panfish	3

About Vasona Lake & Los Gatos Creek: Vasona Lake has resident bass, bluegill, catfish, crappie, carp and koi (dumped here when people tired of caring for them). Los Gatos Creek Peculation Ponds one mile north of Vasona lake have the same species plus trout that are stocked by DFG in pond number one January through May. This is San Jose's most popular general recreation park and fishing is only a part of the activities.

Trout: Trout fishing is fair for eight to 12-inch long trout in Los Gatos Creek Peculation Pond Number One soon after the stocking truck has made its delivery. Use Power Bait or night crawlers floated off the bottom with a marshmallow threaded onto the line just in front of the crawler.

Other Fish: Bass, catfish, panfish and whatever has been dumped from someone's aquarium may be caught but you will get a lot more sunshine and fresh air than fish.

Lake Records: Records have not been kept.

Facilities and Contact: Vasona Lake has a boat launch; paddle boats and rowboats may be rented. Call 408-356-2729 for information.

Cost: Entry and Parking $4.00 per vehicle

Directions to Vasona Lake: This lake is south of San Jose adjacent to Highway 17—you can see the lake from this highway. Follow Highway 17 south from San Jose and take the Lark Avenue exit. Go west on Lark Avenue to University Avenue. Turn south (left) and look for the signs into Vasona Lake County Park. For the Percolation Ponds, take a right (north) on Winchester at the end of Lark Avenue, a right on Division Street and left on Dell Avenue to the Number One pond where trout are stocked.

Regulations: Fishing is permitted during park hours from about 8:00 AM until the park closes at sunset. The limit is five trout and five bass (bass must be 12-inches long or longer), five catfish, 25 crappie and no limit on bluegill and sunfish. Koi are an ornamental fish and should be released. Only non-powered boats may be used.

6. Almaden Lake:

Trout	3
Bass	4
Catfish	3
Panfish	3

About Almaden Lake: This lake is an old rock quarry and is a multi-recreational lake in San Jose with fishing a minor part of the activities. It has resident bass, bluegill, catfish, crappie and carp.

Fishing: Bass are the number one catch here. Catfish and panfish may be caught but only a few are landed. Trout are not stocked but this lake has resident trout that spawn in creeks. Plastic worms and crank baits are basic bass lures and night crawlers are a good all-around bait that will catch the trout as well as the warm water fish.

Lake Records: Records have not been kept.

Facilities and Contact: This reservoir has a dirt boat launch but only rowboats and boats with electric motors may be used. A four wheel drive vehicle is recommended for boat launching. Call Almaden Lake at 408-277-5130 for information.

Cost: Entry and Parking $4.00 per vehicle summer; free in winter
 Boat launch $2.00

Directions to Almaden Lake: From downtown San Jose, take the Almaden Expressway past Blossom Hill Road to Coleman Road. Go past Coleman to the next light, make a "U" turn then make a right turn from the Almaden Expressway to the lake.

Regulations: Fishing is permitted during park hours from 8:00 AM in the summer until the park closes at sunset. During the winter it is open from 7:00 AM and entry is free. The limit is five trout and five bass (bass must be 12-inches long or longer), five catfish, 25 crappie and no limit on bluegill and sunfish. Rowboats, electric powered boats up to 16 feet maximum length, and float tubes are permitted.

7. Guadalupe Reservoir:

Bass	4
Catfish	3
Panfish	4

About Guadalupe Reservoir: This is a second reservoir in Almaden Quicksilver Park south of San Jose. It is not stocked and has only warm water fish. You may catch a few sunfish and occasionally a bass or catfish but it is not a prime fishing area. The fish have accumulated high levels of mercury and should not be eaten.

Fish: Resident warm water fish including bass, catfish and panfish may be caught but only a few fish are caught.

Lake Records: Records have not been kept.

Facilities and Contact: This reservoir has only roadside parking and no facilities so no fees are charged. Call the park at 408-268-3883 for information.

Cost: Entry and Parking No Fee

Directions to Guadalupe Reservoir: This reservoir is in Almaden Quicksilver County Park at the south end of San Jose. From downtown San Jose, take Highway 17 south to Camden. Turn left on Camden Avenue. Turn right onto Hicks Road to the park entrance and continue on this road to the lake.

Health Warning: The DFG warns, because of high mercury levels in their flesh, fish caught from Guadalupe Reservoir should not be eaten.

Regulations: Fishing is permitted when the park is open from 8:00 am until sunset. Since fish caught from this reservoir are not safe to eat, all should be released.

8. Almaden Reservoir:

Bass	3
Catfish	3
Panfish	4

About Almaden Reservoir: This reservoir at Almaden Quicksilver Park south of San Jose is not stocked and has only warm water fish. You may catch a few sunfish and rarely a bass or catfish but it is not a prime fishing area. To make it even less attractive, the fish have accumulated high levels of mercury and should not be eaten. It's fine if you want to get some sunshine on a spring day with an outside chance to catch a few fish but don't count on catching fish and don't eat anything you catch.

Lake Records: Records have not been kept.

Facilities and Contact: This reservoir has only roadside parking and no facilities and no fees are charged. Boats are not permitted. Call the park at 408-268-3883 for information.

Cost: Entry and Parking No Fee

Directions to Almaden Reservoir: This reservoir is in Almaden Quicksilver County Park at the south end of San Jose. From downtown San Jose, take the Almaden Expressway south to Almaden Road. Turn right onto this road and continue to the lake.

Health Warning: The DFG warns, because of high mercury levels in their flesh, fish caught from Almaden Reservoir should not be eaten.

Regulations: Fishing is permitted only during the day when the park is open—from 8:00 AM until sunset. Since fish caught from this reservoir are not safe to eat, all should be released.

9. Parkway Lake:

Trout	9
Catfish	8
Sturgeon	6
After a storm	7
Fly-fishing	6

About Parkway Lake: Parkway Lake south of San Jose has the largest trout in the South Bay Area—many weighing more than 10-pounds are caught. If you want to catch a large trout and don't care that it was probably dumped in the lake by the tanker truck a few days earlier, you would rate this lake a "10" for trout. It is private so anglers don't need fishing licenses and this is a good place to take a friend from out-of-state or someone who only fishes occasionally. The fishing fee costs about the same as a daily license plus a daily fishing fee for other lakes. As in most lakes, catfish are planted in the summer when the lake is too warm for trout. Resident bass and panfish are caught occasionally.

Parkway is the best lake in the Bay Area (really the only lake) to consistently catch sturgeon. Most

lakes aren't allowed to stock sturgeon but this private lake does stock them. Two to half a dozen sturgeon are caught in a typical week depending on how long it has been since sturgeon were planted.

The concessionaire rents boats but shore fishing is as good as fishing from a boat; most trophy trout are landed from shore and most people don't bother with the expense of a boat.

Trout: Parkway Lake is a relatively small put-and-take lake. What you "put" is what you "take". The lake concessionaire plants very large trout so many large trout are caught. Experienced anglers typically catch one to three trout in a half day of fishing; limits are fairly common. Anglers are very successful with Power Bait or night crawlers. The peninsula is a good fishing location. Trout are planted whenever the water is cool—usually from late September to early June so those are good trout fishing times.

Catfish: Catfish are the prime fish during the warm summer and early fall months. Then Parkway Lake is open late hours—as late as midnight—and anglers catch these fish mostly in the evening and at night.

Sturgeon: Sturgeon fishing is very good—1000 to 2000 pounds are stocked every three months and a few are landed most weeks. Grass shrimp is the prime bait but anglers catch them on night crawlers and even Power Bait. Anglers fishing for trout with Power Bait get a surprise when their strong, slow fighting fish turns out to be a sturgeon.

Tips From an Expert: "Most trophy fish are caught from shore," reports lake manager Flint Glines. "A size 14 or 16 treble hook baited with chartreuse or rainbow glitter Power Bait on an 18-24-inch leader fished with a sliding sinker is the way to catch these fish. Inflated night crawlers on the same rig with a single point hook works well." One-quarter ounce gold or silver Kastmasters cast and retrieved from shore have also been doing well for large trout.

Lake Records:

	Trout	19-pounds 6-ounces
	Catfish	20-pounds 8-ounces
	Sturgeon	52-pounds
	Bass	10-pounds

Facilities and Contact: Parkway Lake has a bait and tackle shop and boat rentals. It does not have a boat launching ramp and private boats aren't permitted on this lake. Call the bait shop at the lake at 408-629-9111 or Coyote Discount Bait and Tackle at 408-463-0711 for fishing information.

Cost:

	Entry and fishing	$12.00 per adult, $6.00 for children 12 and under.
	Entry and parking	$3.00 for spectators

Trout like this are the primary catch at several South Bay lakes like Lexington, Coyote and Loch Lomond lakes.

The launch ramp at Lexington Reservoir is a good entry to this lake when the lake is full.

Boat and trolling motor $35.00 per day
Boat only $20.00 per day

Boat rentals with or without a motor are half price Monday through Thursday.

Directions to Parkway Lake: Drive south from San Jose on Highway 101 to Bernal Road. Turn west (right) on Bernal to Monterey Road and turn south (left) onto this road. Make a left turn onto Metcalf Road and get ready to make a left turn to Parkway Lake.

Regulations: This is a day use park in the winter when trout are planted but is open as late as midnight in the summer when night fishing for catfish is popular. Call 408-629-9111 for hours, the latest fees and fishing information. Limits are five trout, five bass (a minimum of 12-inches in length), five catfish, 1 sturgeon, 25 crappie and no limit on bluegill and sunfish.

10. Lexington Reservoir:

Trout	6
Bass	6
Catfish	4
Panfish	5
After a storm	3

About Lexington Reservoir: When the 475 acre Lexington Reservoir south of San Jose just off Highway 17 is full, it is pretty as a picture and looks like it would be a great fishing lake. After a few years of drought, however, water is so low you almost need binoculars to see the water from the launch ramp. It has resident warm water fish including bass, catfish and panfish and has planted trout in the winter and spring. Unfortunately, about the time the lake has been full for a few years and it begins to produce decent catches, a few drought years come along; the lake is almost completely drained and fish are almost wiped out.

Trout: Lexington Reservoir is a good trout lake when DFG is planting these fish. Fish with Power Bait from the dam or shore area or troll from a boat.

Other Fish: Bass, catfish and panfish are caught near the shore and in coves. Use pig and jigs, plastic worms or crank baits for bass.

Lake Records: Records have not been kept.

Facilities and Contact: This lake has a launching ramp that is useable when the lake is nearly full but some years water doesn't even come close to the ramp. For information, call 408-867-0190. Only electric motors are permitted.

Cost:

	Entry and Parking	No fee
	Boat launch	$3.00

Directions to Lexington Reservoir: Drive south on Highway 17 from San Jose and take the Bear Creek Road exit. Drive over the overpass and get back on Highway 17 going north. Turn right on Alma Bridge Road and continue across the dam to the boat launch and picnic area.

Regulations: This park is open from 8:00 AM until sunset. Limits are five trout, five bass (a minimum of 12-inches in length), five catfish, 25 crappie and no limit on bluegill and sunfish. Only non-powered and electric-powered boats are permitted.

11. Calero Reservoir:

Bass	8
Panfish	7
After a storm	6
Fly-fishing	5

About Calero Reservoir: This 325 acre reservoir has been the best bass fishing lake of the South Bay. Bass up to 13 pounds have been landed and anglers can catch a dozen or more on a good fishing day. However, the fish are contaminated with mercury and are not safe to eat but most people release their bass anyway. Maybe that is why it remains such a good fishing lake.

Water skiers are prohibited on this lake and jet skiers were allowed at the beginning of 1998. MTBE (a possible carcinogen added to gasoline to make it burn cleaner and reduce emissions into the air) levels in the water started to climb and soon exceeded the levels recommended as safe. Jet skis were prohibited. Now the lake is open to only slow speed water craft making it ideal for fishing. Changes to boating regulations are being considered so it may be opened to high speed users in the future. The other large recreational lake in the area, Anderson Reservoir, permits water skiers but prohibits jet skiers.

This lake on the southern outskirts of San Jose is not a secret and anyone wishing to launch a boat on the weekend from April through September must call 408-358-3751 to make a reservation. This and Anderson Lake are the only lakes in the Bay Area that require a reservation to launch.

Anderson Lake is busy with boaters and has a reservation system to launch on summer weekends. This is one of two launch ramps at this lake.

Bass: Fishing for bass is best in the early spring when the lake isn't busy but summer was a different story. When jet skiers dominate the main part of the lake many bass anglers left the lake going to Anderson Reservoir. Bass anglers are returning now that these high speed uses have been prohibited. Use traditional plastic worms, lizards, spinner baits and crank baits. If you can, fish on weekdays when the lake is much less crowded.

Tips From an Expert: "Calero Reservoir is big enough to have a lot of good fishing spots but it is small enough to learn every point and every bush in a few trips," says Sam Takemoto, an expert bass angler and fly-fisherman. "It has some tulles, downed trees, and rocky points that drop off to deep water."

"I've had good success fishing plastic worms and curly tail grubs in March and April and have caught a number of fish on surface flies or shallow running flies at that time," Takemoto continues. "Fish your plastic lure very slowly and watch your line. You usually don't feel the bite; lateral movement of the line is the only tip-off that a bass has your lure."

Plastic lures on Carolina rigs fished in deep water can be very good when bass are deeper.

Other Fish: This lake also has crappie, sunfish and bluegill. Use jigs for crappie or worms or Power Bait for all three species. Fly-fishers can also catch these fish on flies including small poppers fished at sunrise or at dusk.

Lake Records: Records have not been kept.

Facilities and Contact: This lake has a launching ramp. For information, call 408-268-3883. Call Coyote Discount Bait and Tackle at 408-463-0711 for fishing information.

Cost: Entry and Parking $4.00 per car
            Boat launch $5.00

Directions to Calero Reservoir: Drive south from San Jose on Highway 101 to Bernal Road. Go west (right) on Bernal to Monterey Road and turn south (left) onto this road. Continue through the town of Coyote (you may want to stop at Coyote Bait and Tackle for bait and information). Make a right turn onto Bailey Road, another right onto McKean Road and follow the signs to the boat launching ramp or to fishing areas.

Health Warning: The DFG warns, because of high mercury levels in their flesh, fish caught from this reservoir should not be eaten.

Regulations: This lake is open from 8:00 AM in the winter and 7:00 AM in the summer until one-half hour after sunset. Since fish caught from this reservoir are not safe to eat, all should be released.

12. Loch Lomond Lake:

Trout	7
Bass	6

Cathy Lambert holds up a small trout. Many Bay Area lakes give up thousands of these fish in a season.

Catfish	2
Panfish	5
Fly-fishing	5

About Loch Lomond Lake: Loch Lomond Lake north of the city of Santa Cruz is a pleasure to visit whether you catch fish or just have an outing at a very pretty mountain lake. Its location in a cool part of the Santa Cruz Mountains at an elevation of 580 feet makes it an enjoyable summer trip to escape the heat of warmer climates. Managed by the City of Santa Cruz Water Department, it is open March 1 to September 15. Anglers make good catches of trout and bass.

Trout: Trout are planted by the DFG from opening day of March 1 until early July. Shore fishing is good using Power Bait, worms or small lures. Trolling with small lures like Needlefish, Triple Teazers, Humdinger or Dick Nites is also a good way to catch these fish.

Bass: "Wild bass are the favorite of many anglers here" said Ranger Tom Gilmore. "Casting lures from shore is almost as good as fishing from a boat. Don't expect giant fish but anglers who have learned the lake can catch a half dozen or more bass in a morning of fishing."

Other Fish: Panfish and channel catfish may also be caught. Use bits of worm on small hooks to catch panfish; try night crawlers on larger hooks for catfish.

Lake Records: Records have not been kept.

Facilities and Contact: Facilities at this lake include a launching ramp for small electric-powered fishing boats and a park store that rents rowboats and electric boats, sells bait, tackle and snacks. Contact Loch Lomond Recreation Area at P. O. Box 682, Santa Cruz, 9060, Phone 408-335-7424

Anglers land a trout.

Cost:	Entry and Parking	$4.00 per car
	Boat launch	$5.00 per day
	Boat and motor	$25.00 per half day
	Boat only	$18.00 per half day

Directions to Loch Lomond Lake: Follow Highway 17 south from San Jose or north from Santa Cruz to Scotts Valley. Go west on Mount Herman Road then north on Zayante Road. When Zayante Road veers right, go straight ahead on Lompico Road and turn left onto West Drive to the park.

Regulations: Loch Lomond Lake is open from March 1 through September 15 from 6:00 AM until sunset. Alcoholic beverages, swimming, wading and float tubes are prohibited. Limits are five trout, five bass (a minimum of 12-inches in length), five catfish, and no limit on bluegill and sunfish. Children under 14 years of age must be accompanied by an adult.

13. Coyote Creek:

| Trout | 5 |
| Fly-fishing | 4 |

About Coyote Creek: Several miles of Coyote Creek below Anderson Reservoir are stocked with trout from April to August. Fishing is permitted from the last Saturday in April to November 15. The creek runs through a day use park just a couple miles east of Highway 101 so is easily accessible.

Fishing: Planted trout from April through August make up the catch.

Lake Records: Records have not been kept—fish are small.

Facilities and Contact: Coyote Creek runs through Coyote Creek County Park below Anderson Reservoir. This park has picnic facilities, restrooms, plenty of shade and is a very pleasant park. During the summer it gets crowded though most people come to picnic and fishing is still reasonable. For information, call the park at 408-779-3634 or the Santa Clara County Parks Dept. at 408-358-3741. Call Coyote Discount Bait and Tackle at 408-463-0711 for fishing information.

Cost: Entry and Parking No fee

Directions to Coyote Creek: Follow Highway 101 south from San Jose almost to Morgan Hill. Take the Cochrane Road exit and go east (left) to the creek below Anderson Reservoir. For a downstream area, take the Cochrane Road exit but go west (right) to Monterey Road and then turn north (right) to the creek.

Regulations: Limits are five trout during the open season from the first Saturday in April through November 15.

14. Anderson Lake:

Bass	9
Catfish	7
Panfish	7
After a storm	4
Fly-fishing	5

About Anderson Lake: Anderson Lake is a 1200 acre lake on Coyote Creek northeast of Gilroy and is the largest lake in Santa Clara County. Water skiers are permitted and they are its predominate users during the warm months. Jet skis have been temporarily banned to reduce the levels of MTBE.

This lake has very good fishing for bass and for crappie particularly in the spring and fall and produces some very large catfish. Anglers fishing during early spring avoid most of the water skiers. Several five mile-per-hour zones around the lake provide relief from high speed users.

Reservations are required to launch a boat here on weekend days from April through September. There is a limit of 160 boats allowed on this lake—but that tells you it is pretty busy in the summer and other lakes are more angler friendly on busy weekends and holidays.

Bass: Black Bass are the number one catch in this lake. When the weather warms and high speed water users take over the lake, fishing is best in coves like Rattlesnake Cove and Packwood Cove at the north and west end of the lake or at the east end of the lake where the speed limit is five mph. This lake has brush and cover and some rocky shores all around the lake where bass are caught. Plastic worms, crankbaits and spinner baits that work well in other lakes and the Delta also entice bass here.

Tips by and Expert: "I would rank Anderson Lake as the number one fishing lake in Santa Clara County," says Denise Bradford from Coyote Bait and Tackle and an expert angler. "Calero ranks a close second."

"Limits of bass are easy at Anderson Lake in the spring and often will include a 5 to 7-pound bass," she says. The lake is full of threadfin shad so lures like Rat-L-Traps or Luhr Jensen Speed Traps are good lures. Plastic worms and lizards are still the number one fish producers in the spring. Green pumpkins or June bug lizards are good patterns. Pig and jigs in browns, blacks or orange or two tone pork rinds are best in the fall."

Panfish: This is an excellent lake for crappie—probably the best in the South Bay Area. Fish with minnows or mini-jigs in brush all-around the lake to catch these fish.

Other Fish: Catfish and bluegill are also caught in this lake.

Lake Records: Lake records have not been kept.

Facilities and Contact: This lake has two launching ramps and a bait and tackle shop but does not have rental boats. Call 408-779-3634 for information or call 408-927-9144 to make a boat launch reservation for the weekend or holiday during the summer. Call the preceding Monday to make a Saturday reservation and call Tuesday to make a reservation for Sunday. Call Coyote Discount Bait and Tackle at 408-463-0711 for fishing information.

Cost: Entry and Parking $4.00 per car
Boat launch $5.00
Boat Reservation Fee $5.00

Directions to Anderson Lake: Travel south from San Jose on Highway 101 to East Dunne Avenue in Morgan Hill. exit the freeway and make a left turn to the lake. A bait shop and launching ramp are in this area. A second launching ramp is off Cochran Road, the next exit north of East Dunne Avenue.

Regulations: This day use lake is open from 8:00 AM in the winter and 7:00 AM in the summer until sunset. Limits are five trout, five bass (a minimum of 12-inches in length), five catfish, 25 crappie and no limit on bluegill and sunfish.

15. Chesbro Reservoir:

Bass	6
Catfish	6
Panfish	4
After a storm	5
Fly-fishing	5

About Chesbro Reservoir: This lake is a long narrow 269 acre lake west of Morgan Hill and is primarily a fishing lake. It is not stocked with fish but has resident warm water fish and is most noted for good bass fishing. Extended years of drought impact fishing but with recent high rainfalls, the lake has remained nearly full and fishing is good. Only rowboats and electric-powered boats are permitted.

Bass: Largemouth bass are the prime sport fish at Chesbro Reservoir and fishing is best in the spring when fish spawn. Fish all along its shoreline with plastic baits, spinner baits or crank baits to catch fish.

Other Fish: Catfish, crappie, bluegill and sunfish may be caught when consistent water levels are maintained. The lake also has carp.

Lake Records: Records have not been kept.

Facilities and Contact: Chesbro Reservoir has a minimum of facilities that include a boat launch ramp, picnic tables and restrooms. For general information call 408-779-9232. Call Coyote Discount Bait and Tackle at 408-463-0711 for fishing information.

Cost: Entry and Parking No fee
Boat launch $3.00

Directions to Chesbro Reservoir: Follow Highway 101 south from San Jose and make a right turn onto Bernal Road. Make a left turn onto the Monterey Highway. Take Bailey Road to the right and turn left onto McKean Road. This road becomes Uvas Road. Turn left onto Oak Glen Avenue and follow the signs to the lake.

Regulations: The park is open and fishing is permitted only from 8:00 AM in the winter and 7:00 AM in the summer to sunset and only non-powered and electric-powered boats are allowed. Limits are five trout, five bass (a minimum of 12-inches in length), five catfish, 25 crappie and no limit on bluegill and sunfish.

16. Uvas Reservoir:

Bass	6
Catfish	6
Crappie	5
After a storm	5
Fly-fishing	4

About Uvas Reservoir: This lake is a long narrow 286 acre lake west of Morgan Hill. It is not stocked with fish but has good fishing for resident warm water fish when the lake remains fairly full. It could be a much better fishing lake but it is often drawn down after bass spawn; their eggs are left high and dry and spawning is unsuccessful. With recent high rainfalls,

it has retained a more consistent water level; bass have spawned successfully, and fishing has improved.

Bass: Resident largemouth bass are the prime fish at Uvas Reservoir and fishing is good particularly in the spring when fish spawn. The long narrow lake has a lot of shoreline and that is the place to catch bass.

Other Fish: This is an excellent lake for crappie, catfish and sunfish when consistent water levels are maintained.

Lake Records: Records have not been kept.

Facilities and Contact: This lake has a minimum of services including a launch ramp, picnic tables and restrooms. For information call 408-779-9232. Call Coyote Discount Bait and Tackle at 408-463-0711 for fishing information.

Cost: Entry and Parking No fee
Boat launch $3.00

Directions to Uvas Reservoir: Take Highway 101 south from San Jose and make a right turn onto Bernal Road. Make a left turn onto the Monterey Highway. Take Bailey Road to the right and turn left onto McKean Road. This road becomes Uvas Road; follow the signs to the lake.

Regulations: The lake is open from 8:00 AM to sunset. Boating and fishing are permitted only during daylight hours and only non-powered or electric-powered boats are allowed. All boats must be off the reservoir one-half hour before sunset. Limits are five bass (a minimum of 12-inches in length), five catfish, 25 crappie and no limit on bluegill and sunfish.

17. Coyote Lake:

Trout	7
Bass	5
Catfish	4
Panfish	5
After a storm	4
Fly-fishing	5

About Coyote Lake: This lake is a long narrow 635 acre lake east of Gilroy. It has planted trout and several species of warm water fish. Water skiing and jet skiing are permitted but both ends of the lake have five mph speed limits and these are the best places to fish on warm days. This is one of the few lakes in Santa Clara County that has camping at the lake.

This lake has had a history of being full one year then almost drained the next—a deterrent to good fishing. With recent high rainfalls, it has retained a decent amount of water. It can be a very good bass lake if water management will keep enough water in the lake for these fish to spawn and to survive throughout the year.

Trout: This lake is stocked with DFG trout from March through June (some years stocking begins earlier) and trout fishing is good every year. Power Bait and night crawlers are the prime baits. Trollers using Needlefish or Krocodile lures make good catches. The face of the dam and near the launch are two good areas for shore anglers. It isn't ranked higher because the fish are small with a 12 to 14-inch trout an above average fish.

Bass: The potential as a good bass lake has been thwarted by full then empty water "management." After a series of wet winters the lake has had a decent water level throughout the year and bass fishing has been good.

Other Fish: Catfish anglers do well when and if a reasonable minimum pool is maintained all year. Crappie, bluegill and sunfish may be caught throughout the year.

Lake Records: Lake records have not been kept.

Facilities and Contact: This is a full service lake with fishing, water skiing and hiking and is one of the few lakes in the area to have camping facilities. It has a boat launch and a small general store but does not have gasoline nor boat rentals. For information call 408-842-7800. Call Coyote Discount Bait and Tackle at 408-463-0711 for fishing information.

Cost: Entry and Parking $4.00 per car
Boat launch $5.00
Camping $10.00 for a tent site, $20 for an RV site

Directions to Coyote Lake: Follow Highway 101 south from San Jose past Morgan Hill. Exit at Leavesley Road and go east (left). Make a left turn onto New Avenue and then a right onto Roop Road. Turn left onto Gilroy Hot Springs Road. Make another left onto Coyote Lake Road to the lake.

Regulations: Boating is permitted from 8:00 AM when the park opens until one half hour before sunset but anglers camping at the lake can fish from shore in the early morning and in the evening. Limits are five trout, five bass (a minimum of 12-inches in length), five catfish, 25 crappie and no limit on bluegill and sunfish.

18. Sprig Lake:

Trout   5

Trent Pridemore fishes for striped bass at O'Neill Forebay. This is an excellent location to catch striped bass bait fishing, fishing with lures or fly fishing.

About Sprig Lake: This very small lake in Mount Madonna County Park is stocked with trout April through June. It is open to fishing for children five to 12 years of age during these months and they may only fish from shore. The park located at the summit of Hecker Pass Road (Highway 152) ten miles west of Gilroy has great views of the area, camping and a variety of activities.

Trout: Small trout are stocked by DFG from April through June.

Lake Records: Records have not been kept.

Facilities and Contact: This park has 100 tent camping sites and 17 RV sites on a first-come-first-served basis. Call Mount Madonna Park at 408-842-2341 for information.

Cost: Entry and Parking $4.00
Camping $10.00 to $20.00

Directions to Sprig Lake: Mount Madonna County Park and Sprig Lake are 10 miles west of Gilroy. Take Highway 152 west from Highway 101 in Gilroy or east from Highway 1 in Watsonville and turn north on Pole Line Road to the park.

Regulations: This lake permits fishing April to June for children ages 5-12. The limit is five trout and boating is not permitted on this lake.

19. Pinto Lake:

Bass	6
Trout	5
Catfish	4
Panfish	4
Fly-fishing	4

About Pinto Lake: This 92 acre lake east of Watsonville managed by this city's parks department has both a public and a private campground.

Trout: Trout are planted by the DFG from fall through early summer and most anglers fish for and catch trout. Power Bait and worms are the favorite bait.

Bass: "We have good fishing and anglers catch large bass," reports John Marmo who owns Marmo's Store here. "I weighed in a 9-pound 2-ounce bass last year." Use plastic baits, crank baits, spinner baits or natural bait.

Other Fish: Catfish and panfish are also caught.

Lake Records: Records have not been kept.

Facilities and Contact: This lake has campsites as part of the park on its east shore. The private concessionaire has a bait shop, launching ramp and campgrounds on its southwest shore. Call the park at 408-722-8129 or the private concessionaire, Marmo's, at 408-722-4533 for information.

Cost: Entry and Parking $5.00 per car
Boat launch $5.00 per day
Boat rental $12 per day

Camping $10 to $18

Directions to Pinto Lake: Drive on Highway 152 east from Highway 1 at Watsonville. Turn left on Green Valley Road. Turn left at Amesti Road and follow the signs to Marmo's or turn left off Green Valley Road onto Behler Road to the public facilities.

Regulations: Limits are five trout, five bass (a minimum of 12-inches in length) and no limit on catfish, bluegill and sunfish. Gas-powered motors may be used but the speed limit is five mph.

20. Henry Coe State Park Lakes:

Bass	9
Panfish	7
Trout	6
Fly-fishing	9

About Lakes at Henry Coe State Park: Henry Coe State Park is the South Bay's wilderness area. Not far in distance from San Jose, it seems like another world. The narrow twisty road after you leave Anderson Lake east of Morgan Hill is less than 10 miles long to this park but it seems much longer and separates the adventurer from the casual camper and angler. The park has more than 70 lakes and about half of these have fish. To get to the best ones you need to hike about 10 miles and the trek includes a lot of climbing—this is not just an afternoon stroll.

Some lakes will produce small bass on almost every cast. This is a great place to get away for a few days and hone your skills with a fly rod.

Bass: Black bass are the prime game fish at this park but it takes a lot of hiking to get to the better lakes. Plan three days to really take advantage of them—one day to hike in, one day to fish and explore and one day to hike out. Fly-fishers do very well fishing poppers in the morning and evening.

Other Fish: Panfish are included in the catch. Small surface lures are great sport for these fish. Trout were here at one time but only a few remain. Wild trout are found in some of the streams. Most are less than 10-inches and a big one is about 16-inches long.

Tips From an Expert: "Henry Coe State Park is one of my favorite places in California," says expert angler Tom Stienstra, author of the book *California Fishing*. "Take at least three days and be prepared with all of the normal backpacking equipment including a water purifier." He says the best lakes are Coit Lake, Hoover Lake and Paradise Lake—all good bass lakes. Rapalas are good lures but any bass lure is a good lure when fish are biting in the early morning and near sunset.

Lake Records: Records have not been kept.

Facilities and Contact: This park has campgrounds for tents and trailers and also has backpack campgrounds. Contact Henry Coe State Park at P. O. Box 846, Morgan Hill, CA 95038 or phone 408-779-2728 or visit web site www.coepark.parks.ca.gov for camping information and ask for a book describing fishing in this park ($1.39 plus tax) and a map. Call Coyote Discount Bait and Tackle at 408-463-0711 for fishing information.

Cost: Entry and Parking $5.00 per car
Camping $16.00 at improved campsites

Directions to Henry Coe State Park: Drive south on Highway 101 to East Dunne Avenue in Morgan Hill. Take this twisty road to the left and continue past Anderson Lake to Henry Coe State Park. The entrance is at 2500 feet elevation 13 miles east of Morgan Hill.

Regulations: Limits are five trout, five bass (a minimum of 12-inches in length), 25 crappie and no limit on bluegill and sunfish.

21. San Luis Reservoir:

Striped Bass	9
Black Bass	6
Catfish	7
Panfish	7
After a storm	4
Fly-fishing	5

About San Luis Reservoir: This 13,800 acre reservoir is a water holding facility for the California Water project. It gets water pumped from the Delta down the California Aqueduct. The water is held until it is needed for crop irrigation, residential, or industrial use. With the water comes striped bass larvae—a very early stage of these fish, too small to be screened out of the water. These larvae thrive and may grow to record size striped bass.

O'Neill Forebay is adjacent to San Luis Reservoir and is all part of the same water holding complex. Both lakes have excellent striped bass fishing. See the next entry for a description of O'Neill Forebay.

Caution: Winds can come up quickly at San Luis Reservoir and O'Neill Forebay. A yellow light flashes to warn caution when winds are 15 to 30 mph. When red flashing lights signal the winds are stronger than 30 mph, the lake is closed and everyone must take their boats off the water.

Striped Bass: This is the premier fish that puts San Luis Reservoir and O'Neill Forebay on the map for fishing. Still fishing with bait, trolling or casting crank baits are all good ways to catch striped bass. Fly-fishers have good success for striped bass using baitfish imitation flies like Lefty Deceivers or Dan Blanton Whistlers.

Other Fish: San Luis Reservoir also has catfish, crappie, shad, perch and bluegill. They hold some salmon and sturgeon brought in with the water pumped from the Delta but anglers rarely catch them. Who wants to fish for them when striped bass fishing is so good?

Tips From an Expert: "My favorite fishing method is jigging," said Perley Spaulding who regularly catches 800 or more striped bass here in a year. "Anglers also catch stripers on bait or by trolling slowly 30 feet deep in the spring to 60 feet deep in the summer."

Lake Records: The 67-pound 8-ounce striped bass caught by Hank Ferguson at O'Neill Forebay is a world record for landlocked striped bass and the size of striped bass in San Luis Reservoir is not far behind.

Facilities and Contact: San Luis Reservoir has two launching ramps and a public campground. It does not have rental boats. Call 1-800-444 7275 to make reservations at a campground. Call 209-826-1196 for general information.

Cost: Entry and Parking $5.00 per car
Boat launch $5.00 per day
Camping $16 per night
Seniors' entry fee is $4.00 and camping for seniors is $14.

Directions to San Luis Reservoir: Drive on Interstate 5 south from Tracy to Highway 152. Exit the freeway, proceed west on this highway and follow the signs to the lake. San Luis Reservoir is a left turn and O'Neill Forebay is to the right. From San Jose, take Highway 101 to Gilroy, turn east on Highway 152 and go most of the way to Los Banos to these lakes.

Regulations: Fishing is permitted from boats during the day and from shore both day and night. Boating is permitted from 1/2-hour before sunrise to sunset—all boats must be off the reservoir by sunset. The daily limit for striped bass is five and they may be any size. A striped bass stamp as well as the normal fishing license is required to take striped bass.

Water skiing is permitted. If the wind is more than 30 mph, the lake is closed to all boating—a red flashing light signals the lake is closed and all boats must be taken off the reservoir.

22. O'Neill Forebay:

Striped Bass	10
Black Bass	5
Catfish	6
After a storm	7
Fly-fishing	8

About O'Neill Forebay: San Luis Reservoir has good striped bass fishing but O'Neill Forebay is where the really big ones seem to be caught. This lake is the perennial producer of record fish and currently holds the record for the largest landlocked striped bass caught in the United States—a 67-pound 8-ounce striper caught in 1992 by Hank Ferguson.

O'Neill Forebay adjacent to San Luis Reservoir, gets water from the Delta. Along with the water it also gets striped bass, catfish, black bass,

An angler shows why O'Neill Forebay is a favorite striped bass fishing lake.

crappies, bluegill and a few salmon and sturgeon but striped bass get most of the attention.

This reservoir is a very good place to catch stripers fly-fishing. This is smaller and shallower than San Luis Reservoir and has better fly-fishing opportunities. A fly tied to imitate a bait fish will catch stripers—a Dan Blanton designed fly called a Whistler tied in light colors is a very good fly for these fish.

Striped Bass: Striped bass are the fish that put O'Neill Forebay and San Luis Reservoir on the map. Bait like live threadfin shad is the number one way to catch these fish. Trolling or casting plugs is also good. Matt Desimone casting his Stud Lure was very successful catching fish. He used both a floating stick bait and a diving lure successfully. Perley Spaulding particularly likes jigging.

Other Fish: Catfish and black bass fishing is good but striped bass dominate fishing here.

Tips From an Expert: "My favorite fishing method is jigging," said Perley Spaulding. "Bait fishing using live shad, mudsuckers or cut anchovies is the favorite fishing method of most anglers although trolling also catches stripers."

Lake Records:	Striped Bass	67-pounds 8-ounces
	Black Bass	Not recorded
	Catfish	Not recorded

Facilities and Contact: O'Neill Forebay has two launching ramps, a public campground with 53 developed campsites with electricity and water and a group campground. Call 1-800-444-7275 to make reservations at a campground. Call 209-826-1196 for maps and general information.

Cost:	Entry and Parking	$5.00 per car
	Boat launch	$5.00 per day
	Camping	$15.00 per night

Seniors' entry fee is $4.00 and camping for seniors is $13.

Directions to O'Neill Forebay: Follow Interstate 5 south from Tracy to Highway 152. Exit the freeway and proceed west on this highway and follow the signs to the lake. O'Neill Forebay is to the right. From the San Jose Area, take Highway 101 to Gilroy and turn east on Highway 152 and go most of the way to Los Banos.

Regulations: Fishing is permitted from shore both day and night but boating is permitted only from 1/2-hour before sunrise to sunset. A striped bass stamp as well as a state fishing license is required to take these fish. The daily limit on striped bass is five and they may be any size.

All boat traffic is to be in a counterclockwise direction. Water skiing is permitted. Winds can come up quickly. A yellow light flashes to warn caution when winds are 15 to 30 mph. Red flashing lights signals winds are greater than 30 mph; the lake is closed; and all boaters must get off the lake.

The author shows off a large striped bass. Stripers up to 40-pounds have been landed from Lake Del Valle and to 67.5-pounds at O'Neill Forebay.

23. California Aqueduct:

Striped Bass	5
Catfish	5
Panfish	3
After a Storm	5

About California Aqueduct: The Delta Mendota Canal and the California Aqueduct are two huge water distribution canals. They take water from Northern California where water is plentiful and move it to the Southern California deserts along with water from other sources and like magic, Palm Springs and Los Angeles are tropical oases. They also move water to the San Joaquin and Sacramento Valleys making these arid lands the most productive agricultural region in the world.

The central control for this is the Delta. Waters are diverted from their natural flow from the Delta to the ocean to be exported south. Pumps that start the water flow are screened to keep fish in the Delta but very small fish pass through the screens. Large numbers of striped bass, some salmon, sturgeon, panfish and catfish all are swept with the waterflow into the canals to wherever this water is delivered.

Some of these fish become residents of the aqueducts and grow to catchable size. While fish are caught, these concrete aqueducts are a sterile fishing environment. No free flowing, meandering rivers, no trees, just all business—let's move the water. It gets very low marks for a pleasant environment that is an important part of most fishing experiences.

The California Aqueduct and the Delta Mendota Canal run parallel from Bethany Lake and from Clifton Court Forebay northwest of Tracy to San Luis Reservoir and continue south toward Southern California.

These concrete banks can be a hazard to anglers. Fall into one and there are no shallows to wade to safety and nothing to grab a hold of to climb back out. It is no place for children to play and adults should use care to not lose their footing and fall into the canal.

Fishing: Catfish are the most common catch but striped bass are also caught in these channels. Some panfish are landed but they are not an important part of the catch.

Records: Records have not been kept.

Facilities and Contact: Parking for this fishing is found at Bethany Reservoir at the north end of the California Aqueduct or where the occasional road crosses these aqueducts. They have bike paths all along their banks so anglers can ride bikes along the aqueducts and stop and fish. Call 925-687-1800 for information.

Cost: Fishing in these aqueducts is free but you may need to pay for parking depending on where you enter the area.

Directions to California Aqueduct: To reach the north end of the California Aqueduct at Bethany Reservoir go east on Interstate 5 from Livermore and take the Grant Line Road Byron exit. Go north on this road and turn left onto Mountain House Road and left onto Kelso Road. Make another left onto Burns Road and follow that road to the reservoir.

Regulations: The daily limit on striped bass taken south of Interstate 580 near Tracy is five and they may be any size. North of this boundary, the normal regulations of a daily limit of two striped bass 18-inches or longer applies. A striped bass stamp as well as a state fishing license are required to take striped bass.

24. San Justo Lake:

Trout	7
Bass	6
Catfish	5
After a Storm	6

About San Justo Lake: This 200 acre lake holds irrigation water south of the town of Hollister. It opened in 1988 and was the first recreational facility of the San Benito County Parks Department. "Swimming is not permitted and only non-powered boats or boats with electric motors may be used so this is primarily a fishing lake," says concessionaire manager Linda Dinkuhn.

It has bass, planted trout, crappie and catfish. Like many lakes in the area, it suffers from water draw-downs in drought years. This lake is open to the public from sunrise to sunset Wednesday through Sunday during

Lures like Dick Nites, Needlefish, and Triple Teazers are good lures for trout in Bay Area lakes.

the summer and Friday through Sunday the rest of the year.

Trout: Planted trout are the most popular fish here. DFG plants their typical pan-sized trout and the concessionaire adds trophy trout for derbies. Trout are stocked twice a month from January through June and once a month in October and November. Use the standard Power Bait or night crawlers or troll or cast small lures like Rapalas, Rat-L-Traps, Needlefish, Cripplures, Triple Teazers or Kastmasters. Bass and catfish are also caught.

Bass: Largemouth bass are popular and anglers have caught bass up to about 11 pounds. The lake has some rock banks along with dirt banks and it has a few submerged trees. Catch bass by fishing by the rocks and off points. Plastic baits are the top bass producers but crankbaits and spinner baits also attract fish.

Other Fish: Crappie, bluegill and catfish are also caught. The largest fish caught from this lake are resident catfish weighing as much as about 30 pounds.

Lake Records:

	Trout	10-pounds 2-ounces
	Catfish	30-pounds
	Bass	11-pounds

Facilities and Contact: San Justo Lake has a paved launch ramp, picnic facilities, restrooms, and a store that sells bait and tackle and snacks. Motels, restaurants and supplies are in nearby Hollister or San Juan Bautista. For information, call the lake at 408-638-3300 or call the San Benito County Parks Department at 408-637-3725.

Cost:

	Entry and parking	$5.00 per vehicle
	Fishing	No additional fee
	Boat Launching	$3.00 per boat

Directions to San Justo Lake: Take Highway 101 south from Gilroy and turn left on Highway 156 through San Juan Bautista toward Hollister. Turn right onto Union Road then turn right again into the park.

Regulations: Limits are five trout, five bass (a minimum of 12-inches in length) and no limit on catfish, bluegill and sunfish. Only non-powered boats and boats with electric motors are allowed.

A large Stud Lure that is good for striped bass is compared with a Pop-R, a typical surface lure for black bass.

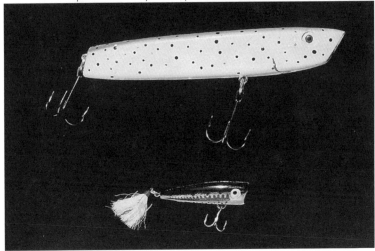

CHAPTER 7

Mississippi River in the Bay Area

The Delta is a maze of 1000 miles of interlaced waterways from Martinez about 40 miles northeast of San Francisco east to Stockton and from Sacramento south to Tracy. It is a place where you can easily imagine yourself transformed back in time 50 or 100 years. Around each bend is a surprise—a ferry, a rustic bait shop, an isolated bar where you can talk with a local field worker, an angler, maybe a vacationing doctor; a fancy restaurant in a grounded paddlewheel ferry looms up in the middle of nowhere. You almost expect to see Huck Finn and Tom Sawyer on a raft around the next corner and Injun Joe could be hiding any place. But this isn't close to the Mississippi River, the settings for Mark Twain's Huck Finn and Tom Sawyer classics. This is inland from the Bay Area at the confluence of the Sacramento and San Joaquin Rivers before they empty into San Pablo Bay.

When you feel certain you have been transformed back to a bygone era, a modern million dollar yacht comes around the corner jolting you into the reality of the time. Earl Stanley Gardner, author and creator of Perry Mason, acknowledged this Delta was his favorite spot on earth and he even wrote a non-fiction book about his ramblings on the Delta.

The Delta has great fishing but it has a lot more. Thousand of boaters cruise the Delta many storing their boats in one of thousands of berths throughout the Delta. The majority of them rarely or never fish—cruising and seeing the Delta is what they are after. Hundreds of houseboats are rented and many more are privately owned.

On a warm day several hundred boaters launch their boats to water ski or jet ski in the Delta. These high speed users as well as high speed fishing boats sometimes collide at blind intersections of crossing waterways with disastrous, sometimes deadly results. Be careful; watch for high speed boaters, and slow down at intersections when you are traveling these waters.

The definition of a delta in my dictionary is the alluvial deposit at the mouth of a river. The delta at the Mississippi River, like most deltas, is adjacent to the ocean. But this California Delta is inland from the San Pablo Bay. Here the deposits carried down the rivers have settled out and this extremely rich peat soil grows bumper crops of vegetables, fruits and flowers. Rivers and canals dug to transport farm products form a maze of interconnecting waterways; dozens of islands are included and ferries still operate as the only means to transport people and equipment to several of these islands. Drawbridges look like they came from another era with three different types of raising or rotating bridges scattered throughout the Delta.

Winds have blown away much of the top soil and the land is as much as 20 feet below the adjacent water level. Levies hold the water back but occasionally a levee fails and an island is flooded. Some are later pumped dry and recovered but one, Frank's Tract east of Bethel Island, was flooded, buildings, farm machinery and all and was not reclaimed. The buildings have decomposed and are gone but foundations and submerged machinery create habitat for fish but are hazardous to boaters. Proceed with caution if you boat in this area. Boaters who have ignored the hazards have been devastated when they impacted a submerged farm implement and their outdrives were ruined.

Shad are a great game fish.

Great Variety of Quality Fish

The water is muddy and you would expect to catch catfish and maybe bass. These are two of the most important fish of the Delta but the fish with real charisma is the striped bass. Some weighing 50 pounds or more have been landed but they range all the way down to 8 to 10 inches. Even a small striper puts up a spirited fight that belies its size (any less than 18 inches must be released). A large one is a powerful fighting machine that must be experienced to be believed.

Anglers looking for even more challenge fish for striped bass with flies and have excellent success. Frank's Tract at Bethel Island is a particularly good place to fish for them with flies. The water is shallow and flows in and out of breaks in embankments. A fly imitating a baitfish cast into this flowing water will often draw a strike from a striped bass waiting to ambush a small fish.

But these aren't the largest fish. Sturgeon are the behemoth fish here and they are the largest fish caught in the United States. The largest freshwater sport caught fish on record in the United States is a 468 pound white sturgeon landed by Joey Pallotta in Carquinez Straits between Vallejo and Martinez.

Catfish are the most abundant fish. Buy a few clams; find a spot on the bank; open a clam with a strong bladed knife. Scrap out the meat; bait your hook with the meat and cast your bait to submerged pilings or piers, to a fallen tree or deep hole. A simple spinning or casting outfit will suffice and soon you should catch a few catfish. For the really large catfish, use chicken liver or turkey liver; fish with heavier tackle and fish at night.

Anglers can catch a mess of panfish from the Delta or a large carp. Carp are very bony, not a favored food fish and earn very low esteem for anglers. It doesn't jump when hooked but is strong and challenging. European anglers prize carp and only in the United States does this fish have such a poor reputation.

The big factor that sets fishing in the Delta off from fishing in other regions is tides. Most of this area is affected by tides as the water reverses direction flowing inland as the tide rises and then flows in its normal direction toward the ocean as the tide recedes. Most fish respond to the flowing water and feed as the water is moving either in or out but seem to take a siesta when water is calm. Because of the distance from the ocean and the choked flow through the Carquinez Strait, high and low tides may be delayed by as much as eight or ten hours from the times published in the tide tables for the Golden Gate Bridge. These tables have the appropriate correction factors so you can adjust the times, calculate when water will be flowing at any location and know when to fish.

The water below about Antioch is partially saltwater during normal flows and water inland from this point is generally freshwater. In a dry year, saltwater intrusion may extend farther inland and heavy water flow after winter storms may push freshwater into San Pablo Bay.

Health Warning:

Due to elevated levels of mercury, PCB and other chemicals, the DFG warns people to limit the amount of Delta caught fish they eat so catch-and-release is a good fishing plan. DFG warns adults should eat no more than two meals of fish caught from the Delta or the Bay in a month. Furthermore adults should not eat any striped bass over 35 inches long. DFG also warns that women who are pregnant or expect to get pregnant, nursing mothers and children under six years old should not consume more than one meal of fish caught from these areas in a month nor should they eat any striper more than 27 inches long or shark more than 24 inches long. This warning does not apply to transitory fish like salmon and shad.

Facilities

The Delta is largely private property peppered with resorts, launching ramps—some free public ramps but most launch ramps are pay-to -launch at a resort—and an occasional public park. You can camp at many private campgrounds or a few state facilities like Brannan Island State Recreation Area southeast of Rio Vista. Typical private and public facilities are listed under the description for each area but these are just a sampling of the better known places. For each one listed, a half dozen or more are not

listed so explore the region to find other resorts, launching ramps and campgrounds that are best for you.

Houseboats are a perfect way to lazily explore the area and they are very popular. The slow pace of a houseboat gives you time to look and see what you miss in a high speed boat. Ride on top of a houseboat and its high profile lets you see over the levies to survey the farms, buildings and resorts that make up this land. Most houseboat rentals are at inland locations in the Stockton to Bethel Island area. A few of the many resorts that have houseboats for rent are identified.

The Delta is divided into 10 areas. The boundaries between them are fuzzy so read about adjacent areas to get a complete view of the area you will be exploring and its fishing opportunities.

Regulations

Fishing is permitted in the Delta all year. The limit for fish throughout the Delta is two striped bass and they must be a minimum of 18 inches, two salmon a minimum of 24 inches long, one sturgeon between 46 and 72 inches long, five black bass 12 inches minimum length, 25 shad and no limit on catfish, panfish and crayfish. Anglers must catch all of the fish with rod and reel or handlines but can set traps for crayfish. An angler must wear a fishing license visible on the upper part of his or her body. A striped bass stamp is required to fish for and keep striped bass.

1. Sacramento Area:

Salmon	9
Steelhead	8
Shad	8
Black Bass	7
Striped Bass	6
Panfish	6
After a storm	7
Fly Fishing	8

About Sacramento Area: Sacramento, our state capital on the northeast corner of the area covered in this book, (I am actually stretching the boundary a little to include Sacramento) is where the American River joins the Sacramento River. The short 22 mile long stretch of the American River from its mouth at the Sacramento River to the Nimbus Dam in Fair Oaks has excellent fishing and good public access along its full length, a rarity in the Delta. Anglers make good catches of salmon and shad and pretty good catches of steelhead in these rivers most years. In drought years, waterflow is down and other fishing locations are better.

With the best public access anywhere in the greater Delta Area you would expect this river to be crowded and it is at times. When salmon are there, anglers come in droves to catch them. When shad are running, the best bite is in the evening after people get off work. You can expect shoulder to shoulder fishing at the best holes when the shad run is good. At other times you have plenty of fishing space.

Discovery Park where the American joins the Sacramento River has a good launching ramp with docks. Car-top boat access and drift boat and raft launch and retrieval sites are found at frequent intervals along the river. The Sacramento River has good fishing particularly downstream from the mouth of the American River.

Salmon: The premier fish in this area is salmon. The Nimbus fish hatchery at the upper end of this section of river draws returning salmon and they can be caught all along the American River. Natural spawners in the upper section of this area add to the number of fish. During the fall when chinook salmon are running, anglers in driftboats bouncing roe or lures off the bottom catch a lot of these fish. Shore anglers also catch some fish. Salmon migrate to this area in the fall and late September through November; these are the best months to catch them. After the salmon run, steelhead show up for a few months in the winter.

Steelhead: Anglers catch steelhead trout beginning in January. Like salmon, some spawn in this river and others return to the Nimbus Fish Hatchery at the eastern boundary of this section. Anglers in drift boats

Anglers fish for American Shad from boats and from shore at Freeport on the Sacramento River.

Three different types of drawbridges like this one that opens from one end are used in the Delta.

have a definite advantage over shore anglers for steelhead but anglers from the bank catch them as well. Steelhead need good water flows and average to wet years produce more returning fish.

Shad: The American River and the Sacramento River at Freeport are two of the few places shad are caught in the Greater Bay Area. Drifting small leadhead jigs like teeny rounders or shad-darts or bead-head flies from shore or from a boat are successful. Shad start arriving here in late April or May; catches peak in May or June and it is over about a month later. Fly fishers wading and casting sinking lines make excellent catches of shad on the American River.

Tips from an Expert: "The American River is really a neat fishery with great fishing access," says Dan Bacher, who grew up fishing this river and is now Senior Editor of the Fish Sniffer biweekly fishing newspaper. "It flows through the middle of Sacramento—you catch big salmon and steelhead around the corner from metropolitan Sacramento."

"Steelhead are my favorite fish on the American River," says Bacher. "Most anglers start fishing with orange corkys and yarn when the season opens the first of January—the dirtier the water, the bigger the corky. In February we switch to power eggs, night crawlers, hotshots, or salmon roe. For salmon, fish roe, Kwikfish or Flatfish from a drift boat. "

"While the American River has the best bank fishing access in the state, anglers in boats do best for salmon and steelhead. But anglers fishing from shore have a realistic chance to catch these fish. Shore-anglers and waders do almost as well on shad as anglers fishing from a boat. In wet years when water is really rolling in the river, shore anglers can't get to some of the best spots and catches suffer but anglers from boats continue to catch shad."

Striped Bass: Striped bass are caught frequently from the American River and the Sacramento River near the mouth of the American River. Bait or lures are both effective for these fish. Bacher says anglers catch stripers fishing live jumbo minnows in the American River above Discovery Park. Stripers migrate to this river in the spring and summer months and that is when anglers catch most of them.

Black Bass: Smallmouth and largemouth bass fishing is good along the American and Sacramento River in this area. Early mornings in the spring are the best times to fish for them and surface lures, deep diving crank baits that bump along rocky bottoms and plastic baits are good ways to catch both smallmouth and largemouth bass.

Other Fish: Bluegill, sturgeon and catfish are caught in this area but are not the primary fish. Catfish are also landed—coves and backwaters away from the main channel produce most of the catfish.

Facilities and Contact: For bait, tackle, guides and information call the Freeport Marina at 916-665-1555 or Fran & Eddy's Sports Den at 916-363-6885. For guides call Rob Bonslett at 916-781-3474, Bob Sparre at 916-863-5866, or Rene Villanueva at 916 684-7148.

Cost: Boat launch free to $10

Directions to Sacramento Fishing: The Discovery Park Launching

Ramp is a good location to begin a fishing trip on either the American or the Sacramento Rivers. From Interstate 5 in Sacramento, take the Richards Boulevard exit. Turn west (left when you are traveling from the south) then take a right on Jibboom Street, cross the American River and follow the signs to the launch ramp. Parks make up most of the length of the American River and the remaining areas have river access. Launching places for rafts, drift boats and car-top boats are found at frequent intervals along the river.

Regulations: The American River from the Hazel Avenue Bridge just below Nimbus Dam to the power lines crossing the river at the downstream end of Ancil Hoffman Park is closed to trout and salmon fishing January 1 through March 31. Further restrictions are summarized in the introduction to this chapter and the "Waters with Special Restrictions" section of the *California Sport Fishing Regulations*.

2. North Delta:

Black Bass	8
Catfish	8
Striped Bass	7
Shad	7
Panfish	7
Sturgeon	5
Fly Fishing	5

About the North Delta: The North Delta is from Walnut Grove and Locke to Freeport. It is primarily the Sacramento River, and small side streams. Here black bass are likely to be smallmouth bass whereas the southerly part of the Delta has mostly largemouth bass. Shad migrate through the San Francisco Bay, the San Pablo Bay, through Carquinez Strait and up the Sacramento River. Few are caught until they get to Freeport at the northern end of this area where anglers fishing from shore and from boats near Freeport catch them. Even here the catch doesn't match the upriver catch above Sacramento and the river is too large for good success fly fishing. Striped bass, black bass, catfish, and panfish along with a few sturgeon are caught here.

This area is far enough from the ocean that tides play only a small role in fishing. Water levels and flows are more important. It has several private marinas with launching ramps but limited public access for shore fishing.

Striped Bass: The premier fish of this area as well as for most of the Delta is striped bass. Fewer stripers are caught from this area than from other areas but striped bass are caught—some of the best catches are made out of Freeport. Butterfly-cut threadfin shad is a preferred bait. The bait is fished right on the bottom with the boat at anchor or fished from shore.

Black Bass: Both largemouth and smallmouth bass are caught in the Delta but in this northern area, smallmouth bass are likely to make up

Several marinas in the Delta rent house boats like these.

The author caught this sturgeon on the Sacramento River south of Rio Vista.

half or more of the catch. Fish rocky shorelines, tulles, docks and pilings using plastic worms, crayfish imitations, crankbaits or use real live crayfish. Fly-anglers are successful in the early morning using popper flies and bait casters fishing with popping lures or stick baits (like Zara Spooks) catch fish.

Catfish: Catfish are abundant everywhere in the freshwater part of the Delta. Fish with clams, liver, cut mackerel, anchovies or prepared bait. Look for some structure like pilings or a dock and cast your bait right into the pilings from shore or from an anchored boat to catch these fish.

Shad: Most Bay Area anglers won't travel to fish this area because they will find equal fishing closer to home. But they will come as far as Freeport for shad. Anglers use lead-headed shad darts plus heavy weights and make long casts from the west shore of the Sacramento River below Freeport. The river is wide and anglers in boats anchored in the middle of the river have the best success. Shad are great fish on fly rods but this big water isn't conducive to good fly fishing—for that go to the American River or farther up the Sacramento River.

Other Fish: Sturgeon are caught but the numbers are down compared with the lower Delta and they don't get the emphasis here. Panfish are caught in sloughs that have slow flowing water.

Facilities and Contact: For bait, tackle, guides and information call First Mate Bait in Freeport at 916-665-1322 or Bridge Tender Bait Shop in Walnut Grove at 916-776-3969. For a full service marina with houseboat rentals, call New Hope Landing at 209-794-2627. Launching ramps are at Freeport, Clarksburg, Courtland and Walnut Grove.

Cost: Boat launch   Free to about $10

Directions to the North Delta: To get to Walnut Grove, take Interstate 5 north from Stockton and take the Walnut Grove Road (J11) west to that city. To get to the more northerly areas take Highway 160 north along the Sacramento River. To get to the Freeport Marina launching ramp from the North Bay, take Interstate 80 to Sacramento then take Interstate 5 south. Exit at Meadow View Road and go east then make a right turn onto Freeport Boulevard (Highway 160). For the New Hope Landing, take Walnut Grove Road (Highway J11) west from Interstate 5. Go north on Highway E13 along the Mokelumne River to this resort.

3. Rio Vista Area:

Striped Bass	10
Catfish	8
Sturgeon	7
Black Bass	6

About Rio Vista Area: Rio Vista on the west side of the Delta is on the main channel of the Sacramento River. Tens of thousands of salmon swim by here on their way to spawn in the Sacramento, Feather and Yuba Rivers but few are caught. That doesn't make Rio Vista a poor fishing destination because it is one of the best in the Delta. Here striped bass are number one and hundreds, probably thousands are caught in a typical year with hot spots above the Rio Vista Bridge south to Decker Island and Horseshoe Bend.

Brannan Island State Recreation Area southeast of Rio Vista is a great starting spot with camping, boat camping and launching ramps. Three launching ramps and several marinas in the city of Rio Vista provide access to these fish and guides in the area will show you how to catch them.

Striped Bass: The most important fish of this area is striped bass. Each year a few in the 30 to 50 pound range are caught. The main channel of the Sacramento above the Rio Vista Bridge south past Decker Island and Horseshoe Bend, a channel that goes around Decker Island, are prime fishing areas. Butterfly-cut threadfin shad is the prime bait.

Tips from an Expert: "Bait always is effective for stripers but trolling is another way to fish for striped bass when the water is warm and the fish are active," says Guide Jack Findelton. "I troll lures when the water temperature is 55 degrees or warmer then switch to bait in the winter months when the water is cool."

Catfish: Catfish are found throughout the Delta. Side channels where the water flow is moderated are better than the main river channel for these fish.

Sturgeon: Sturgeon are caught all along the Sacramento River but their numbers decline as you travel away from saltwater. Fishing for these prehistoric monsters is good in this region but is better in the bays and around Martinez. Last year I caught a 48 inch sturgeon from this area while fishing for striped bass with Guide Jack Findelton.

Black Bass: Black Bass catches are best in sloughs and slower flowing waters away from the Sacramento River. Spring when these fish are moving into shallow water to spawn and fall are the best times to catch them.

Facilities and Contact: For bait, tackle, guides and information call Haps Baitshop at 707-374-2372 or The Trap at 374-374-5554. For guides call Jack Findelton at 800-344-4871 or Jay Sorensen at 209-478-6645. For camping information at Brannan Island State Recreation Area, call 916-777-6671.

Special Programs: Rio Vista has a striped bass derby in early October that has been operating for many years. Today this derby has expanded to a big celebration with a princess, a carnival, pancake breakfasts and lots of special events in addition to fishing.

Cost: Boat launch   Free to about $10

Directions to Rio Vista: From the North Bay, take Highway 80 north to Fairfield then Highway 12 east to Rio Vista. From the East Bay take Highway 24 east to Walnut Creek then take Interstate 680 north to Highway 4. Turn east on this highway to the Antioch Bridge and take Highway 160 across this bridge and north to Rio Vista. From the south, take Interstate 680 north to Highway 24 then follow the above directions to Antioch and north on Highway 160 to Rio Vista.

4. Stockton Area:

Striped Bass	8
Black Bass	8
Catfish	8

About Stockton Area: Stockton on the east side of the Delta is a port for large ships that carry agricultural products to people around the world. It seems so incongruous with large modern ocean vessels in one area and a maze of sloughs and islands where it is easy to get lost only a short boat ride away.

This area has several of the largest, full-service resorts in the area. Resorts like Tower Park have docks, boat launching, campgrounds, general stores, bars and recreation halls. Herman and Helen's rents all kinds of boats including four sizes of houseboat, a runabout, two sizes of water-ski boats, patio boats and larger party boats as well as fishing boats with or without motors. Several other resorts have similar facilities and boat rentals.

This area is also a good fishing location particularly for black bass and striped bass where many professional tournaments are held each year. Even the downtown Stockton port has fair fishing—you might catch a 30 pound or larger striped bass.

Striped Bass: The premier fish of this area as well as in most of the Delta is striped bass. Each year a few in the 30 to 50 pound range are caught. Trolling or bait casting lures are good ways to catch striped bass but butterfly-cut shad is the prime bait. Fly anglers catch them on large flies that imitate bait fish.

Tips by an Expert: "I will only bait fish with fresh threadfin shad," says guide Jay Sorensen. "The butterfly-cut shad releases lots of flavor into the water and attracts these fish better than any other bait." Sorensen fishes with a sliding sinker and when a fish bites, he feeds out line to allow the fish to swallow the bait before he sets the hook.

To prepare a butterfly-cut shad, fillet each side of the shad but leave each fillet attached at the tail. Punch the hook through both fillets then the body of the bait. Sorensen and other experts have a particular way to fold the fillets to make them look like a butterfly but the main idea is to expose a lot of surface and milk a lot of flavor into the water.

Catfish: Catfish are a primary catch in this area from either a boat or the shore. You want relaxation, peace and quiet as well as fishing when you go after catfish. Choose a place off the main channel where water is flowing slowly and you aren't likely to see many boats; cast to a piling or deep hole; sit back on the bank and get lost in the solitude. That's what fishing for catfish is all about.

Black Bass: The shores of the rivers and sloughs in this area are covered with tulles, hydrilla, docks and pilings—ideal habitat for black bass. Weedless pig and jigs are great for getting into this heavy cover. Plastic baits, crank baits and spinners are good ways to catch them in more open areas.

Other Fish: Panfish and carp are caught throughout this freshwater part of the Delta. Sturgeon are also landed but this is outside the primary area where these fish are caught.

Facilities and Contact: Many marinas throughout the area have camping, launch ramps and houseboat rentals and a few rent fishing boats. For bait, tackle, guides and information call Island Bait and Tackle at 209-933-6905. For camping reservations call Tower Park Marina at 800-778-6937. For full service marinas and houseboat rentals call Herman and Helen's at 209-951-4634 or King Island Resort at 209-951-2188. For general information, call the Delta Chamber of Commerce at 209-466-7066.

Cost:	Boat launch	Free to about $12
	Boat and motor	$60 per day at Herman and Helen's
	Boat only	$27 per day at Herman and Helen's
	Camping	$10 to $15 per night is typical

Directions to Marinas near Stockton: Stockton is on Interstate 5. Marinas in the area are west of Stockton. Take Eight Mile Road west from Interstate 5 north of Stockton to Herman and Helen's Marina at the end of the road. Follow the same directions except turn left from Eight Mile Road onto Atherton Road to King Island Resort. Tower Park Marina and Resort is on the east shore of the Mokelumne River north of Highway 12. Take Highway 12 west from Interstate 5 near Lodi to the resort.

5. Pittsburg - Antioch:

Striped Bass	9
Sturgeon	8
Catfish	6
Black Bass	6

Butterfly cut threadfin shad is a favorite bait for striped bass.

About Pittsburg-Antioch Area: This area on the west side of the Delta is from the Benicia Martinez Bridge on the west to the confluence of the Sacramento and San Joaquin Rivers just east of Antioch. It includes the mothballed fleet of navy ships just above the Benicia Bridge, Grizzly Bay, Suisun Bay, Honker Bay, the middle ground and the channel from Pittsburg to Antioch.

Pittsburg has recently upgraded its launch and marina and has clean, modern facilities with berths for 500 boats. Respected guide Barry Canevaro has relocated here during the winter season—he said that he usually has motored to this area to fish so it is better to start there minutes from where he catches striped bass and sturgeon.

Tens of thousands of salmon swim by here on their way to spawn in the Sacramento, San Joaquin, Feather and Yuba Rivers and anglers catch some but not many of them. Anglers in boats catch most of the fish but anglers fishing from shore and from public piers catch catfish, flounder, black bass, a few striped bass, salmon and may even catch a sturgeon.

Most of the Delta is protected channels and is okay for aluminum fishing boats if anglers are careful. But winds can come up quickly here; this area can get really rough and anyone taking out a small boat must be very careful. A friend bought a 15 foot aluminum boat and fished his favorite spot on Hooker Bay. After a few trips he had caught several stripers but he went out one day when he should have stayed home. The afternoon winds came up; his boat capsized; he lost his fishing tackle and a camera as well as his boat and motor. He survived the cold water only because he is a strong swimmer and a nearby boat rescued him.

Being on a big boat doesn't guarantee you will be safe. Another time four friends spent the night anchored on a 22 foot cruiser. The anchor didn't hold and the boat drifted into submerged pilings while they slept. As the tide went out the boat settled on pilings that punctured the hull. It hung on the pilings until the tide came in; then it floated off; the hole was exposed and the boat filled with water and sank. Everyone had donned life jackets; the ones that were the weakest swimmers got two life jackets. The next morning the coast guard picked them up clinging to bridge pilings and whatever else they could get ahold of. They were chilled but thankfully they were all okay.

Striped Bass: This area has excellent fishing for striped bass. Each year a few in the 30 to 50 pound range are caught. Honker Bay and the middle ground just down river from Pittsburg are two favorite places to catch stripers. Bullheads (staghorn sculpin) and mudsuckers along with threadfin shad are the best baits here.

Tips by an Expert: "An effective fishing technique in using bait is the toothpick trick," says striper fishing fanatic Keith Rogers. "Attach a toothpick along the grip of the rod just beyond the reel using rubber bands. Tuck the line under the end of the toothpick and leave the reel in free spool. When a striper pulls on the bait, the line snaps free from the toothpick and the bait drifts freely. Thumb the spool very lightly and wait for the fish to stop and swallow the bait. When it takes off the second time, set the hook."

"Don't change the bait if it has gotten bit," Rogers adds. "This is the bait the next striper will usually bite."

Sturgeon: The mothball fleet is an excellent place to catch sturgeon. Use bait like grass, mud or ghost shrimp, mudsuckers, or herring fillets for bait. The three kinds of shrimp are the best baits but you must watch the tip of your rod like a hawk. You get one, sometimes two and maybe three pumps of the rod to set the hook. If you miss those bites, you won't get another chance.

Other Fish: Catfish and black bass are found in this area but it is salty water when the river flows are down and inland areas are better fishing spots for these fish. Starry flounder were once an almost sure catch here but their populations are way down. Better catches recently suggest they may be coming back. Only time will tell if this is just a little blip on their recovery or if they are on an upward trend.

Tips from an Expert: "This area has brackish water and bait and game fish hang in that area longer than any place else," guide Barry Canevaro says. "It is great for both striper and sturgeon."

"Fishing is good at the beginning and end of tides and small tide changes are very good. Both striper and sturgeon fishing is best on incoming tides from October through December but in the spring fishing is much better on outgoing tide," Canevaro says. "The flow at the mouths of sloughs like Little Sloughs, Middle Slough and Broad Slough are slower and these are good places to fish during big tides."

Canevaro uses whole live bullheads or filleted fresh shad when the water temperature is above the mid 50's and cuts the heads off bullheads and fishes with just the body when the temperature is below the mid 50's. A lot of anglers use mudsuckers but Canevaro believes bullheads are better bait.

"Fish with the reel in free spool," Canevaro suggests. "Stripers take the bait, start running, then seem to pick up speed and that is the time to set the hook. I use a limerick double hook when fishing with bullheads and they have proven to be very good at hooking fish."

Facilities and Contact: Launching ramps are found in the metropolitan area of both Pittsburg and Antioch. Call 925-439-4958 for the Pittsburg Marina and Launch and 925-779-6957 for the Antioch Launch. For bait, tackle and information call Kings Bait and Tackle in Pittsburg at 925-432-8466 or the Antioch Marina at 925-779-6957. For a guided fishing trip call Barry Canevero at the Fish Hookers Guide Service at 916-777-6498. Canevaro and his wife Diana both operate boats out of the Pittsburg Marina in the winter.

Cost: Boat launch   Free to about $10

Directions to Pittsburg and Antioch Launching Ramps: Both of these cities are east of Walnut Creek and Concord off Highway 4. Take Highway 4 east from Concord to Pittsburg. Take the Railroad Avenue exit north off this road to its end. Make a left turn onto 3d Street then a right onto Marina Boulevard and another right on Cutter to the Pittsburg launching ramp. For the Antioch ramp, take Highway 4 to Antioch and take the Somerville Road northeast. This road turns right and becomes 4th street. Where this street ends, turn left one block to the marina.

Bethel Island has several launching ramps.

Guide Barry Canevaro holds up a striped bass.

6. Big Break :

Black Bass	9
Catfish	8
Striped Bass	7
Sturgeon	6
Fly Fishing	7

About Big Break Area: Big Break east of Antioch has a different character. It is full of tulles, sunken ships, barges and pilings and has lots of crayfish—all the things black bass thrive on. Consequently most of the bass in this area are largemouth bass rather than striped bass.

Black Bass: Black bass fishing is excellent. When I fished here with Dave Byers, we caught fish on 10 inch long Berkeley Power Worms, imitation crawfish and on spinnerbaits fished through the tulles. Pitching into the tulles or at the edges of wrecks produced the majority of our fish.

Tips from an Expert: "Look for lanes in the tulles and cast spinner bait down those lanes," said bass pro fisherman Dave Byers. "Retrieve the lure just slow enough so you can't see the lure in the water."

"Use something out of the ordinary like large or small worms," Byers said. "Dee Thomas won one tournament using very small four inch plastic worms and I placed second using very large 10 inch Power Worms."

"Plan your fishing around the tides. Know when areas will be deep enough to fish on an incoming tide and be there at that time. Fish will hold at the up-current area of tulles and wrecks waiting for food. Fish the side where water is flowing into the area."

Striped Bass: Bait is a good fishing method for stripers but here casting lures like Rat-L-Traps or Rapalas and Rebels or trolling these same lures will catch fish. Some stripers are caught fishing for black bass.

Catfish: The same features that make this good for black bass, particularly pilings and wrecked ships, also makes it good for catfish. Clams, anchovies, mackerel, liver or prepared baits are good bait for these fish. Live crayfish are also work well and may garner a black bass as an incidental catch.

Other Fish: Sturgeon, panfish and carp are caught in this area.

Facilities and Contact: The Big Break Marina has good launching ramps and caters to all anglers but particularly to ones going after black bass. Call Hook, Line and Sinker Bait and Tackle at this marina at 925-625-2441 for boat launching, bait, tackle, guides and information.

Cost: Boat launch   Free to about $10

Directions to Big Break: Big Break Marina is on Big Break Road between Antioch and Oakley. Take Highway 4 east through Antioch. Turn left onto Big Break Road to this private marina.

7. Bethel Island and Franks Tract:

Striped Bass	9
Black Bass	8

Discovery Bay is a large community where each home is on the water and has a boat dock at its back door.

Catfish   8
Fly Fishing   9

About Bethel Island: Bethel Island in the heart of the Delta really looks like Tom Sawyer and Huck Finn country. It has marinas with conventional launching ramps and with platform launches (you back your boat and trailer onto the platform and it is lowered into the water) bait shops, and campgrounds. Sunken barges and boats, piers and pilings in all states of repair and disrepair give it character.

When you cross the bridge onto this island, it as if you were magically transported into a time gone by. The people are friendly and helpful but the pace is slow and customs and laws outside the island may or may not be observed here. When I visited on a weekday morning in May, the island seemed almost deserted—very different from the hectic summer scene. Locals were shooting pool around a pool table on a covered patio at a bar in a resort. Laws prohibiting smoking in bars had been in effect for five months but when I went in, the bar had only one patron inside and an acting bartender—both were smoking. Somehow I wasn't surprised.

Franks Tract State Recreation Area adjacent to Bethel Island can only be reached by boat. It is an island that was flooded many years ago when a levee failed. Too expensive to reclaim, it is now a recreation area. Be aware that the machinery and buildings were left intact. The structures except for foundations are deteriorated and gone but the machinery is still there. High speed boaters in this area have had their day ruined when their outboard motor caught a solid piece of a submerged plow or tractor and was wrecked. Go slow and watch for obstacles here.

Striped Bass: Striped bass is the premier fish but fishing for them is a little different. Bait is always a good way to catch stripers but casting to spots that probably hold stripers, particularly flowing water through breaks in levees around Franks Tract, is a good fishing method. You can baitfish from shore but you will be much more successful for stripers and black bass with a boat and a trolling motor to silently glide along the tulles and shorelines and work a large area. This is probably the best place to fly fish for stripers and black bass in the Delta.

Black Bass: This area is filled with tulles, breaks with flowing water—cast to the edges of these breaks—and docks, pilings and structure. All are ideal hiding places for black bass. The best times to catch them is spawn time from March through May and again in September through November but anglers catch these fish all year.

Tips from an Expert: "September, October and November are my absolute favorite times to [fly] fish the Delta," says famous fly fisherman, Dan Blanton, who has caught dozens of five pound bass on flies here. "Water is lower so anglers need not cast into overhangs to get to the fish and the winds are generally nil, a great asset for fly fishers and most water skiers and jet skiers have left the water."

"Striped bass and largemouth bass aggressively key in on threadfin shad and any variety of flies that simulate bait fish will work. If I were to limit myself to one pattern for bass, it would be my Flash Tail Whistler pattern, tied in a variety of color combinations. I tie all my flies for the Delta with double wire (#7) snag guards so they can be fished in weeds or trees. Of course these fish love all the great streamers, bucktails, Sar-Mul-Macs, Flashtails Clousers, Deceivers and they also have a penchant for poppers at times."

Blanton recommends a 8 or 9 weight fly rod and a 10 or 11 weight shooting head line. "The effective flies here are quite large and it takes this size rod with the extra heavy line to handle them. You will want a rod at least that heavy if you hook into a 20 pound striped bass."

"Use a type 4 (sink rate) shooting head for water that is six to 10 feet deep and a lead-core line like Cortland's LC-13 for deeper water. Of course, for surface flies, you will want a floating line."

Catfish: This is excellent catfish territory. Use clams, chicken liver, night crawlers, anchovies, mackerel or prepared bait to catch them.

Other Fish: This is not a primary area for sturgeon fishing but you never know when one might take your bait. If you want something big and strong, go after the plentiful carp.

Facilities and Contact: For bait, tackle, camping reservations, boat launch, fishing boat rental, guides and information call Chuck's Bait & Tackle and Russo's Marina both at 510-684-0668. Call the houseboat rental hotline at 209-447-1840 for a packet of boat rental brochures from all members of this association.

Cost: Boat launch   Free to about $10.00
        Camping $15 at Russo's Marina

Directions to Bethel Island: Take Highway 4 east through Oakley then make a left turn onto Cypress Road. This road turns north becomes Bethel Island Road and crosses the bridge to Bethel Island. Take Gateway Road east (right) then Piper Road north (left) to Russo's Marina or spend a few minutes exploring the island to find other marinas, campgrounds and facilities.

8. Discovery Bay:

Black Bass   9
Striped Bass   8
Catfish   8

About Discovery Bay Area: Discovery Bay is the largest on-water development in the Delta. More than 1000 homes have been built mostly along channels that connect to Indian Slough east of Brentwood. This is for people who love the water. Here anglers have their boats at their own dock a few feet from their back door. The development is so large that people away from the entrance to Indian Slough may have to run through the development at the five mph speed limit for 20 minutes to get out to open water.

Anglers keep bass in their live wells and release them at their dock in Discovery Bay. From these "plants" bass fishing is fair around the docks and channels in this development but the really good fishing is in the channels throughout this part of the Delta. Black bass are tops followed by striped bass, catfish and panfish. Sturgeon are rarely caught.

Black Bass: Black Bass fishing is excellent in this area. They are predominately largemouth bass and are caught on plastic baits, spinner baits, crank baits and real live crawdads. Tulles, rock walls, docks and points are the primary fishing locations.

Tips from an Expert: "Flip a plastic worm into the breaks in the tulles and work it slowly" Discovery Bay resident and expert bass fisherman Mike Peila says. "Cast a plastic worm or crank bait to flowing water at the edges of breaks in a berm and stop and fish all the water return pipes that you come across. Cast a plastic bait to the edge of pilings and docks and fish points and rock walls. The Delta is so full of good bass fishing habitat you never run out of places to fish."

Striped Bass: Fish the breaks in the berms when the tide is flowing bringing food to these fish. The same tactics and lures that catch black bass are good for stripers. Also, anchor and fish the holes with fresh butterfly-cut shad. Night fishing using bait is good here and anglers who fish all night and take turns sleeping on a boat catch very large stripers.

Catfish: Catfish are caught by the hundreds here. In fact anglers may fish a few hours in the morning or evening and catch 100 eight to 12 inch cats with an occasional large one. The only problem is cleaning that many fish so don't keep too many.

Clams are my favorite bait but mackerel, anchovies, liver and pre-pared bait are all good for catfish. Serious anglers that go for large catfish usually fish at night using turkey liver or mackerel and often catch catfish weighing in the tens of pounds.

Facilities and Contact: For general information call the Discovery Bay Yacht Harbor at 925-634-5928. For bait, tackle, guides and camping information call Orwood Resort at 925-634-5928.

Cost: Boat launch   Free to about $10

Camping $10 to $15 per night

Directions to Discovery Bay: Take Highway 4 east from Concord past Pittsburg and Antioch. This road starts out as a divided highway but at Antioch it deteriorates to a two lane road. Continue through Oakley and Brentwood. Discovery Bay is a left turn. Discovery Bay has a boat launching ramp for its residents so you can use it if you know someone there. Otherwise the nearest ramp is at Orwood Resort. The route to this resort is Sunset Road east from Highway 4 north of Brentwood. Take a right turn when this road dead ends into Byron Road then a left turn onto Orwood Road to the resort.

9. Clifton Court Forebay:

Striped Bass	8
Black Bass	8
Catfish	9
Fly Fishing	7

About Clifton Court Forebay: Clifton Court Forebay on the southwest side of the Delta is a water holding lake for the water that flows south through the aqueducts. The surrounding area has excellent fishing for black bass, striped bass and it is usually easy to catch a stringer of catfish.

Striped Bass: Like the rest of the Delta, the premier fish of this area is striped bass. Each year a few giant stripers are caught and it is common to catch and release lots of stripers far smaller than the legal 18 inch size limit. The entrance to Clifton Court Forebay is an excellent place to catch large stripers when water is flowing either in or out.

Black Bass: Black bass fishing in this area is excellent. Work Italian Slough or the waters around Coney Island, a development with lots of homes and docks. Tulles along the rivers, sloughs, docks and irrigation returns with flowing water throughout the area are good bass locations.

Catfish: Fish for catfish with clams or other traditional catfish bait around pilings or in a deep hole. You can usually land a mess of catfish and you may also hook into a large, powerful carp.

Other Fish: Panfish and carp are caught throughout this area.

Facilities and Contact: To launch a boat in the Delta (you can't boat on Clifton Court Forebay) contact the Lazy M Marina at 925-634-4555 or Del's at 209-835-8365. The Lazy M Marina has a low bridge that you must cross under and Del's has a rather small launch ramp. Both are suitable for most fishing and ski boats but not for high top cruisers. Stop at Geno's General Store in Livermore just north of Interstate Highway 580 on Vasco Road or call them at 925-449-3838 for fresh bait.

Cost: Boat launch $10 typical

Directions to Clifton Court Forebay: To reach Clifton Court Forebay, go east on Interstate 580 through Livermore and over the Altamont Pass. Take the Grant Line Road/Byron exit north. Turn left on Mountain House Road then left again onto Highway 4 (Byron Road). Take the second right (at the Lazy M Marina sign) to this marina and for limited shore access.

10. South Delta:

Black Bass	8
Catfish	8
Striped Bass	7

About South Delta Area: This area north of Tracy includes the Grant

Mossdale Recreation Area has a launch ramp on the San Joaqum River

Line Canal, (every spring a few really large striped bass seem to come from this canal), Old River, the San Joaquin River and Middle River. It is well away from saltwater but it is still influenced by tides though high and low tides may be as much as eight to 10 hours later than the ones in the tide tables for the Golden Gate Bridge. Here many of the channels are narrow and winding. You can always duck in behind a levee and find a fishing spot out of the wind.

Most of the shoreline is private so you need to look to find public access. I have fished from shore along the Grant Line Canal west of Tracy Boulevard and off levees near bridge crossings.

Striped Bass: The hot time to fish this area far into the Delta is spawning time in April or May. Some really large spawner bass are caught on a variety of baits including anchovies, threadfin shad and mudsuckers. Crank baits trolled or cast to these holding spots can also produce stripers.

Black Bass: This area is laced with channels with tulles, tree roots, docks and pilings that have bass. Pitching is a good fishing method using plastic baits and crank baits are good lures to catch these fish. Spinner baits are particularly effective fishing through tulles because they are weedless lures and can get into the areas that would snag most lures.

Catfish: Catfish are found throughout the Delta and the South Delta laced with channels is an excellent place to go after these fish.

Other Fish: Though not considered a game fish, carp are plentiful, large and strong. When my seven year old son caught a 10 pound carp from this area on one of his first fishing trips he didn't mind that it didn't have the reputation of a sought-after gamefish.

Facilities and Contact: Contact the Tracy Oasis Marina at 209-835-3182 for fishing information, for camping or to launch a boat. Contact Geno's Shell Station in Livermore at 925-449-3838 for bait and information.

Cost: Boat launch $6 to $14 at Oasis Marina; $4 to $8 at Mossdale

Directions to South Delta: Take Interstate 205 east from Tracy to the bridge over the San Joaquin River to the Mossdale boat launching ramp. The ramp is on the north side of the Interstate on the east side of the river. To get to the ramp, take Interstate 5 north toward Stockton and take the Louise Avenue exit. Turn left under the freeway then make an immediate left turn to the frontage road and follow it back to the Mossdale County Park and the launch ramp. This ramp has a dock but since it is on the main channel of the San Joaquin River it has a current. For the Tracy Oasis Marina turn north on Tracy Boulevard off Interstate 205 in Tracy then turn left on Grimes Road just south of the Grant Line Canal to the Marina. They have a ramp and a platform launch and also have bait, tackle and camping.

Section III
Saltwater

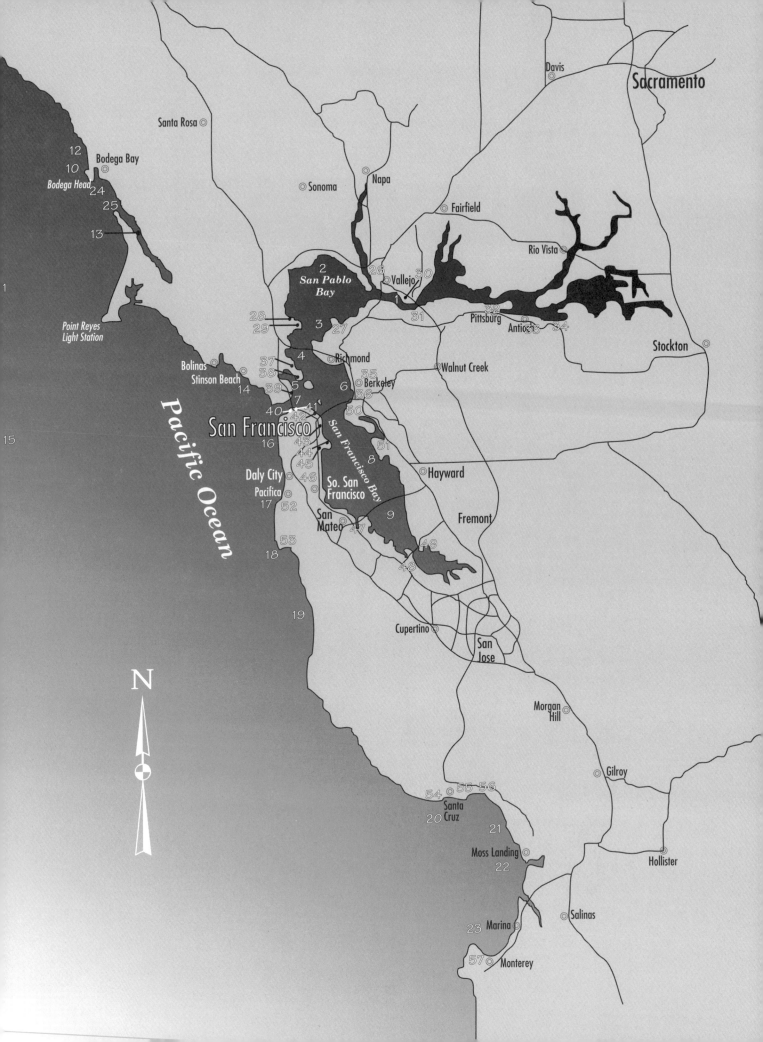

CHAPTER 8:

Bays of Plenty

The San Francisco and San Pablo Bays more than anything else set off the Bay Area as a great fishing location. Anglers catch striped bass, halibut, sturgeon, shark and many other fish in these saltwater estuaries. Together with the Delta and the rivers that feed this system, there is more water with excellent fishing than any angler can explore in a lifetime. Moreover, many fish caught in the ocean and rivers depend on these bays. They are the nursery or the rearing location for fish like striped bass and sturgeon and are the channels that most of California's salmon, shad and some steelhead pass through when they return from the ocean to spawn.

Striped bass were the premium summer fish for years. But as these fish declined, anglers turned to halibut and now these flatfish are a very important fish for anglers working these bays. Anglers who were spoiled by super striper fishing have readjusted their thinking and realize, though not as fabulous as it was 20 years ago, striped bass fishing is still very good. When you think the great striper fishing is gone and forgotten, a year like 1998 rolls around where limits of stripers are caught from the bays and beaches and you think it is just like old times. Surfperch are caught throughout these bays. When nothing else seems to bite (at least in the winter and spring) anglers can usually catch surfperch, sharks, skates, flounder, jacksmelt and kingfish.

Small shiner surfperch are sometimes so pesky, you can't seem to get your bait through them to catch larger fish. But that isn't always a bad thing. Catch shiner surfperch then use them as bait to go for striped bass or halibut. They are more hardy than live anchovies you purchase (the usual live bait) so are easier to keep alive and lively. Put a few in a five gallon bucket half full of water and they will stay alive if you change the water frequently. You may want to catch your own bait when the best tides are mid-morning or later. This gives you time to fish an hour or two to catch bait and still fish the best tides. Purchase bait when the best tides are early and you want to start fishing for bass and halibut as soon as you can get to them.

One or more quality fish are always biting in the bays. From April to about November, concentrate on striped bass and halibut; in late summer you can catch salmon in the bays; in the winter turn to sturgeon and surfperch. Stripers are an important part of the catch all year—striper fishing is good near San Francisco in the spring and summer, in San Pablo Bay in the fall and winter and in the Delta in the fall, winter and spring.

You can fish from your own boat if it is seaworthy and can handle winds and waves in the bay with a margin of safety in case wind and waves increase suddenly; you can fish from a charter boat from several locations around the bay; or you can fish from piers or the shore. Piers are located in some very good fishing locations so you have a chance to catch a large fish including sturgeon, striped bass, salmon and halibut. (Chapter 10 is a guide to piers and pier fishing.)

Fishing can be combat type fishing on an outgoing tide at the south tower of the Golden Gate Bridge with boats jockeying for positions. Striped bass school at the outside of the large concrete pier that anchors the south tower of this bridge and fishing boats sweep by the south face of the structure drifting with the current while anglers drop their live bait right next to the pier to sink to the fish. You have only seconds—a cable from the center of the tower will snag your rig if you drop too early—but get the timing right so the bait is at the right depth and you will hook stripers frequently. You land the fish then go back to cue up in line for the next pass. Charter boats and private boats jockey for position but the regulars know the procedure and take their turn in line. I was on one charter boat that had an altercation with a private boat and the two boats collided but usually it goes smoothly.

Charter Boats: While these waters are generally okay for moderate sized private boaters and catching these fish from a private boat is great sport, many people fish from commercial sport fishing boats called charter or party boats. (I'll call them charter boats but that includes open charter where many individuals or several small groups fish together on one boat.)

The skippers and crew fish almost every day, networking with other skippers to locate and catch fish, becoming very skilled at knowing where to find fish. A trip on one of these boats is a very good way to catch fish

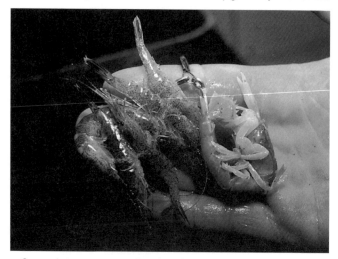

Grass shrimp are an excellent bait for striped bass and sturgeon.

and is a fishing education. Some friends have boats that are perfectly suitable for fishing in these bays or in the ocean but leave them home and fish from charter boats to take advantage of the skipper's knowledge and fishing skills. Fishing from a charter boat also avoids the cleanup and the saltwater degradation to their boats.

These charter boats may be the 50 feet or longer vee-hull boats, or recently introduced catamarans of similar size both holding 20 to 40 people. Or they may be six-pack boats, generally about 25 feet long, that fish with four to six anglers. The large charter boats cost about $45 to $55 per person for a day of fishing while the six-packs typically cost $100 for each angler. An advantage of the six-pack is you can reserve one for a group of four to six friends, get individual attention and call all the shots—what fish you will go after, where you will fish and how long you will fish. The large boats handle rough seas better; the skippers may be more experienced and you learn from other anglers. The skippers on most six-packs and large charter boats are experienced, skilled anglers

An angler caught and released this green sturgeon. These are much more rare and smaller than the common white sturgeon.

and both normally make good catches.

Health Warning: Due to elevated levels of mercury, PCB and other chemicals, people should limit the amount of bay-caught fish they eat so catch-and-release is a good fishing plan. The DFG warns that adults should eat no more than two meals of fish caught from the Delta or the Bay in a month. Furthermore adults should not eat any striped bass over 35 inches long. Women who are pregnant or expect to get pregnant, nursing mothers and children under six years old should not consume more than one meal of fish caught from these areas in a month nor should they eat any striper more than 27 inches long or shark more than 24 inches long. Resident fish caught from the Richmond Channel should not be eaten. This warning does not apply to transitory fish like salmon and shad.

1. Carquinez Strait:
    Sturgeon   10
    Stripers   7
    Flounder   4

About Carquinez Strait: Carquinez Strait will long be remembered in the record books of fishing. In 1983 Joey Pallotta landed the largest sports-caught fish ever recorded in fresh or brackish water in the United States from this short channel between the Delta and San Pablo Bay. His 468-pound sturgeon is expected to be the largest freshwater fish on record for the foreseeable future. This isn't because there aren't larger fish to be caught—it is because the laws no longer allow anglers to keep these very large fish.

White sturgeon, the kind Pallotta caught, are the only fish in freshwater that attain such huge size. Actually these are anadromous fish but most are caught in saltwater bays and freshwater. Most states (perhaps all states) that have these fish have a slot limit with an upper limit of 72 inches total length—about 100-pounds. In theory, you could catch, weigh on a certified scale, measure, photograph and release the fish and get a record but that isn't practical with a 10-foot long 500-pound class fish.

The Carquinez Strait is the transition from saltwater in the San Pablo Bay west of the Carquinez Bridge at Vallejo to generally freshwater inland from the Martinez Bridge. The salt content varies from year to year, season to season and even hour to hour. After heavy rains on low tide, the water in the strait has a low salt content. When water flowing into the bays is low, the salt content above the Martinez bridge is high. During high tides, saltwater flows farther inland and at low tide the transition areas are less salty. Freshwater fish begin to show up above Martinez but it is inland from Antioch when all of the freshwater fish including black bass and catfish are abundant.

Sturgeon: Sturgeon are the number one fish caught in this strait. This is generally deep water fishing. Anchor on the edge of the channel and cast mud shrimp, ghost shrimp, grass shrimp, a mudsucker baitfish, or a strip of herring and watch the rod tip.

Striped Bass: Striped bass are caught in large numbers in San Pablo Bay just below Carquinez Strait and in the Delta leading into Carquinez Strait but not as many are caught in this channel. A better plan to catch striped bass is to launch in this area and run to San Pablo Bay or above the Martinez Bridge (see the section on the Delta that covers fishing in this area). Flounder and other small fish are also caught.

Tips from an expert: Joey Palotta who landed a 468-pound sturgeon, the largest sports caught fish ever landed in fresh or brackish water tells how he caught this fish.

"I was headed for the mothball fleet but saw sturgeon jumping near Benicia so I stopped, anchored and started fishing," Pallotta said. "I hooked the fish right away. I hadn't been fishing more than 5 or 10 minutes. The fish was about to spool me so I yelled for a friend, Tom Glaklin, fishing nearby for help. He motored over; I stepped on his boat and we started following the fish. Glaklin probably had no idea what he had committed himself for. It took six hours to land the fish."

Palotta was fishing alone using grass shrimp for bait with an 80 pound test outfit. Since then he has purchased a charter boat and appropriately named it the Sturgeon King. He operates the charter boat out of Crockett.

"Get your bait on the bottom—that is where the sturgeon feed," says Palotta. "Use every clue you can including looking for fish on your fish finder [sturgeon are large and show up like logs on your finder] and don't bypass jumping stripers. That really paid off for me."

Facilities and Contact: Launching ramps in Martinez, Benicia and Vallejo provide access for private boaters. For information call the Martinez Marina at 925-229-9420, the Benicia Marina at 707-745-2628 or the Vallejo Muni Marina at 707-648-4370. Norm's Bait Shop and Brinkman's Marine at 707-642-7521 are next to the Vallejo launch.

The Crockett Marina has three charter boats. The Happy Hooker moves to the Martinez Marina for the sturgeon and striped bass fishing in the winter. For information and reservations on charter boats, call the Martinez Marina Bait and Tackle at 925-229-9420 or Crockett Sportfishing at 510-787-1047.

Cost: Cost for charter boats is about $50 for an all day trip. Six-packs

The Carquinez Bridge at Vallejo is a good sturgeon fishing spot.

cost about $100 per person. Boat launching and parking is $4.00 to $10.00.

Directions to Marinas: For the Martinez Marina, take Highway 680 north out of Walnut Creek and take the Marina Vista exit to downtown Martinez. Turn right at Ferry Street (just past the train depot), turn right onto Joe DiMaggio Drive then left onto North Court Street and follow the signs to the marina. For Benicia, take the East 5th Street exit off Interstate 780 and go south to the marina. The single lane ramp is off 5th Street. For the Vallejo ramp, take the Interstate 780 exit from Interstate 80 and go west. Turn left on Curtola Parkway and watch for Brinkman's Marine. The ramp is next to this store.

2. North San Pablo Bay:

Sturgeon 9
Stripers 7
Shark 6
Surfperch 4

About North San Pablo Bay: San Pablo Bay is large so I have divided it into a northern and southern half. No feature divides this bay but the exact location of the line is not very important because there is a gradual change in fishing as you travel north to south. Cities on this part of the bay include Vallejo on its northeastern shore, Rodeo and Pinole on its eastern shore.

After heavy winter rains when water is almost thick from all of the sediment in the water sturgeon fishing is excellent. Choose a moderate or large tide for the best fishing and be sure to fish the last half of the outgoing tide for the best fishing.

Sturgeon: Ghost shrimp, mud shrimp and grass shrimp are favorite baits. The take is very delicate and you must react quickly as the sturgeon picks up the bait, crushes it and spits out the shells. It is usually quick and you must be ready to set the hook.

Lisa Gillis landed this sturgeon in the North San Pablo Bay.

Loch Lomond Marina at San Rafael has a good bait shop and is a favorite launching site for sturgeon anglers.

A small bait fish called a mudsucker is less effective but it is hard to steal; a herring filet can also be good at times. You don't get as many bites on these baits as on shrimp but it is easier to hook a sturgeon when it does bite. Buoy 7, the mouth of Sonoma Creek and the mouth of Carquinez Strait are sturgeon hot spots.

Striped Bass: Striped bass are caught in large numbers in San Pablo Bay. Farther south striper fishing is good in the early summer but the best time to catch them in this part of San Pablo Bay is in the fall and many are caught throughout the winter by anglers fishing for sturgeon. The same bait used for sturgeon is good for striped bass. In addition, trolling or casting white or yellow lead-head jigs or lures like Rapalas and Rat-L-Traps is particularly good when stripers are in schools.

Other Fish: Surfperch fishing is good though water is becoming less salty and here these fish are not as plentiful as in other parts of the bay. At one time a good catch of flounder was almost a sure thing; now they are sparse but are caught occasionally. Shark, rays and a variety of other small fish are landed. Crabs are skilled bait stealers—you can let them drive you crazy or you can move to a different spot.

Tips from an expert: "The San Pablo Bay is the best place to catch sturgeon in the Bay Area," says Jim Smith who along with his son James operates the 58 foot long Happy Hooker charter boat. "We move our boat from its summer berth in the Berkeley Marina to the Martinez Marina in the winter to be near this area when sturgeon fishing is best."

"Really skilled anglers who watch their rod tip constantly and set the hook in an instant will catch more sturgeon on mud shrimp or ghost shrimp. Novice anglers will miss bites and will probably catch more sturgeon on bait that is harder to steal like whole, fresh mudsuckers or herring fillets. Unless you are an experienced sturgeon angler, take a trip or two on a charter boat to learn how to rig and how to fish; then you can start fishing from your own boat."

Facilities and Contact: Boat launches that are convenient to this area include Vallejo, Benicia and Martinez described in the previous Carquinez Strait section as well as the Rodeo Marina, Loch Lomond Marina in San Rafael and the Black Point Launch Ramp under the Highway 37 bridge in the Petaluma River (phone 707-778-8055).

Charter boats from Martinez and Crockett (see the previous section) spend most of their fishing time in the north San Pablo Bay. For information and reservations on these charter boats, call the Martinez Marina Bait and Tackle at 925-229-9420 or Crockett Sportfishing at 510-787-1047. Boats from Loch Lomond Marina in San Rafael 415-456-0321 and the Fury out of the Point San Pablo Yacht Harbor 510-237-4880 also fish this area. Berkeley and Emeryville boats may come this far when the bite is hot. For information call the Berkeley Marina at 510-849-2727 or the Emeryville Marina at 510-654-6040.

Cost: Boat Launching $5.00 at Black Point Ramp, Free to about $10 at other ramps

Charter Boat   Typical cost is about $50 per person

Directions to Marinas: Directions to the Vallejo Marina are covered in the last section and the Loch Lomond Marina is described in the South San Pablo Bay section. To get to the Rodeo Marina (510-799-4436) drive north from Berkeley on Interstate 80 and take the Willow Avenue exit. Go west, veer left onto Pacific and follow the signs to the marina. The Black Point Launch Ramp is a Marin County Launch Ramp under the Highway 37 bridge over the Petaluma River. Take Highway 37 west from Vallejo or east from Highway 101 at Novato. Turn south off this highway west of the Petaluma River Bridge.

3. South San Pablo Bay:

Sturgeon	10
Stripers	9
Shark	7
Surfperch	4

About South San Pablo Bay: This area from the Richmond-San Rafael Bridge to a line half way up San Pablo Bay is prime sturgeon fishing. Famous sturgeon spots like China Camp, Buoy 5, The Pump House and the Richmond San Rafael Bridge are all in this region. It also has great striped bass fishing spots like The Brothers, The Sisters (both are pairs of islands) and Red Rock off Richmond just north of the Richmond San Rafael Bridge.

For a romantic non-fishing weekend, make a reservation to stay overnight in the Brother's Lighthouse. This is a bed and breakfast in the middle of the ship traffic lanes in this part of San Pablo Bay on one of the Brothers Islands. But when you do, pray for a clear night. On a foggy night, the fog horn is automatically activated and sleeping is tough when the fog horn is blasting every few seconds.

Sturgeon: This area has great sturgeon fishing when conditions are right—lot of rain and flowing muddy water. Incoming flows as waters come up to a large high tide are good but fishing the outgoing tide is better. Expert sturgeon angler Keith Fraser says the last half of a moderate to high outgoing tide is the best fishing time.

A young angler shows off a sturgeon caught from San Pablo Bay.

The Pump House on San Pablo Bay is a noted landmark for sturgeon anglers.

You want a rod with some heft to its main shaft but with a flexible tip. The light tip doesn't alert the sturgeon when it picks up the bait but the rod flexes and gives you a signal of a sturgeon bite.

Tips from an expert: "Use mud, ghost or grass shrimp for bait; lean your rod on a sturgeon cradle or in the corner of the boat and watch the tip of your rod like a hawk. Don't use a conventional rod holder—you want to be able to pick up your rod instantly and be ready to set the hook," instructs Keith Fraser, sturgeon guru, proprietor of Loch Lomond Live Bait in San Rafael and author of the book, Keith Fraser's *Guide to Sturgeon Fishing.* "The bite of a 200-pound sturgeon is a light tugging, pumping motion on your rod tip. A sturgeon may give you only a couple of chances to set the hook. You must be ready and react quickly to hook the fish. Set the hook as the rod tip goes down; you will be too late and miss a lot of fish if you wait until the rod tip is down."

Other tips from Fraser include, "Keep your bait cool—let the beer get warm," and, "If Miss America floats by on a piece of balsa wood, don't take your eyes off the tip of your rod." And a final plea to conserve sturgeon fishing, "If you kept a nice fish yesterday, release your catch today."

Striped Bass: Striped bass are caught in large numbers in San Pablo Bay—fall is the best striper season here. Sometimes anglers go specifically for them and other times catch them when fishing for sturgeon—the favorite sturgeon bait is also excellent striper bait.

Anglers may also catch stripers casting or trolling lures. Tom Glasser fishing with Mike Mcollum landed 100 stripers from this area on lures on a fall day in 1997. "We pulled into Red Rock; a school of bass had anchovies trapped on the beach and they were all over," Glasser said. "We started casting chartreuse worm-tail jigs; the lure would hit the water and we would have a fish on. Whenever the bite slowed, we just moved and found them again. We were really ready to quit after about 75 fish but decided maybe we could catch 100 so we kept fishing until we caught and released 100 striped bass. What a day of fishing."

Fraser said anglers usually catch the largest stripers with bait from anchor or drifting live bait. But they have very impressive numbers casting or trolling. Drift with shiner surfperch over rocky reefs or troll or cast 1/2 or 1-ounce chartreuse or white worm tail jig or bucktail jigs.

Other fish: Surfperch, shark, rays and a variety of small fish are caught.

Facilities and Contact: This area has boat launch ramps and bait shops on both sides of the bay. Keith Fraser's bait shop at Loch Lomond Marina in San Rafael (415-456-0321) has a variety of fresh bait and good information particularly for sturgeon anglers. That marina also has a launching ramp. The Rodeo Marina and the Richmond Marina although outside this area, are close and have convenient launch sites for East Bay residents.

Charter boats in this area include boats at Loch Lomond Marina in San Rafael at 415-456-0321 and the New Keesa at 510-787-172 in the Point San Pablo Yacht Harbor north of Richmond. Boats from Emeryville, Berkeley, San Francisco, Crockett and Sausalito may travel to this area to fish for sturgeon and striped bass in the winter.

Cost:	Boat Launching:	Free to about $10.00
	Charter Boat:	Typical cost is $50.00 per person

Ghost shrimp (top) and mud shrimp are two favorite sturgeon baits.

Directions to Marinas: For the Loch Lomond Marina in San Rafael take Highway 101 north to San Rafael and take the Central San Rafael exit. Go east (right) on 2nd Street which combines with 3rd Street and then becomes Point San Pedro Road. Look for the Loch Lomond Marina on the right. From the East Bay, cross the Richmond-San Rafael Bridge. Turn north (right) on Highway 101, take the first exit (the 2nd Street exit) into San Rafael and follow the above directions. For other marinas, see the preceding and following sections.

4. California City to Richmond Bridge:

Sturgeon	9
Halibut	6
Stripers	7
Salmon	6
Shark	5
Surfperch	6

About California City to Richmond Bridge: The northern end of this region at the Richmond Bridge is noted for sturgeon. The southern end at California City (at Bluff Point just north of Raccoon Strait) is most famous for salmon. This is the place in the bay to troll for salmon as they come through in August and September on their runs up the Sacramento River. Striped bass and halibut fishing is also good.

Sturgeon: Use mud shrimp, ghost shrimp or grass shrimp and the same methods as described in the previous sections to catch sturgeon at the edge of the shipping channel north and south of the Richmond San Rafael Bridge.

Striped Bass: Stripers and halibut are caught along the west shoreline along Paradise Cay and Point Chauncay. Live bait is best but some are caught trolling or casting lures.

Salmon: When salmon swim under the Golden Gate Bridge and head inland, they swim around the point northeast of Angel Island and lull in a protected cusp of the bay at California City. If you want to catch salmon without getting out on the open ocean, you can catch them here during August and into September.

Tips From an Expert: "Troll parallel to the shore off California City to catch salmon," says Glenn Peck, skipper of the six-pack boat, the Reel Lady. "Fishing isn't usually fast but the fish are large—most weigh 20-pounds or more. Persistent anglers will often get their two fish limits."

"Troll back and forth near the shoreline from Bluff Point south of California City north to the channel marker buoy," Peck advises. "Fish with anchovies and use flashers in front of your bait."

Other Fish: Shark, surfperch and small fish may be caught but most people catch them while fishing for the premiere fish already discussed.

Facilities and Contact: Anglers can launch from many ramps around the bay and make a short run to this area. Richmond Marina in the East Bay, the Berkeley Marina and Lock Lomond Marina in San Rafael are all close to this area and all have launching ramps.

Contact six-pack boat skipper Glenn Peck at 415-499-5768 for information and to make reservations on his boat. For bait, tackle, and reservations on a charter boat, call the Loch Lomond Marina in San Rafael at 415-456-0321. Boats that often fish in this part of the bay include the Captain Hook from Loch Lomond Marina in San Rafael at 415-456-0321, the Happy Hooker out of Berkeley at 510-849-2727 and the Huck Finn out of Emeryville at 510-654-6040.

Cost: Boat Launching   Free to about $10.00
Charter Boat   Typical cost is $50.00 per person

Directions to Marinas: Directions to the Loch Lomond Marina are included in the preceding South San Pablo Bay section; directions to the Berkeley and Richmond marinas are in the Berkeley Flats section.

5. Raccoon Strait & Richardson Bay:

Stripers	8
Sturgeon	6
Halibut	4
Shark	4
Surfperch	3

About Raccoon Strait & Richardson Bay: Raccoon Strait and Angel Island are premier places to fish. I've had good days catching stripers drifting live bait near the bottom at the west end of Raccoon Strait. You can take a break and visit Angel Island (their harbor is on the north side of the island), and get a sandwich at their dining room.

Striped Bass: Raccoon Strait between Angel Island and the Tiburon shore is a choke point where food is brought in by the incoming tide. The best fishing here is on a moderate incoming tide in June and July.

One day drifting live bait off the west end of the this strait on a private boat I found the secret to catching stripers (stumbled onto the secret may be more accurate) and it didn't last long. As our boat drifted through the channel on an incoming tide, the bottom came up quickly and the stripers were tight against the face of the incline. I found I hooked a fish on almost every drift by reacting quickly to "walk" my live bait along the slope. I alternately reeled in line and lowered my rod tip bouncing bottom. If I reacted too slowly, my rig hung up on the bottom and I usually lost a rig but get it right and a fish would almost always take the bait. I caught my two striped bass in successive drifts. I hooked another two drifts later and handed the rod off to another angler. Then the tide flow slowed and it was over.

Sturgeon: Sturgeon fishing is good at the mouth of Richardson Bay and off Tiburon north of Angel Island near the shore during the herring spawn. Fishing can be very good using herring roe scrapped off pilings at

The Richmond San Rafael Bridge is a good sturgeon fishing location.

Anglers launch their boat at the Richmond launch ramp. This free launch is close to most of the bay fishing.

low tide. In fact, it is so good the season is closed in this area from January 1 through March 15. In years with a good herring spawn, right after sturgeon fishing reopens can be a good time to fish in this area.

The northern boundary for this sturgeon closure is Point Richmond at the southwest corner of the city of Richmond southwest across the bay to Point Chauncy; its southern boundary is the Oakland Bay Bridge and its western boundary is a line between Point Lobos and Point Bonitos at the entrance to the Golden Gate Channel well outside the Golden Gate Bridge.

Other Fish: Halibut as well as striped bass are caught drifting live bait off the west side of Angel Island. Bounce the weight on a sandy bottom to put a live bait right in front of the eyes of a halibut buried in the sand and he will often take it.

Facilities and Contact: Sausalito has two launching ramps (call 415-332-3500 for the Clipper Yacht Harbor). A good bait shop is Caruso's Charter Center in Sausalito at 415-332-1015. Live bait is available at Sea K Fish Dock in Sausalito and Fisherman's Wharf at J&P Bait from the end of April until fall. Live bait seems to come and go so check to see if these operators are still selling bait before you finalize your plans to get bait.

The closest boat ramp is at Sausalito but anglers in the East Bay may launch at Richmond or Berkeley, and North Bay anglers may start at San Rafael. Most launching points on the main bay are not too far from this area. Charter boats fish this area from marinas at Fisherman's Wharf in San Francisco, Sausalito, San Rafael, Berkeley and Emeryville.

Cost: Boat Launching   Ranges from free to about $15.00
        Charter Boat   Typical cost for a day trip is $50.00 per person

Directions to Marinas: To get to the Clipper Yacht Harbor in Sausalito, take the Sausalito-Marin exit, make a left and go under the highway. Turn right on Bridgeway and then left on Harbor to the Yacht Harbor (phone 415-332-3500 for information). A Sausalito public launch ramp is at the end of Tunney street. Directions to the Loch Lomond Marina are included in the South San Pablo Bay section; directions to the Berkeley and Richmond marinas are in the Berkeley Flats section.

6. Berkeley Flats:

Halibut	9
Stripers	7
Shark	7
Sturgeon	4
Surfperch	8

About Berkeley Flats: Shallow mud flats extending from the east shoreline of San Francisco Bay to Berkeley, Richmond, Emeryville and off Treasure Island are very good fishing spots. These have perfect habitat for

halibut to half bury themselves and ambush small bait fish making it one of the best places to catch halibut in California. Striped bass also wait here on incoming tides to eat small fish and are often caught.

Halibut: Drift mooching—bouncing the bait along the bottom—is the typical way to catch halibut and striped bass. Most halibut are caught on live anchovies purchased from one of the bait suppliers. Live shiner perch you catch or can purchase occasionally are excellent bait when you can find it. Trolling live bait or a jig or lure weighted so it is right on the bottom also catches these fish. Most halibut are caught off sandy or mud bottoms so you can fish right on the bottom and not lose much tackle.

Tips from an Expert: "Tie halibut rigs on a three-way-swivel with a snap for a weight on a short 10 inch leg and a size 2 to 1/0 live bait hook on a six foot long leader," says Art Roby, long time halibut angler and skipper of the New Huck Finn charter boat operating out of Emeryville Sport Fishing. "Choose a lively live bait from the bait tank; lightly nose hook it and drop it to the bottom. A lively bait that is swimming naturally will consistently catch halibut and striped bass."

Bounce your weight along the bottom, lifting and lowering your rod tip. "You must drop your weight onto the halibut to get its attention," Roby says only half in jest. "When you get a take, drop your rod tip; wait for the line to tighten up and set the hook." If you think you may have a bite, drop your rod, then set the hook. If it wasn't a fish you will need to reel in and get a new bait but that is better than taking a chance on missing a bite.

Striped Bass: Striped bass are caught in large numbers in the spring, sum-

A white sturgeon is in the net. These are the ultimate fish for many Bay anglers.

mer and early fall. Usually live bait is best but dead bait will work fine sometimes. One afternoon John Marion, his son, and I had caught only one striper when we saw birds working the surface off the Berkeley flats. We motored to the edge of the commotion and cast our fresh but dead anchovies into the area. I gave my bait an irregular retrieve trying to make it swim like a wounded bait. Wham! A fish had my bait. I landed that ten-pound class striper, rebaited and cast again. After a couple pumps on the bait, I had another fish that I landed and released. A third cast and I had another one to play and release. Then the school was gone and action was over but what a time it was while it lasted.

Other Fish: This is an excellent location for surfperch that are landed around almost any pier or structure. Look for pilings that have mussels; anchor 30 to 40 feet from the piling positioning your boat so the current will take your bait to the piling. Cast a live grass shrimp to the base of the pilings and get ready for a take.

Facilities and Contact: Boat launching ramps with direct access to this area include the Berkeley Marina at 510-644-6376, the Richmond Marina at 510-236-1013, and the Emeryville Marina at 510-654-6040. The historical source of live bait has been at Fisherman's Wharf in San Francisco but now live anchovies may be purchased at Berkeley or

Anglers fish for surfperch at San Francisco piers.

Sausalito. Or you can catch your own shiner surfperch and have even better bait.

The new Huck Finn out of Emeryville Marina 510-654-6040, the Happy Hooker out of Berkeley Marina at 510-849-2727, and the Bass Tub out of San Francisco at 415-456-9055 are all noted for live bait fishing. Many other charter boats from throughout the bay fish this area.

Cost: Boat launching   free at Richmond, $2 in quarters at Berkeley
    Charter Boats   About $50 for a day trip

Directions to Berkeley Flats Marinas: Take Interstate 80 north out of Oakland and turn on the Powell Street exit to the Emeryville and Berkeley marinas. Go west on Powell to the Emeryville Marina. For the Berkeley Marina, go north on West Frontage Road west of the freeway and make a left turn onto University. Turn right on Marina Boulevard to the boat launch or go straight on University Avenue to the charter boats. For the launching ramp at the Richmond Marina take Interstate 580 west toward the Richmond San Rafael Bridge, turn south on Harbour Boulevard (this is tricky after you get off the freeway so pay close attention to the signs), and make a left turn at Hall Street to the launching ramp.

7. West Bay:

Stripers	10
Halibut	6
Sturgeon	5
Shark	7
Surfperch	6

About West Bay: This is the part of the bay that everyone knows. Bound by the famous Golden Gate Bridge on the west, Alcatraz to the east, the San Francisco Shoreline and Fisherman's Wharf to the south. It contains great fishing areas like Alcatraz Island, Harding Rock, Shag Rock and the south tower of the Golden Gate Bridge. Striped bass are the number one fish caught here and it ranks as one of the best places to catch them. Large shark, halibut and a variety of fish are landed in this area of the bay.

Striped Bass: My first serious striped bass fishing trip was one June afternoon on a party boat trip on the Wild Wave out of the Berkeley Marina with skipper Bill Beckett. Ex-party boat skipper and skilled fisherman, Ray Bertolotti gave me directions on how to fish the south tower of the Golden Gate Bridge. The tides weren't right at the bridge when we started fishing so we fished the shoals off Alcatraz Island waiting for the tide to shift so we could go to the south tower of the Golden Gate Bridge, the hot fishing spot.

Fishing started slow off Alcatraz; a couple of fish were caught but I figured these were the skilled striper anglers and I wasn't even close to that category. When my reel started spinning fast, I flipped the reel into gear, and set the hook. A strong fish took off under the boat and just kept going. Eventually it sawed my line in two. Despite my disappointment at losing the fish I begin to think that I really could catch them and I realized what a strong, exciting fish they are.

When the tide changed we drifted near the south Golden Gate tower. On the fourth drift I hooked my first fish and it was a rocket. It went deep

taking me from the bow to the stern; a deckhand was at my side giving me instructions. When the fish reversed its direction; I reeled like crazy until the fish went behind the boat and line started screaming off my reel again. The deckhand helped me get across the stern to the starboard side clearing the lines of other fishermen. Once more the fish tried the other direction taking me back to the port corner. This time it stayed on that side and eventually tired.

When the deckhand saw the fish, he yelled at another deckhand, "This one's a hog. Get another gaff." With two gaffs in the fish they lifted it aboard as I stood in awe. This 32-pound fish was a third larger than any fish I had ever caught and was the largest on the boat that day. Sometimes there is a lot to be said for beginner's luck.

The south tower (of the Golden Gate Bridge) is famous for striped bass on outgoing tides. Shag Rock, Harding Rock, the channel under the south end of the Golden Gate Bridge and Alcatraz Island are other good fishing locations.

Other Fish: Halibut are caught with the striped bass when fishing on the bottom of the bay but they are not as numerous as stripers here—this isn't the best area for halibut. Anglers catch surfperch, rockfish and shark but who wants to fish for them when you have a chance at striped bass.

Tip from the Author: If you are fishing the south tower of the Golden Gate Bridge in a private boat, you can cooperate with the large charter boats and catch fish. Get in line and take your turn fishing but remember your boat is much more maneuverable than these big boats so work with them; keep out of the big boats way, and everyone will catch fish.

Facilities and Contact: Live bait can be purchased at Fisherman's Wharf, Sausalito, and Berkeley. Boat launches near this area are at Sausalito, Berkeley, Richmond and San Francisco south of the Oakland Bay Bridge. Any charter boat on the San Francisco or South San Pablo Bay isn't far from this area. Call boat operators like the Bass Tub at 415-456-9055 or call Hi's Tackle Box at 415-221-3825 for information and reservations on a number of boats.

Cost: Boat Launching   Ranges from free to about $10
    Charter Boat   Typical cost for a day trip is $50

Directions to Marinas: See Raccoon Strait, Mid-Bay and Berkeley Flats sections for directions to boat launches close to this area.

8. Mid Bay:

Sturgeon	8
Halibut	8
Stripers	6
Shark	7

Anglers crowd the front of the boat trying to put
their bait right against the south tower of the Golden Gate Bridge.

Halibut are another prized fish caught in the San Francisco Bay.

Surfperch 7
Fly Fishing 6

About Mid Bay: The Mid San Francisco Bay region is from the Oakland Bay Bridge to the San Mateo Bridge. It has several great sturgeon spots. Many halibut and sturgeon are landed from the main channel and numerous piers and pilings are good for surfperch.

Sturgeon: The Alameda Rock Wall, Candlestick Point and the edges of the shipping channel are good spots to catch sturgeon. One of this area's advantages is that it is open to sturgeon fishing from January 1 to March 15 and fishing can be good here during the herring spawn.

Striped Bass: Striped bass and halibut are caught in the spring and summer using live anchovies or shiner surfperch, or trolling. The flats off Alameda and the region off the San Francisco airport are good for striped bass. Anglers wading and fishing the flats with flies catch a few stripers here.

Other fish: Surfperch fishing is very good here in the winter months. Live grass shrimp is the top bait. Shark are also caught in large numbers.

Facilities and Contact: Several bait shops including Sun Valley Bait and Tackle in San Mateo (415-343-6837) and Central Bait and Tackle in Alameda (510-510-522-6731) have good information about current fishing conditions here and usually have fresh bait. Several boat launching ramps in this area include Coyote Point on the west shore of the bay at San Mateo, China Basin in San Francisco, the Alameda Municipal Launching Ramp and the San Leandro Marina (510-357-7447).

No charter boats operate out of this area but many are close-by and fish here. Boats from the Emeryville Marina (510-654-6040) the Berkeley Marina (510-849-2727) and the San Francisco wharves frequently fish this area.

Cost: Boat Launching   Free to about $10
          Charter Boat   Typical cost for a day trip is $45 to $55
Directions to Mid Bay Marinas: For the Coyote Point Marina, take the Coyote Point Drive off Highway 101 at the boundary between San Mateo and Burlingame. Follow this road east to the marina. The China Basin Ramp is just north of Pier 54 south of the Oakland Bay Bridge off China Basin Boulevard. For the Alameda launch, take the Highway 61 exit west from Interstate 880 through the Webster Street Tube. Turn right on Pacific Avenue then left on Main Street and continue straight to the launching ramp. For the San Leandro Marina, take the Marina exit west off Interstate 880 in San Leandro. Take the sweeping turn left as Marina approaches the bay then make a right turn onto North Dike Road to the Marina.

9. South San Francisco Bay:

Sturgeon   7
Shark   7
Stripers   5
Surfperch   5

About South San Francisco Bay: The part of the San Francisco Bay south of the San Mateo Bridge has very good sturgeon fishing during winter and into the spring months. It also has good fishing for surfperch and shark. It is far south of the migratory routes of salmon and shad so doesn't have these fish and doesn't have many striped bass or halibut.

Sturgeon: Sturgeon are caught along the edges of the shipping channel during incoming or outgoing tides. Mud shrimp, ghost shrimp, and grass shrimp are good bait.

Shark: The south end of the bay is a good place to catch many small shark. Squid or cut bait like anchovies or sardines are good bait.

Striped Bass: These fish reach their peak in the South Bay a little later than in the main bay. Look for them here from August to October.

Surfperch: Surfperch and other small fish along with skates and rays are caught in this area.

Where to fish: Find the edges of the shipping channels that run under the high rise sections of the San Mateo and Dumbarton Bridges. Buoys and your depth finder will locate the slope. Meter the bottom to find sturgeon or anchor near these edges and fish the incline part of the channel. Fishing can be good at the bridges and all the way south to the southern end of the bay and into Coyote Creek.

Tips from an expert: "Watch for jumping sturgeon to find a good fish-

Alcatraz Island is a landmark in the Bay and a good striped bass fishing location.

ing location," says renown angler and sturgeon book author Abe Cuanang. "If you see jumpers in the same place, they are probably holding there and that is the place to fish. If you see them in different places, try to figure out which way they are moving so you can intercept them— they move along rip tides or with the current."

Facilities and Contact: A good bait shop that keeps tabs on fishing in this area is Sun Valley Bait & Tackle, at 610 South Norfolk Street in San Mateo (415-343-6837). You can launch your boat at the Port of Redwood City (415-306-4150) midway between the San Mateo and Dumbarton Bridge. Or you can launch north of this area at the Coyote Point Launching Ramp or the San Leando Marina Ramp on the east shore of the bay and run south to this area. This part of the bay doesn't have commercial charter boat operators and these boats rarely if ever go this far south.

Cost: Boat Launching ranges from free to about $10.00
Directions to Launching Ramp: The Port of Redwood City boat launch is in the middle of this area. Take Highway 101 to the Seaport Boulevard exit in this city and go east on Seaport Boulevard. Turn left on Chesapeake Street and follow the signs to the launching area. See the previous sections for directions to the Coyote Point Marina and the San Leandro Marina in the mid-bay where you can launch a boat and run to this part of the bay.

CHAPTER 9:

Giant Pond Full of Fish

The best ocean fishing along our entire West Coast is off the San Francisco Bay Area. Salmon are the favorite Pacific Ocean fish and one statistic stands out—in recent years more than seven out of ten salmon caught off our West Coast have been caught out of the Greater San Francisco Bay Area (from Monterey to Bodega Bay). That statistic is particularly impressive when you consider the Bay Area makes up about one-tenth of the shoreline off our West Coast.

The abundance of these favorite saltwater fish is a big part in declaring the San Francisco Area the premiere area for ocean fishing off our West Coast but there is a lot more. The Farallon Islands, Cordell Bank and Point Sur are three of the best areas for lingcod and rockfish anywhere. Reefs close to harbors provide additional opportunity to catch these fish.

When waters are warmed by El Nino as in 1997, all kinds of warm-water fish are caught. Waters were several degrees above normal bringing these fish north and near shore. Albacore were caught by the thousands in 1997. There is no limit and, on a one day trip out of Pillar Point, 21 anglers on the Wild Wave landed 432 albacore. On other trips Blue-fin tuna and Dorado were caught and marlin were sighted in the ocean off San Francisco.

The bays and beaches out of San Francisco offer yet another reason to choose this area as the best saltwater fishing area off our coast. A lot of striped bass and some halibut are caught along the beaches, from the rocks and off piers outside San Francisco. California Halibut are caught in Monterey Bay, in Bodega Bay and both inside and outside Tomales Bay. A few Pacific Halibut are caught in the ocean off San Francisco.

Charter boats out of Bodega Bay, Berkeley and Emeryville take combination trips for crab and whatever fish is in season. Usually rockfish and lingcod are caught on these trips but it may be salmon when these fish are in season. Anglers set crab-pots in the morning, fish all morning and come back in the afternoon to tend the pots or they tend pots previously set by the charter boat crew. A limit of Dungeness Crab and a good catch of rockfish or salmon make delectable table fare.

At low tides, many beaches are filled with clams from the small razor clams to large geoducks. The most famous place to go for these is Tomales Bay. For a fee, the clam barge at Lawson Landing on this bay delivers you to islands or areas inaccessible by roads and experienced clammers have little trouble digging limits of clams. Bodega Harbor (inside the breakwater) and beaches all along our coast also yield clams at low tide.

Divers go after abalone. What a gourmet treat!. These must be gathered by free diving (without air tanks) and regulations are complicated. One deterrent is that part of the prime abalone diving area is the breeding grounds for great white sharks. In this case the prize (abalone) goes to the brave (or foolhardy) who are willing to dive in areas frequented by Great Whites. Even abalone aren't that valuable to me.

Regulations: The limit is two salmon 24 inches minimum length except during July, August, and early September anglers fishing in the Bay area north of Pigeon Point must keep their first two salmon regardless of size. Anglers may use only one rod when fishing for salmon. Only barbless circle hooks are permitted when drift mooching for salmon when using bait and only single point barbless hooks are permitted when trolling or when mooching with lures without bait. Fishing for salmon in the Bay Area is permitted from mid-March south of Pigeon Point and from the end of

Dawn Leibold lands a string of blue rockfish.

March north of that point. The season closes in early September south of Pigeon Point and the first of November in the rest of the Bay Area. The season and regulations for salmon change often so see the latest DFG regulations for the exact dates and the latest regulations.

The striped bass limit is two and they must be at least 18 inches total length. Three California Halibut may be taken and they must be 22 inches minimum length. However, only one Pacific Halibut may be kept; it must be a minimum of 32 inches long and open season for this species of halibut is May 1 through September 30. The limit is two lingcod and they must be a minimum of 24 inches long. No more than 20 fish may be taken and no more than 10 may be the same species. However, 15 rockfish may be kept and generally they may all be the same species. But that isn't all—no more than three bocaccio may be taken and there is no limit on albacore and some of the smaller fish. See the Department of Fish and Game *Sport Fishing Regulations* for additional restrictions.

Dungeness crab taken from a charter boat must be at least 6-inches across and the limit is six. From a private boat the limit is 10 and the minimum width is 5-3/4 inches. The width is the shortest distance across the width of the shell measured in front of the lateral spines. The season in the ocean off the Bay Area is the Saturday preceding the second Tuesday in November through July 30. Taking of Dungeness Crab is prohibited inside the Bay (inside the Golden Gate Bridge). Rock crab and other crab have a more generous season and limit. See the California *Sport Fishing Regulations* for details for crab, clams and abalone.

Marine Protection: The decline in fishing every place has been severe. We have long understood that freshwater catch is limited but we are just beginning to comprehend the devastation to ocean fishing. Now we have some reason for optimism for these fish in the future in the Bay Area. Three National Marine Sanctuaries have been established off the Bay Area providing some protection for its marine life.

The Farallon Islands and Cordell Bank are National Marine Sanctuaries protecting these bastions of fishing. The largest marine sanctuary off the nation's coasts is the Monterey Bay National Marine Sanctuary. This 200 mile long area from Marin County to Cambria just north of Morro Bay is protected from harmful development such as oil drilling and sets limits on commercial fishing.

Monterey Bay is a unique deep water canyon full of marine life. The Monterey Aquarium, a world renown facility that displays the varied marine life of this area in a natural setting, and the associated research has given the people of the world an understanding of the unique and fragile nature of this ecosystem. It deserves a large part of the credit for bringing this to the attention of policy makers and the protection of this area as a marine sanctuary.

A New Kind of Charter boat: Charter boats have evolved from old, slow wooden charter boats with top speeds of six to eight knots with only a compass and stop watch to navigate and to find fish. Skippers often missed their intended spot but fish were abundant and the catch was often still very good. Today's fiberglass and metal versions have double and triple the cruising speed and an array of navigational and fish finding electronics. The next upgrade arrived when Jim Robertson brought the Outer Limits, a new catamaran charter boat to Sausalito in June 1998. Two other catamarans are to be delivered to skippers in Berkeley and one to Fisherman's Wharf in San Francisco. These charter boats are 50 to 65 feet long and 20 to 22 feet wide—about 50 percent wider than a conventional charter boat of the same length. They are faster, more stable in rough seas and smoother riding than conventional Vee hull fishing boats.

A catamaran is a type of boat built on two narrow hulls that go into the water on each side of the boat. These narrow hulls cut through the water while the cabin and most of the rest of the boat stays above the water. The catamarans have minimum water resistance and high speed—about 20 knots or more—with low fuel consumption. When the bow of a conventional boat heaves up over a wave and slaps down hard on the

Seven of every 10 salmon caught off our West Coast in recent years have been caught out of the San Francisco Bay Area.

water, a catamaran smoothes out the wave and drops down on a cushion of air in the tunnel under the boat. The bow on a normal boat is very bouncy and is pointed but a catamaran is more rectangular with a wider bow and room for several extra anglers. Since the bow doesn't slap down spraying water to the side, it has a dryer ride.

Equally important, when the boat is drifting like mooching for salmon, bait fishing for albacore or drifting for rockfish and lingcod, the narrow twin hulls cuts through the water and the ride is smoother. I've seen many anglers handle the trip to the fishing grounds while the boat is moving but when it stops and rhythmically rocks to and fro, anglers succumb to the action and get seasick. These more stable boats smooth out this boat motion and anglers have less tendency to become seasick. They don't prevent all cases of motion sickness but anglers who can't quite handle the rolling motion on a conventional boat may feel okay on a catamaran.

1. Bodega Bay:

Salmon	9
Rockfish	7
Lingcod	5
Halibut	4
Albacore	3

About Bodega Bay: Bodega Bay has the look and feel of a quaint New England fishing town. With new upscale motels and restaurants in the area, its character is changing but it is still basically a fishing village. The creators of the Alfred Hitchcock's movie, *Birds,* found it was just the look they were after for their movie and filmed much of it on site at Bodega Bay.

But its real attraction is its setting as a safe harbor for anglers in private boats and excellent salmon fishing only a few miles from the entrance to its harbor. It has a good launching ramp (at Westside Park) and good but crowded camping—crowded to overflowing when salmon are being caught. This combination makes Bodega Bay the best place in the area to camp and spend a weekend, or a week or longer fishing and exploring. When salmon catches peak during the month of July, fishing here definitely rates a 10.

You almost need an atlas to keep the terms straight. Bodega Bay is the name of the town. The large bay protected from the ocean by a rock wall that includes all the wharves and the harbor is called Bodega Harbor. Bodega Bay is also the large open bay in the ocean. Bodega Head is the large hill that you pass after you exit the harbor and head southwest to sea. The town of Bodega is a few miles inland from Bodega Bay.

Best Fishing: Salmon is what draws anglers to Bodega Bay but it has other good options. Local rock fishing is good and this includes some lingcod but most fish are small. A trip 19 miles north by boat to Fort Ross garners larger fish and easy limits of rockfish with a few lingcod. A trip on a charter boat to Cordell Bank puts you in arguably the finest fishing for rockfish off this area and perhaps off the whole California Coast. These fish are large and your catch may be a burlap bag of fish filled to overflowing.

Another feature of this area is charter boat trips for crab and rockfish or salmon and crab combinations. You can often catch a limit of Dungeness Crab and a limit of rockfish—maybe even a couple of lingcod or a salmon or two along with crab. Dungeness Crab and chinook salmon—WOW, what a gourmet combination.

Salmon: Salmon fishing out of Bodega Bay ranges from slow to excellent. July is usually the best month to get really excellent catches of salmon. I have caught salmon there from March into October but my best salmon catches have been in July.

Anglers have bragged about catching and releasing 15 to 20 salmon in a day to sort out large 20 pound plus fish. I am ashamed today to say I did that 15 years ago but I would never do it now. That was trolling and we carefully released the fish but even then statistics show about 14% of the released fish die. Two legal salmon of any size is fine with me. I fish enough that eventually I'll get some big ones and I won't kill excess fish.

Good fishing spots include the whistle buoy, Tomales Head and near the mouth of the Russian River 12 miles north of Bodega Head. The whistle buoy is two miles southwest of the entrance to Bodega Harbor. Some anglers use this buoy as a reference fishing north, west or south of the buoy, always keeping the buoy in sight. On windy days, when it is too rough to be out in the open ocean, the seas inside Bodega Bay may be protected from the wind and swell and fishing can be okay. One morning when seas were rough, two friends and I caught one 23 inch salmon and one 23 pound salmon in that protected area.

Lingcod & Rockfish: Local fishing for rockfish and lingcod is good but most fish are small. Anglers go on charter boats to Cordell Bank for premium rockfish and lingcod. Reefs out from Muscle Point and off Salmon Creek north of Bodega Bay are good local spots. A trip to Fort Ross usually produces larger fish and more lingcod.

Tips from an Expert: "Charter boats carry a lot of passengers and have good success mooching for salmon but trolling is usually a better fishing method for anglers in a private boat," says Jim Cramer, an expert angler who lives in Bodega Bay and fishes for salmon frequently. "Mooching works better on charter boats because a lot of anglers are fishing. On a private boat with a two to four anglers you can fish some lines almost straight down with downriggers or heavy weights on sinker releases and other lines with lighter weights far behind the boat. Lines are separated and don't tangled." Author's note—See my book, *The Troller's Handbook* to learn how to get your bait or lure to the fish's depth using a weight on a conventional line.

Albacore: Bodega Bay is being developed as a good albacore fishing location now that boats have started fishing for albacore. Just like every place in this area, albacore fishing is only really good when the ocean is warm and their natural bait is near shore as in El Nino years.

Crab Combos: The Dungeness Crab season out of the Bay Area is open from the Saturday preceding the second Tuesday in November through June 30 in all the ocean areas near the Bay Area. Most sports fishing boats go for crab, then rockfish and lingcod but sometimes they go after salmon and crab.

Bob Tockey made two crab traps from steel bar and we would set those then fish for salmon. At the end of the day we would pull the crab traps and always have some rock crab and occasionally score with a legal Dungeness Crab. Both made great appetizers before dinner.

Other Sealife: Halibut are landed from sandy areas in Tomales Bay or in Bodega Harbor. Abalone abound here and divers can get them. However,

A crab pot full of Dungeness Crab make a combination crab/salmon or crab/rockfish trip an excellent charter boat trip.

Lingcod like this one are a premium catch from Cordell Bank, the Farallon Islands and any other fishing spot along our coast.

shark are always around—these are breeding grounds for great white shark—so diving for abalone is risky.

Facilities and Contact: The best camping facilities are at Westside County Park and Doran County Park. Both have boat launching ramps but the Westside Park ramp has docks and is much better for launching larger boats. Neither accept camping reservations but private campgrounds in town and Sonoma Coast State Beach just north of Bodega Bay make camping reservations (phone 707-875-3483 for information at the state beach). For reservations on a charter boat, call the New Sea Angler at 707-875-3495, Bodega Bay Sport Fishing Center at 707-875-3344 or Wil's Fishing Adventures at 707-875-2323.

Cost: Charter boats $45 to $55 per person
Boat Launch   Free at the County Parks
Camping $14 to $18 at County & State Parks

Directions to Bodega Bay: Take Highway 101 to Petaluma and turn west on Washington Avenue. Follow Bodega Bay Avenue turning right in the town of Two Rock and continue on to Bodega Bay. Go north almost through town and, after you go around the hairpin curves at the north end of town, turn left onto Eastshore Road. Turn right at the stop sign at the bottom of the hill to get to Westside Park or go straight ahead to the Bodega Bay Sport Fishing Center and charter boats. The State Recreation Area with camping is off Highway 1 north of town.

2. Cordell Bank:

Rockfish   10
Lingcod   9
Salmon   5
Albacore   4

About Cordell: Cordell Bank, located at the northern end of the Gulf of the Farallons is probably the best place off California to catch large rockfish. It is also very good for lingcod but Fanny Shoals, the Farallon Islands and Point Sur south of Monterey are also excellent places for large lingcod. Cordell Bank is a range of underwater mountains with their peaks about 180 feet deep.

Several charter boats from Bodega Bay travel to Cordell Bank if the seas are low but don't always count on getting out to Cordell Bank. Often it is a choice of being tossed around in a bouncing boat with a fast drift so another fishing spot closer to shore is a better destination on windy days. But get to Cordell Bank with calm seas and a slow drift and you have a recipe for outstanding rockfish and lingcod. While many locations yield 20 to 30 pound bags of bottom fish, Cordell Bank sacks may weigh 50 to 100 pounds.

Rockfish and Lingcod: Rockfish and lingcod are caught all year. In the fall, seas are often calm; lingcod move into shallow water to spawn and fishing for these large bottom dwellers is very productive. Bait or jigs will catch them.

Tips from an Expert: "Anglers will catch a lot of fish on our trips to Cordell Bank," says Rick Powers, skipper of the New Sea Angler charter boat out of Bodega Bay. "But for the best chance to catch large lingcod try a jig special or lingcod special trip. Several skippers offer these trips. I run a trip going after lingcod every Monday and Friday from September to January when the weather is suitable."

"Tie a shrimp fly or grub tail on a drop loop 18 inches above a jig," Powers says. "Not only will you catch fish on the grub or fly, including some large fish, you will catch more fish on the jig."

Facilities and Contact: See the preceding section on Bodega Bay for the charter boats that operate to Cordell Bank, and for facilities and costs.

Directions: Cordell Bank is 28 miles southwest of Bodega Bay at 123.25 degrees west longitude and 38.01 degrees north latitude. If you don't have a Global Positioning Satellite (GPS) unit, get one to find these positions before you even think about traveling to this or any off-shore locations on a private boat. Many days are too rough to fish Cordell Bank from a 65 foot charter boat. A private boat should be very seaworthy to even think about Cordell Bank and a trip there should only be attempted when both the weather and the weather forecast are very good.

3. Sonoma County Beaches:

Surfperch 8
Rockfish 5
Fly-fishing 6

About Sonoma Beaches: The Sonoma Beaches from Bodega Bay to Jenner give you a feeling of being in a different world. You wonder where all of the people went particularly before or after the summer vacation season. The sandy beaches and rocky surf make a picture card scene around every corner. This is one of the few places along the Bay Area Coast where people can find mile after mile of unspoiled beach with good public access and relatively uncrowded camping.

Surfperch: The public beaches north of Bodega Bay have good fishing for surfperch. Try Shell Beach south of Jenner and Salmon Creek Beach near Bodega Bay, both state beaches, or other public beaches all along this stretch. Sand crabs dug up from the beach, pile worms, grass shrimp or white or yellow plastic grubs on lead-head jigs are all good attractors. Fly-fishers using shrimp or bait fish imitations find this one of their best places to catch surfperch.

Other Fish: Some of the rocky areas have rockfish, eels and cabezon and poke poling is a good method to catch them. This is fishing with a long pole with a two foot long wire tip extending from the pole and a short six to 12 inch leader. Poke a piece of squid or a worm into rocks and crevasses and be ready to set the hook on a fish or eel..

Facilities and Contact: The state beaches have excellent campgrounds

Sonoma Coast has good fishing for surfperch in a remote setting.

and good access to the beaches. Call the state beaches at 707-875-3483 for camping information. Call Bodega Bay Sport Fishing Center at 707-875-3344 for fishing information, bait and tackle.

Directions: Several Sonoma State Beaches are off Highway 1 north of Bodega Bay. Look for signs and turnoffs to them as you drive along this highway. Bodega Dunes State Beach just north of Bodega Bay has a large campground.

4. Tomales Bay:

Clams 10
Surfperch 7
Halibut 5
Rockfish 3

About Tomales Bay: Tomales Bay is a long narrow bay running along the San Andreas Fault. It has launching at Inverness for small boats and larger boats can be launched at Dillon Beach and north of Marshall. This is not a good location to enter the ocean. The entrance to this bay is shallow and sneaker waves always pose a threat to boaters. It has fair halibut fishing but its claim to fame is based more on clams than on fish.

Clams: The clam barge operates from Lawson Landing south of Dillon

Anglers can have the Lawson Landing tractor launch their boat or launch it with their own four-wheel drive vehicle.

Beach when clam season is open and low tides make for good claming. It will drop you at an island or sandy beach where those in the know can get limits of horseneck or other clams. A game warden often checks for limits and may interpret the laws rigorously. One person got fined for having an extra clam neck; the rest of the clam escaped but any part of a clam counts and can cost you. A fishing license is required to take clams.

Charter boats used to operate out of Dillion Beach but found the shallow mouth of the bay a challenge in bad weather and moved their operations to Bodega Bay.

Tips from an Expert: Large clams have long necks, can be a foot or more below the surface and move before you can dig down to them. "Take a PVC plastic clam pipe to get the large geoducks," Bill Karr, Editor of *Western Outdoor News* who goes every year to collect clams said. The clam pipe looks like a large stove pipe. "When you see the spout of a clam or see the large almost square indentation in the sand that marks a breathing hole for one of them, push the pipe straight down into the sand to enclose the clam. Now it can't move away and you dig down as much as 18-inches or two-feet to find the clam inside the pipe." The pipe contains the clam and keeps the walls from caving in as you dig inside the pipe.

Fish: Tomales Bay has good fishing for halibut in the warm months and for surfperch in the cool months. If you aren't having success on these fish, you can usually catch a few shark.

Facilities and Contact: The Clam Barge at Lawson Landing will take you to islands to dig clams. You can also launch your boat from the sand beach (Use your own four wheel drive vehicle to launch or have them back your trailer into the water with their tractor) and camp. Call them at 707-878-2443 to get a schedule of low tides and when they operate.

Directions: For the Clam Barge or other facilities at Lawson Landing follow Highway 1 north to Tomales and make a left turn to Dillion Beach. In Dillion Beach, continue on the main road south to Lawson Landing. You will go through gates and a campground to get to a boat launch on the beach and the clam barge.

To get to the boat launch at Inverness, follow Highway 1 north out of San Francisco past Olemay and look for the signs to this town. It is a left turn. A surfaced boat ramp with docks at Miller Park off Highway 1 three miles north of Marshall puts you in the northern part of Tomales Bay.

5. Marin County Beaches:

Salmon   10
Surfperch   7
Rockfish   5
Fly-fishing   5

About Marin County: The Marin coast includes Point Reyes National Seashore, Stinson State Beach and part of the Golden Gate Recreational area. Combined, these make up most of the seashore and are a great recreational area with a lot of fishing opportunity. Much of the shoreline is steep and treacherous. Large sneaker waves occasionally wash unsuspecting people off apparently safe beaches and rocks. Be very careful.

The best fishing is offshore with salmon the number one catch. The largest salmon ever caught off the California coast, a 52.2 pound salmon,

Anglers fish off the back of the charter fishing boat Cobra in the shallow water at the Farallon Islands.

was caught here. Anglers looking for large fish usually go north from the Golden Gate to this area.

Salmon: On a good weather weekend day in the late spring or summer, an armada of boats are usually fishing off this coast. Many of the Bay Areas' charter boats will be here but for each of them, there may be 10 private boats—this is the place to go for the largest salmon. Anglers from charter boats usually mooch with frozen and thawed anchovies; anglers on private boats mooch or troll using the same anchovies. Trollers may also use lures like Apex lures, Krocodiles or plug-cut herring imitations.

Tips From an Expert: Charter boat skippers switched from trolling for salmon with heavy three pound weights and heavy tackle to mooching with six or eight ounce weights about a decade ago and that has made profound changes. "Mooching has changed the way we fish," says Tony Broglio who has been a deckhand and a skipper on Bay Area charter boats for a couple of decades. "With the light weights with mooching, anglers can use light sporting rods and salmon fishing has become a lot more fun. Many of our anglers won't even think about trolling (some charter boats still troll with heavy weights when fish are scattered and trolling is catch-

The Farallon Islands are one of the very best locations to catch rockfish and large lingcod.

ing more fish)."

"With circle hooks you have to be extra patient when you get a bite. Just wait for a steady pull. Don't set the hook, just lift your rod and reel. If your line goes slack, a salmon has probably grabbed your bait and is swimming up toward the boat. Reel fast until you feel weight on your line and continue to reel. You will probably get a salmon."

Surfperch: Sandy beaches along this shoreline are great for a variety of surfperch during the cool months from about November to May. Use pileworms, sand crabs dug from the sand, live grass shrimp or white or yellow plastic grubs on a lead-headed jig. Fly anglers can catch these fish on flies that imitate small bait fish.

Rockfish: Fishing along rocky walls can produce a variety of rockfish, eels, cabezon and maybe a lingcod. These latter fish must be at least 24 inches in length or they must be released.

Facilities and Contact: Point Reyes National Seashore has camping and is large enough to take several days to explore. It has a general store but few services. Olema has private campgrounds and this area has a few motels, bed and breakfasts and restaurants in the larger towns. Services are scattered but they are generally small, personable and interesting. For information call Hi's Tackle Box at 415-221-3825 or any Bay Area charter boat operator for offshore fishing, Point Reyes National Seashore at (415) 663-1092 or Marin County Parks Department at 415-499-6387 for on shore fishing.

Directions: Most of the beaches in this county are along Highway 1. Stinson Beach is just off the highway west of Mill Valley. Point Reyes National Seashore is a very large park off this highway at Point Reyes Station but you must drive several miles into the park to get to any beaches.

6. Farallon Islands:

Lingcod   10
Rockfish   9
Salmon   8
Albacore   7
Halibut   4

About The Farallon Islands: The Farallon Islands and Fanny Shoals are rich in marine life. The islands and surrounding seas are sanctuaries for all sorts of wildlife including sea lions, white shark and many species of birds and are off limits to people.

This is an excellent place to catch territorial fish like lingcod and rockfish as well as migratory fish like salmon and albacore. Anglers occasional catch a large Pacific Halibut. Charter boats from Pillar Point, Berkeley and Emeryville and the 94 foot long Cobra out of Richmond travel to the Farallon Islands if the seas are low.

Rockfish and Lingcod: Rockfish and lingcod are caught all year. In the fall when seas are often calm; lingcod move into shallow water to spawn and fishing for these large bottom dwellers is the best of the year. Fanny Shoals, Noonday Rock and Soap Bank north west of the Farallons are some of the best ling spots. They are shallow enough (usually less than 200 feet deep) to use a jig effectively. Live bait, when it is available, is great for all anglers and jigs are great lures in the hands of experienced ling anglers.

Tips from an Expert: "Experienced lingcod anglers will catch a lot of fish on jigs but people that haven't caught many lingcod can catch them on live bait," advises Don Wong, a skipper who operates frequent trips to the Farallons on the charter boat, C-Gull, out of the Emeryville Sportfishing Center. "Bait up; drop it to the bottom; crank your line up a few feet off the bottom and be ready for a take. If you don't get bit after a couple of minutes, drop back down to the bottom. If others are getting fish and you aren't, you probably aren't on the bottom or a fish has stolen your bait."

Albacore: On El Nino years, the water is warm and albacore fishing can be fantastic. The Farallons and beyond are good for these fish but other areas near port are often better.

Halibut: Anglers rarely catch halibut from the offshore ocean areas but the few I have seen caught have been Pacific Halibut including one from the Farallons that weighed 53 pounds. Most are caught accidentally while bait fishing for lingcod.

Facilities and Contact: Charter boats to the Farallon Islands operate regularly from Richmond, Berkeley, Emeryville, and Pillar Point and occasionally from Sausalito and San Francisco. Charter boat operators who send boats to the Farallons include Cobra Sport Fishing out of Richmond at 925-283-6773, Emeryville Sportfishing out of the East Bay city of the same name at 510-654-6040, Berkeley Marina at 510-849-2727, Huck Finn Sportfishing out of Pillar Point at 650-726-7133 and Captain John's also out of Pillar Point at 650-726-2913. For other boats, call Hi's Tackle Box at 415-221-3825.

The launching ramp closest to these islands is at Pillar Point. Anglers may also launch their boats at any of the launching facilities in the San Francisco Bay but it is not safe to make a trip to these islands from any port unless your boat is very seaworthy, has good navigational equipment including GPS and the weather and weather forecast are very good.

Directions: The main Farallon Islands are 28 miles west of the San Francisco coast. The southern end of this chain is at 123 degrees west longitude and 37.41.40 degrees latitude. The center of Fanny Shoals at the northern end of these islands is 123.11 degrees west longitude and 37.47 degrees latitude. This area has several islands, shoals and shallow areas that have excellent fishing.

7. San Francisco Coast:

Salmon	9
Striped Bass	8
Halibut	8
Rockfish	6
Lingcod	5

A salmon fishing boat motors out from San Francisco. Note Coit Tower in the background.

The Point Bonito lighthouse marks the northern entrance to San Franciso Bay.

About San Francisco Coast: An old photo by Ansel Adams shows the entrance to the San Francisco Bay before the San Francisco Golden Gate Bridge was under construction. In that photo there is no break where you can easily say the bay ends and the ocean begins. At that time I would have considered the three miles outside the Golden Gate Bridge all the way to the mouth of the inlet from Seal Rock to Point Bonito part of the bay. Now the Golden Gate Bridge forms a break and that is where the bay ends and the ocean begins. The DFG sets their limits and fishing criteria for the bay inside the bridge and ocean rules apply outside the bridge.

The Golden Gate entrance to the Bay is a rich area with tides constantly flowing in and out bringing food on each exchange of water. The tides are so strong and so constant, wardens at Alcatraz Island Prison had little concern that an escaping prisoner could successfully swim to shore only one mile away. Now strong swimmers have made that swim but they chose their time with the most favorable current and they have a rescue boat almost at their side to pull them out of the water if they should get into trouble.

This flowing water brings bait while striped bass wait on the lee side of the south tower that supports the Golden Gate Bridge on an outgoing tide. Anglers take advantage of this by drifting live anchovies or shiners in the current past this tower, hooking many stripers.

Bakers Beach on the south side of the channel just outside of the Golden Gate has excellent fishing. I have caught salmon, striped bass and halibut on live anchovies all on the same day in the same area. Drop the bait to the bottom and you may add lingcod and rockfish to the catch. Seal Rock just off the beach from the Cliff House is an excellent area to catch halibut. On windy days the north side of the channel provides protection from the wind and anglers may catch some fish. Trolling the south side of this channel just outside of the Golden Gate produces some salmon.

Fishing from the beach can be good and the techniques discussed in the Pacifica Beach section apply along this beach. For this section I will concentrate on fishing from a boat and will emphasize beach or small craft fishing in the next section.

Salmon: The channel outside the Golden Gate Bridge has fair salmon fishing and it is a place to duck in away from high seas to get a chance to fish. The ocean west of San Francisco is a very good area to fish for salmon. It is noted for frequent limits of fish but the largest salmon are usually caught north off the Marin Coast.

Halibut: Anglers drift fishing along the bottom with live bait make very good halibut catches off Seal Rock. This is just off the cliffs from the Cliff House at the south entrance to the Golden Gate channel. They also catch halibut all along Baker Beach at the south side of this channel from the Golden Gate Bridge to Seal Rock.

Rockfish and Lingcod: Rockfish and lingcod are caught inside and outside the Golden Gate Bridge all year. The swift current here makes it

A deckhand holds up an albacore caught out of Pillar Point.

difficult fishing so this is not the best place to catch these bottom fish.

Facilities and Contact: These are sand and rock beaches. Anglers need only a long casting rod but waders or a wet suit can be very helpful. Call Hi's Tackle Box in San Francisco at 415-221-3825 for information.

Directions: San Francisco beaches are from the Golden Gate Bridge to the entrance of this channel then south along the beach to the southern limit of San Francisco. It includes the waters up to several miles off shore.

8. Pacifica Beach:

Striped Bass	9
Salmon	7
Surfperch	7
Halibut	6
Lingcod	4
Rockfish	4

About Pacifica Beach: The beach off Pacifica south of San Francisco has a great variety of fish from small shiners, surfperch and smelt to salmon, striped bass and halibut. When striped bass are close to shore, this is a very exciting place. Anglers catch fish from charter boats or private boats, from shore, from the Pacifica Pier, from small boats launched at the beach and anglers even fish from surfboards.

Striped Bass: Many anglers including those on charter boats use mostly live bait lightly nose hooked to catch striped bass. More anglers casting from shore or working from small beach launched boats fish with hair-raiser jigs, surface lures like pencil poppers or with crank baits. Really good anglers may catch and release 10 or 20 stripers in a day.

When schools of striped bass are holding against beaches, a conflict arises between anglers in boats, particularly charter boats and shore anglers. These boats bring many scoops of live anchovies so they start chumming to draw the school of stripers to the boat. In the process, the fish move out from shore, out of range of the shore anglers.

Shore anglers don't take kindly to anglers in boats moving fish away from where they can catch them. One charter boat skipper said he was happy to stay in close enough to shore for anglers casting from the beach to reach the fish but it isn't safe. He has had lures with two or three treble hooks cast from shore hit the deck and they might just as well end up with their hooks in an angler on his boat.

Striped bass may be in this area in late June, July and August. Some years they never show up in numbers.

Tips from an Expert: "When the seas are almost flat, the winds calm and the tides right, my friends and I launch aluminum fishing boats from the sandy beach just north of Pedro Point at Pacifica," Angeleo Cuanang says. "We fish with hair raiser jigs with barbless hooks to catch striped

bass very near the beach. A good angler may catch and release more than a dozen stripers in a few hours."

Author's note: Fishing in the ocean from a small boat can be very dangerous and is not for the novice. Be certain the seas are calm, the weather forecast is good, you have all of the necessary safety equipment and you are skilled in operating a boat off the beach before you try this.

Salmon: Salmon may be there at any time and seem to be there every September. Weather is usually good this time of year and this is a good time to take a private boat out of Pillar Point to catch them. Check to be sure salmon are being caught then plan your fishing trip.

Who To Contact: Boats from Pillar Point and from the San Francisco Bay Area fish for striped bass and for salmon in this area. Contact the Pillar Point boats listed under that section, the San Francisco Bay boats listed at the end of this section or Hi's Tackle Box at 415-221-3825. Call the Pacifica Pier Bait and Tackle at 415-355-0690 (they are located at the Pacific Pier and know what angers are catching) for local sea conditions and a fishing report.

Directions: The Pacifica beaches are at the city of Pacifica about five miles south of the southern boundary of San Francisco. Striped bass are usually found south of the Pacifica Pier and salmon are found in a large area both north and south of this protrusion into the ocean. Anglers can launch small boats from a sandy beach just north of Point Pedros to go after these fish on very calm days.

9. Pillar Point:

Salmon	10
Rockfish	9
Lingcod	8
Albacore	8
Surfperch	8
Striped Bass	7

About Pillar Point: Pillar Point is at an excellent harbor facing onto the ocean south of San Francisco at the town of El Granada. It has a new, eight-lane launching ramp with good parking and about 10 charter boats. All the facilities are enclosed in a well-protected rock wall harbor. It does have a shallow, hazardous reef outside the protected harbor so you must become familiar with the hazard and follow the marked channel when exiting the harbor.

The primary advantage of this harbor is its location right on the ocean near the fish with excellent fishing for salmon, rockfish and lingcod near the harbor. It is a good place to start an albacore trip from a charter boat

Jigbars like these are excellent lures to catch lingcod.

Anglers leave their rods in rod holders waiting for a salmon to bite.

or from a very seaworthy private boat. A five year old, six lane launching ramp has good docks and adequate parking except on weekends when salmon fishing is very good. Anglers who launch here avoid the long, sometimes rough ride out of San Francisco Bay. In short, it is one of the best ports for anglers in private boats in the area.

Best Fishing: Historically rockfish and lingcod drew anglers to Pillar Point. Three hundred feet deep Deep Reef 14 miles south has been an excellent fishing location yielding many large lingcod. Fifteen to twenty years ago when this reef didn't get as much pressure and the limit was 10 lingcod per day, I've had days where I have caught seven lings including some 20 pound class lings fishing from a private boat. Today the limit has been reduced to two lings with a minimum length of 24 inches and one or two legal lingcod is a good catch. This is a very rocky structure and has claimed many rigs—sometimes half a dozen or more in a day of fishing.

One time, Price Hennan snagged the bottom in his private boat and was holding the boat in perfect position over Deep Reef. Dick Fiel and I were catching lingcod as quickly as we could get sanddab bait to the bottom. Hennan tied his line off on a cleat on the boat, grabbed another rod and started catching them as well. We took time out from catching fish for a quick radio call to our friends in another boat telling them we already had six large lingcod in the boat and two more on our lines. They weren't having much success and didn't believe us. Eventually we convinced them to come join us. We caught 11 lings all in the 15 to 25 pound range and our friends caught three before the line anchoring our boat broke and we lost that great location.

Today salmon get equal attention; striped bass may be caught on boats going north to Pacifica and albacore are an important fish in El Nino years when these fish come close to shore. Anglers going after lingcod and rockfish often take trips to the Farallon Islands or may go on a light tackle trip. Slow wooden boats have been replaced by fast fiberglass and metal boats and anglers from this port fish a large area.

Salmon: Salmon fishing out of Pillar Point can be very good most of the season. Anglers get a jump on the season when it opens south of Pigeon Point in mid March, two weeks ahead of the opener north of this line. Pigeon Point is about 17 miles south of Pillar Point—within reasonable range for today's fast charter boats out of Pillar Point.

Good fishing spots include the Deep Reef, Pacifica Beach, Montara north of town, Pigeon Point to the south and the Farallon Islands. Occasionally salmon are found just outside the entrance buoy and limits may be landed within a couple hours from leaving the dock.

Lingcod & Rockfish: Local fishing for rockfish and lingcod is good. The Deep Reef 14 miles south of the harbor and local reefs are good for these fish though the size and quality of fish has declined over the years. Anglers go on charter boats to the Farallon Islands for premium rockfish and lingcod where large fish are landed. Some boats like the Queen of Hearts specialize in light tackle rockfish.

Tip from the Author: Local reefs are so rocky that a high price is paid in lost tackle. The ticket price for a trip to the Farallons is more than a local trip but you usually lose less tackle. The overall cost may be about the same for the two trips and you usually catch larger fish at the Farallons so think seriously about a trip to these islands.

Albacore: Pillar Point is in an excellent location to catch albacore. The Wild Wave is one of a few boats set up for long trips often required to reach these fish with 20 bunks for anglers and a hot galley. The 601 spot where albacore are often found is about 40 miles southwest of Half Moon Bay. Boats also fish the Farallon Island area when albacore are in this area. On good years, albacore rate a 10 out of this harbor—albacore catches were so good in 1997 that it should rate a 12.

Other Fish: The beach off Pacifica about seven miles north of Pillar Point is a famous place to catch striped bass. When fish are there, boats from Pillar Point are closest to these fish and anglers launching private boats here have only a short run to these fish.

Tips from an Expert: "Mooching is a great way to catch salmon," says Dennis Baxter, skipper of the charter boat, the New Captain Pete out of Pillar Point Harbor. "You need to get your bait to the right depth. You can use reels with line counters, mark your line or use color coded line. But most anglers learn to pull out one foot at a time and count the number of pulls to get to the proper depth."

"Don't move your rod tip when you have a bite. If you pull the bait away from the fish, it will probably look someplace else for its meal and you will miss a good chance to catch a salmon."

Facilities and Contact: Two charter boat operators work out of the wharf at Pillar Point. Captain John's (phone 415-726-2913) who was the first charter boat operator in the area has been in business for more than 40 years. Huck Finn Sport Fishing (415-726-7133) is a couple of doors down from Captain John's.

Cost:	Entry and Parking	No fee
	Boat Launch	About $10
	Typical charter boat	$45 for rockfish to $55 for salmon
		Albacore trips cost $150 to $185.

Directions to Pillar Point: This harbor is about 14 miles south of the city limits of San Francisco off Highway 1. Turn right at the stop light at El Granada then turn left into the harbor area. From the east, go west across the San Mateo Bridge and continue west on Highway 92 to Half Moon Bay. Turn north on Highway 1 to El Granada. Turn left at the stop light and left again to enter the harbor area.

10. San Mateo Beaches:

Surfperch 7
Rockfish 4
Lingcod 3

About San Mateo Beaches: San Mateo County that borders San Francisco and runs almost to Santa Cruz is as different from San Francisco as sunny weather is different from a heavy storm. It is remote and isolated and full of natural splendor from beaches to small towns with character, remote lighthouses and many miles of undeveloped shoreline. Sprinkled along Highway 1 are about a dozen state beaches and two lighthouses that operate as youth hostels. There are tens of miles of sandy beaches to fish for striped bass, surfperch or other near-shore fish. The Pacifica beaches discussed earlier are part of the San Mateo beaches but this section will concentrate on the remote part of these shores south of Pillar Point.

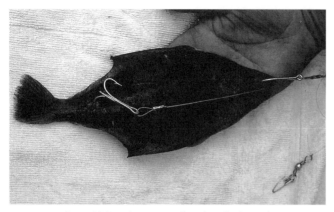

A sanddab makes an excellent bait for lingcod.

Ana Nuevo Island along this shore is a very good fishing location for anglers fishing for lingcod and rockfish from a boat but is most famous as a breeding location for elephant seals. You can arrange a tour to see these huge mammals when they are in the area during the winter months by calling 415-879-0227.

Pigeon Point 17 miles south of Pillar Point is the boundary for the salmon season openers. South of this point, the salmon season opens on the Saturday nearest mid-March; north of this boundary salmon season opens the last Saturday in March, about two weeks later. Anglers from boats have very good salmon fishing but shore anglers rarely catch one.

Santa Cruz small boat harbor has a good launching ramp but limited parking.

Surfperch: Beaches off this part of the San Mateo county coast are good places to catch surfperch. Fish with grass shrimp (live shrimp if you can get it), sand crabs, anchovies or mackerel and wait for the fish to take your bait. Or cast and retrieve plastic grubs on lead-head jigs.

Other Fish: This area has good fishing for lingcod and rockfish and some striped bass fishing. Shore angling for these fish is only fair but anglers can catch a few from rocks and reefs at the shoreline. Anglers may also catch cabezon, eels, smelt and kingfish. Poke pole fishing where the bait is pushed into crevasses that are exposed at low tide is a good fishing method.

Facilities and Contact: The beaches south of Half Moon Bay are in a remote area and have very little commercial development. Youth hostels at Montara Light Station (415-728-7177) and Pigeon Point Lighthouse (415-879-0633) are great, adventurous places to stay for the young at heart. For information on the state beaches call 415-726-8819. For bait and tackle, stop at Pillar Point harbor. The town of Pescadero a few miles inland on Highway 84 has a good local restaurant.

Directions to San Mateo Beaches: State beaches are located along

Highway 1 every few miles from San Francisco to Santa Cruz. From the east, go west across the San Mateo Bridge and continue west on Highway 92 to Half Moon Bay. Turn south on Highway 1. Watch for public beaches all along the way and take time to explore and fish for surfperch in the winter and smelt and rockfish the rest of the year.

11. Santa Cruz:

Salmon	10
Rockfish	9
Lingcod	8
Albacore	7
Halibut	4

About Santa Cruz: Santa Cruz, located at the northern end of Monterey Bay, has many options for offshore anglers starting with great salmon fishing from March through June or July. Rockfish and lingcod are caught in this area all year. Albacore make their annual circuit staying in the warm water offshore. Some years albacore fishing is good and other years these fish travel too far from shore for anglers to reach in a day.

Several charter boats operate out of Santa Cruz; a good although crowded launch ramp, and even boat rentals give Santa Cruz anglers many options. Shore bound anglers can fish off the Santa Cruz Wharf, the Capitola Wharf or many beaches. This is the closest port for anglers in the San Jose area.

If you don't get enough thrills fishing, you can ride the Big Dipper roller coaster or the other thrill rides at the Boardwalk. The roller coaster, built in 1924, is one of the 10 best roller coasters in the nation according to American Coaster Enthusiasts organization and is a national historic landmark. If you are still wobbly from a day rocking on the ocean, forego the ride on the roller coaster and avoid the fun house with its distorted mirrors and dizzying illusions.

Salmon: Salmon season south of Pigeon Point opens in mid-March, a couple weeks ahead of the San Francisco opening. Catches during the early season out of this port are great with frequent limits of salmon. The Monterey Bay catch is often the best along the coast through April; fishing remains good through June and sometimes into July. After the commercial season opens, usually May 1, salmon scatter and fishing may be more difficult. Concentrate your salmon trips to Santa Cruz in March and April but go anytime fishing reports are good.

Tips from an Expert: "Work your bait. You will catch twice as many fish if you will drop your bait to the maximum depth you want to fish then slowly crank it up through the fishing zone," instructs Tim Zoliniak, skipper of the Makaira sport fishing boat. He also warns salmon fishermen to gear up with fairly heavy tackle until sea lions leave the area in May or June. The cute but pesky mammals may take half the hooked fish. "Tighten your drag a notch; put a bend in your rod and hurry the salmon to the boat when these mammals are a threat to take your fish," Zoliniak says.

"Mark your depth by carefully counting out 100 feet of line," says Tim's father, Ed. Loop a small rubber band around the line; pull one end

Live mackerel like this and live sardines are excellent lingcod bait.

Sea lions have had a population explosion and now take many hooked salmon from anglers' lines.

of the rubber band through the loop in the other end and pull it tight around the line." The next time you can just let out line to the rubber band and know you are at 100 feet."

Rockfish and Lingcod: Rockfish and lingcod are caught all year. In the fall, when seas are often calm, lingcod move into shallow water to spawn and fishing for these large bottom dwellers is very productive. Charter boats usually go north to Davenport or to Point Ana Nuevo but anglers in private boats can find some of these fish a short distance from the harbor. Anglers can even rent small boats at the Santa Cruz or Capitola wharf. A map is provided with the rental boat to direct anglers to good, close-to-shore fishing locations protected from the prevailing northwesterly wind. Anglers may catch rockfish, an occasional halibut and maybe even a salmon.

Albacore: When albacore are found off our coast, there is no other fish that compares. This is one of the best ports to go after albacore in the Bay Area.

Tips from an Expert: "You can catch a lot of albacore from a private boat just trolling and you don't need super heavy tackle," says expert angler and pending world record holder Don Giberson. When El Nino started showing in 1997, Giberson knew that could mean albacore and took the summer off so he could fish out of Santa Cruz on his own boat almost every day. He landed more than 700 albacore including a pending world record 90 pound albacore he caught on October 21, 1997 trolling a Zucchini Zuker ZG17 lime colored head, orange & yellow body trolling lure.

On charter boats, getting the troll-caught fish to the boat quickly brings the school to the boat so other anglers may catch perhaps dozens of fish on live bait or lures. Anglers use heavy troll tackle to land the albacore quickly. But on a private boat you catch your fish on troll and don't need to hurry the fish to the boat. "From a private boat, use a heavy leader but use a rig with 40-pound, maybe even 25-pound test line and play each fish carefully," Giberson says. "For large fish, concentrate on fishing the end of the season," says Giberson. "Albacore counts are down, but many large ones are caught."

Facilities and Contact: Three charter boat operators take trips out of Santa Cruz. The Makaira fishes from the small boat harbor (phone 831-426-4690); Shamrock Charters has two boats operating out of the small boat harbor (831-476-2648) and Stagnaro's operates off the wharf. The first two have fast, modern fiberglass boats. Stagnaro's (831-425-7003) has older, slower wooden boats but charges less for a trip. Make reservations well in advance during salmon season. Weekend trips may be booked full weeks in advance when salmon fishing is good and even on weekdays may fill up a week or more before the departure date.

Santa Cruz Boat Rental rents 16 foot boats with motors at the Santa

Cruz Wharf (831-423-1739) and Capitola Boat and Bait (831-462-2208) rents similar boats from the Capitola Wharf. For beach and roller coaster information, call 831-423-5590.

Santa Cruz has a variety of motels for every budget, camping at New Brighton Beach, Seacliff State Beach or at private campgrounds, shops, swimming and surfing beaches, the Boardwalk with many rides and a wharf with many restaurants, shops and fish markets. It is a favorite weekend getaway place for Bay Area people in the spring, summer and fall so be prepared for crowds on the weekends. Stop downtown for a delicious cookie with a scoop of ice cream at the Pacific Cookie Factory. For general information, call the Conference and Visitor Council at 800-833-3494. For an elegant gourmet meal, make reservations at Shadow Brook Restaurant in Capitola at 831-475-1222—you won't be disappointed.

Cost: Typical charter boat fee $45.00-$55.00
Rod and Reel Rental $6.00
Boat launch $8.00
Boat and motor rental $32.00 per half day

Directions: The Santa Cruz Wharf is on the beach west of the Boardwalk. Go south on Highway 17 until it intersects Highway 1. Continue into Santa Cruz on Ocean Street, turn right on Soquel and left on Front Street. When that deadends, turn left to the wharf. Stagnaro's operates off the wharf. The charter boats Makaira and Shamrock Charters both operate out of the small boat harbor on the boundary between Santa Cruz and Capitola. The boat launching ramp is at this harbor. Take Highway 17 south from San Jose and continue east on Highway 1 to Soquel Avenue. Turn (right) south on Soquel then turn left onto 7th street. For Shamrock Charters or for boat launching continue on 7th Street. For the Makaira, turn right on Brommer Street and follow the street around the harbor to H dock. For Capitola Boat and Bait, take Highway 1 east to Bay Street. Turn south on Bay and follow the signs to the wharf. Parking is very limited.

12. Monterey Bay Beaches:
Surfperch 8
Halibut 3
Fly-fishing 5

About Monterey Beaches: Monterey Bay stretches about 40 miles from Santa Cruz to the city of Monterey. Its beaches are sandy and smooth—good swimming beaches. Anglers catch fish along these beaches but the lack of structure means they don't have the fish found in caves and

An angler fishes the surf on the Monterey Bay shore. Surfperch are the primary catch in this area.

This commercial wharf in Monterey Harbor is the best fishing location in the harbor.

crevasses along rocky beaches. Surfperch find this a perfect place to forage for food and spawn and they are the primary focus of anglers.

This area is blessed with a great abundance and variety of sea mammals like otters, sea lions and birds. Elkhorn Slough at Moss Landing and the Salinas River State Wildlife Area south of Castroville are two of the best places to view wildlife in the Bay Area.

Surfperch: Surfperch are the number one target for anglers along these beaches. Bring bait like grass shrimp, pile worms or anchovy filets or dig sand crabs from the beach. Cast your bait and wait for a bite. You can cast and retrieve grub tails on lead-head jigs or fly-fish with shrimp or small baitfish imitations.

Facilities and Contact: Most of the Monterey Bay shore has public access including several state beaches, some with campgrounds. To the north anglers fish off the surf along the public beaches from Santa Cruz, Capitola, New Brighton and Seacliff State Beach. Southern beaches from Sunset State Beach near Watsonville to Marina State Beach north of Monterey have good fishing. For information about state beaches including camping call 408-384-7695.

Directions: Monterey Bay Beaches include New Brighton Beach and Seacliff Beach just south of Capitola, Manessa and Sunset State Beaches at Watsonville, Salinas River State Wildlife Area just south of Castroville and Marina Dunes State Beach at Marina north of Monterey. Most beaches are adjacent to Highway 1. For Sunset Beach that has camping, take Beach Road west off Highway 1 at Watsonville. Turn right onto Shell Drive to the park. Ask locally for directions to other beaches.

13. Moss Landing:

Salmon	10
Albacore	7
Rockfish	7
Lingcod	6

About Moss Landing: Moss Landing is on the shore of Monterey Bay midway between Monterey and Santa Cruz. Large smoke stacks from the power generating plant in this town can be seen for miles. Elkhorn Slough in this town has a tremendous variety of wildlife—a two hour tour on a boat on weekends gets you close to these mammals and birds.

The waters off Moss Landing have very good salmon fishing from March through June or July. Rockfish are caught all year. Often salmon are found very near this launching point making it a good location to start a trip in a private boat or from the one charter boat fishing this area.

Salmon: The Moss Landing area salmon season opens in mid-March, a couple weeks ahead of the San Francisco opening. The early season out of

this port is great with frequent limits of salmon. On opening day 1997, Tom Jones, skipper of the charter boat Kahuna, made a short run straight out from port, found a school of hungry fish and had limits of salmon for his 22 anglers an hour and 15 minutes from the time he left port.

Albacore: Fishing for albacore is only good on El Nino years when water temperatures are unusually high. Then these fast, strong, exciting fish are the rage—anglers can't get enough of them. Most are far offshore and anglers pursue them from charter fishing boats like the Kahuna out of Moss Beach or large, seaworthy private boats.

Rockfish and Lingcod: Rockfish and lingcod are caught all year. In the fall, seas are often calm; lingcod begin to move into shallow water to spawn and fishing for these large bottom dwellers with jigs or bait, particularly live bait you catch, is very productive.

Facilities and Contact: One charter boat, the Kahuna, operates out of Moss Landing (call 408-633-2564). Two launching ramps are available for anglers in small boats. When salmon are running, parking is full early on weekends.

Moss Landing is a small town midway between Monterey and Santa Cruz with only a few services. The area in and south of Moss Landing has a variety of motels and nearby Monterey and Watsonville have all the services you could want. For general information, call the Monterey County Conference and Visitor Bureau at 408-649-1770.

Cost:	Typical charter boat fee	$50.00
	Rod and Reel Rental	$6.00
	Boat launch	$5.00

Directions: The Moss Landing public launch is off Highway 1 at the north end of town. It is a good launch with good but limited parking. Come early to get a parking spot on a weekend when salmon are running.

14. Monterey:

Salmon	9
Lingcod	8

Bill Nebo shows a large red rockfish landed at Point Sur out of Monterey.

Seafood markets are found on the Monterey Wharf.

Rockfish 8
Albacore 7

About Monterey: Monterey, located in a protected cusp at the southern end of Monterey Bay, has very good salmon fishing from March through June or July. Rockfish and lingcod are caught all year but local charter boat operators have agreed not to target lingcod until October. Albacore make their annual circuit staying in the warm water offshore. Monterey is a good port to fish for albacore as the fish come close in here and charter boat skippers go after these fish when they are within range. Albacore fishing can be very good but only two or three out of ten years has good action for these fish.

All the Monterey charter boats operate out of Fisherman's Wharf—a tourist attraction if there ever was one. Most visitors to the wharf come to see the waterfront area, eat a fresh fish lunch or dinner, buy caramel corn or saltwater taffy, tee shirts or a variety of souvenirs, feed the sea lions and maybe take a whale watching trip.

The most famous attraction in Monterey is the aquarium. It is so well done it is a "must see" for anglers after a day of fishing or take an extra day to explore it. The Monterey Bay National Marine Sanctuary from Marin County north of San Francisco to Cambria protects the ocean along about 200 miles of shoreline.

Monterey is steeped in history. On July 7, 1846 Captain John Sloat won California for the United States without firing a shot. He simply sailed into the harbor and hoisted the American flag with acquiescence if not enthusiastic support of the mostly Spanish residents. Colton Hall where the constitution for California was ratified and many other official buildings and homes are restored to that era and are open for tours.

Salmon: The Monterey area salmon season opens in mid-March, a couple weeks ahead of the San Francisco opening. The early season out of this port is great with frequent limits of salmon. The Monterey Bay catch is often the best along the coast through April and fishing may remain good into July.

Sea lions may take half your hooked fish so use heavy tackle and a fairly tight drag to try to land your salmon before a sea lion homes in on it.

Rockfish and Lingcod: Rockfish and lingcod are caught all year. In the fall, seas are usually calm; lingcod begin to move into shallow water to spawn and fishing for these large bottom dwellers is very productive. Trips to Point Sur 20 miles south produce some of the best catches including large lingcod.

Albacore: Albacore are the fastest, strongest, most exciting game fish off Northern California. They are warm water fish often following the off shore warm currents too far away for day boats to reach. But when these currents move close to shore under El Nino conditions, albacore fishing can be great. On a good year they rank a 10 out of Monterey but only two or three out of ten years are good for them so they get a lower overall rating. These fish usually appear in July and reach a peak in August or September. In a very good year fishing may start in June and may continue into December. A catch of two albacore in a day is good but a catch of six to 10 or more is possible.

Tips from an Expert: "Act quickly when someone gets a hookup when trolling for albacore," advises Richard Turnello, skipper of the Point Sur Clipper out of Sams Sportfishing in Monterey. "Get a good lively anchovy and hook it under the bony collar behind its gills using a small live bait hook. Don't use a weight but let the bait swim naturally. If the bait will dive down, keep your reel in free spool and slowly feed out line to let it dive but keep the line tight enough to feel the beat of its tail before feeding out more line. If the bait isn't swimming down, get a new bait.

"When you get a take, count slowly to three, put the reel in gear and lift your rod. Preset the drag on your reel before you start fishing. It is too late to set your drag when you try to hook a fish. If your drag is too tight, you break your line before you can react and if it is too loose you will miss the fish or end up with a backlash on your reel—probably both. Then be patient fighting your fish. They are so strong and have such good

Rockfish like this are only one of many attractions
in the Monterey Bay Aquarium.

endurance you think you will never land the fish but it will tire eventually and you can land it."

"Carry extra hooks and rubber core twist on weights in a 35 mm film canister in your pocket. After every fish, cut off your hook and about three feet of line then tie on a new hook. The end of the line gets frayed from abrading against the fish and you risk loosing your next fish. If you need to get deeper to the fish, quickly twist on a small sinker about two feet above the hook and feed out line slowly."

Facilities and Contact: Four charter boat operators work out of Monterey and each has three to five boats. Chris's, (408-375-5951) Monterey Sportfishing (408-372-2203), Randys (408-372-7440) and Sams (408-372-0577) all fish for salmon, rockfish, lingcod and albacore. Make early reservations during salmon season. Weekend trips may be booked weeks in advance but you can usually find a boat with space on a weekday at the last minute.

Monterey has a variety of motels for every budget, camping, shops, many historic attractions and the aquarium. This city is a favorite weekend getaway for Bay Area people so be prepared for crowds during the summer and on weekends all year. For information on the aquarium, call 408-648-4888. For general information, call the Conference and Visitor Bureau at 408-649-1770.

Cost: Typical charter boat fee $50.00
Rod and Reel Rental $6.00
Boat launch $8.00

Directions: The scenic route to Monterey is through Santa Cruz on Highway 17 then south on Highway 1. The quick route is Highway 101 south of San Jose to Prunedale. Then take Highway 56 west to Highway 1 and go south on Highway 1 to Monterey.

The Monterey Fisherman's Wharf where the charter boats are located is off downtown Monterey. Go south on Highway 1 and turn right on Del Monte Avenue (there is a Del Monte Avenue north of Monterey so bypass that one and wait until you are in Monterey). Turn right on Washington into the parking lot. Go to the long term parking part of the parking lot and bring lots of quarters to feed the meters. Covered garage parking is available at the corner of Del Monte Avenue and Tyler Street. Both launching ramps are in this area.

CHAPTER 10:

Pier Pressure Game Fish

Fishing from piers can be an art. Serious anglers study tides, the fishes' schedule and develop a set of techniques. They fish when the tide is flowing and conditions are right for good fishing. They have their favorite spot on a pier and know exactly where they will cast, what bait they will use and how long they will fish.

Other anglers have a different motivation for fishing from piers. For them it is the fresh air and the sunshine, the companionship of talking with Joe or Shirley at the pier and catching fish is secondary. They time their trips by the warmth and sunshine, not the tides and the fishes' schedule.

The common catches from piers are small fish—surfperch, jacksmelt, kingfish (croaker), sardines but really quality catches are made from many piers. Notable is the Pacific Pier jetting out into the ocean from the city of Pacifica. During a typical year more than 1000 salmon and a few hundred striped bass will be taken and thousands of other smaller fish will be landed from this 1100 foot long pier. Some piers in the bays yield an occasional salmon, striped bass and rarely a sturgeon.

Fishing License is Not Required

All adult anglers must have fishing licenses except for the two days designated free fishing days and when fishing from public saltwater piers any day of the year. That's right, anglers can fish every day without a license from public saltwater piers. Phil Nelms, of the DFG responded to my request for clarification of where saltwater ended said the ocean and any slough or estuary in the San Francisco and San Pablo Bays and Carquinez Strait to the Benicia-Martinez Bridge are considered saltwater so public piers in these areas are exempt from license requirements. However, anglers are responsible to know the rules and all rules are enforced.

Piers above the Benicia-Martinez Bridge are considered freshwater piers and licenses are required. Piers at Pittsburg, Antioch and throughout the Delta fall into the freshwater category, and all adult anglers must have licenses. Many lakes and some rivers have piers where anglers can fish but they will be covered in the sections on those waters.

An angler I met on a charter boat fishing for salmon told me about

A bait fished under a float is the way to catch salmon and striped bass from Piers.

the last time he fished for salmon. He took a day off work, spent about $60 and fished hard all day. A few anglers caught a salmon but he didn't catch one. When he got home, two fresh salmon were waiting for him in an ice chest. His son had gone out on the Pacifica Pier, spent a couple bucks for bait and caught his limit of salmon.

The piers listed are primarily fishing piers or fishing has become an important part of their use. Other piers may also permit fishing or sometimes at least tolerate kid's fishing. When several piers are close together, a typical pier has been included and fishing at close-by piers is similar. The major game fish and surfperch are rated but many anglers rarely catch one of these. They catch smaller fish like jacksmelt, anchovies, kingfish, flounder and sanddabs and go away happy.

Fishing

A variety of small fish is a typical catch from a pier but anglers also catch salmon, striped bass, and halibut including some large fish. Surfperch, a small scrappy and delicious food fish, is one of the most plentiful and favorite fish. Anglers catch sturgeon up to 190 pounds, shark including the good eating leopard shark, skates, rays, lingcod, a dozen or more species of rockfish, flounder, jacksmelt, kingfish (croaker), mackerel, sardines, anchovies and the list goes on and on.

Some critters are not so desirable. Crabs steal bait and you almost never hook one. Sometimes one will hold onto your bait and you can retrieve it all the way up to the pier so you know what is pilfering your bait. For a while, crabs keep your interest up but soon you tire of them and may move to a different area on the pier to avoid them. A skate or ray may go for your bait at any time and while not a primary food fish, they sure are strong fighters and are exciting at least until you see that it is not the game fish you were hoping for.

Special landing methods are required from a pier. Imagine you have a tired 10 pound salmon at the surface 20 feet below you at the end of a pier. You can't walk the fish to a beach—it may be several hundred yards away and several dozen anglers' lines block your path. The procedure is to drop a flat circular crab net down, play the fish to the net and lift the net with the salmon on it. It sounds precarious but it works. Oh yes, when fishing from a pier with dozens of other lines to tangle in and pilings for the fish to circle, the lost fish rate is high but many are also landed. If you hook a large fish you have a good fish story even if you lose it and chances are reasonably good, with help from nearby anglers, you will land the fish.

The favorite baits are pileworms, bits of anchovie, sand crabs dug from the beach and grass shrimp for most of the smaller fish. Live grass shrimp, mud shrimp and ghost shrimp are excellent for sturgeon and lures sometimes catch salmon; plastic grubs may entice surfperch. Live bait fish, particularly shiner surfperch, are great bait for striped bass, salmon and halibut; mudsuckers attract stripers and sturgeon and staghorn sculpin (called bullheads) catch striped bass. Cut anchovies, mackerel, sardines or herring, strips of squid and any bait you can think of will probably work at one time or another. Berkeley Power Bait which has become the standard for trout in freshwater is now being formulated for saltwater fish and may replace at least part of these natural baits. Culprit Lures makes a

A lady and her daughters come to the pier to fish.

variety of plastic baits with fish attractants for saltwater and they will catch fish.

The rod can be a spinning outfit that you might choose for trout with six to 10 pound line. That is good for surfperch and small fish though you always run the risk of hooking a large fish that will quickly spool you and be gone. Or it can be a surf spinning rod with a 10 to 12 foot long rod using 15 to 30 pound test line or heavier. Spinning reels are the norm because they cast more easily and farther, often important when fishing from a pier, but some anglers prefer conventional revolving spool reels for their superior drags and more rugged character. A good all around rod for pier fishing is a seven to eight foot long rod with a medium to heavy weight spinning reel filled with 15 to 20 pound test line.

Light tackle is the fun way to catch these fish but don't go too light. You always have a chance of hooking a large fish and you can kiss it good-bye with light tackle. You have a real chance of hooking a salmon or striped bass from some piers notably the Pacifica Pier and there you need to gear up with heavier tackle. I favor the light, fun tackle unless the pier I am fishing has a reputation for large fish.

Each pier has its own character and an important part of learning to fish from a pier is watching and remembering. See how the most successful anglers are fishing, what bait they are using, where they are fishing. There may be one deep hole or a tide flow that brings food and fish to a certain area. The regulars know just where that is. Cast to that spot and you catch lots of fish; miss the spot even a few feet and fishing isn't nearly as productive. Learn the tricks of the regulars and you will soon match their fishing success.

Ratings

Fishing for each major species from each pier is rated. This is rated against all kinds of fishing including someone fishing from a boat. The angler in the boat can move around, meter fish, anchor above them and fish anyplace. They can also move as the tide changes and have a definite advantage over someone confined to one general spot not always in the best fishing location. Consequently pier fishing doesn't rate as high as fishing from a boat. A seven is an excellent rating and a five or higher is a good rating for pier fishing.

Regulations

While you don't need a fishing license to fish from a public pier, you do need one if the pier is private. You are also responsible to know and obey all of the state fishing regulations. Striped bass must be a minimum of 18 inches in length and the limit is two. California Halibut must be at least 22 inches long and the limit is three. Sturgeon must be between 46 and 72 inches and the limit is one. Salmon must be at least 24 inches long and the limit is two (except anglers must keep the first two salmon they catch from July 1 to early September between Point Reyes and Pigeon Point).

Lingcod must be at least 24 inches long and the limit is two. Leopard shark must be 36 inches long and the limit is three. When fishing from a boat in the San Francisco and San Pablo Bay, you are restricted to one rod but when fishing from public piers you may fish with two rods.

You can't gaff sturgeon. You should have a large landing net so you can land all species gently and release them unharmed if they do not meet the size restriction.

These are just the highlights of the fishing regulations that are in effect in 1998 and 99. They change frequently and other regulations may apply to other fish so get a free copy of the Fishing Regulations available wherever fishing licenses are sold and be familiar with its provisions.

1. Bodega Bay Wharves:
Surfperch 4
Other Fish 4

About Bodega Bay Wharves: Bodega Bay is a great place to fish but the real fishing is for salmon from your own boat and salmon, rockfish and lingcod from a charter fishing boat. A public fishing pier at Doran Park and two private wharves, Lucas Wharf and the Tides, permit fishing. The catch is primarily surfperch and kingfish or other small fish.

Fishing: Use pile worms or sand crabs to catch surfperch. Jacksmelt, kingfish and occasionally a skate, ray or shark may also be caught.

Facilities and Contact: Camping is north of town at Bodega Dunes State Beach (make reservations through the State Park system) or in Sonoma County Doran Park or Westside Campground (these are first-come-first-served). Several motels are located in Bodega Bay. Contact the Tides at 707-875-2777 for fishing information and Sonoma Coast State Beach at 707-875-3483 for camping information.

Cost: Camping fees $12 to $16 at the state beaches and the county parks.

Directions to Bodega Bay Wharves: Take Highway 1 north into Bodega Bay and look for the left turn to Doran Park at the south end of town. Lucas Wharf is a little farther on the left side of the road and the Tides is on the left soon after Lucas Wharf.

Regulations: You can fish from public piers like Doran Beach Pier without a fishing license. If you are 16 year old or older, you must have a fishing license to fish from the Tides and Lucas Wharf because they are private piers. Since they are private, they can change their fishing policies so ask before you fish from their piers.

2. Miller Park Pier:
Surfperch 2
Other Fish 2

About Miller Park Pier: This pier on Tomales Bay about 45 miles north of San Francisco is next to a commercial oyster farm. The pier ends in shallow water and isn't in a great fishing location (hence the poor rating). "You can fish from the beach north and south of the pier and be more successful but you need a fishing license where fishing from the pier is free," says Ed Hulme, Chief Park Ranger for Marin County. You don't have to catch fish here to have a delicious seafood dinner. Visit the oyster farm and buy some of these bivalves for oysters on the half shell, fried oysters or stew.

This is a pleasant rural area surrounded by green pastures and maybe some cows or sheep, away from tall buildings and traffic. Perhaps it would be too much to expect good fishing as well.

Fishing: The premium catch here is an occasional halibut but remember it must be at least 22 inches long to be legal. Use pile worms or sand crabs to catch surfperch and try squid strips or cut anchovies for jacksmelt, kingfish and maybe a skate, ray or shark.

Facilities and Contact: This pier has fish cleaning stations with running water, restrooms and a snack bar nearby. It is operated by the Marin County Department of Parks. Call the office at 415-499-6387 or the park ranger station at 415-499-6405 for information.

Cost: Entry and Parking $5.00 per vehicle
Boat launching is included in the entry fee.

Directions to Miller Park Pier: Follow Highway 1 three miles north of Marshall and turn left into the Miller Park entrance.

3. Vallejo Pier:

Sturgeon	7
Striped Bass	5
Other Fish	3

About Vallejo Pier: The Vallejo Pier had always been thought of as a hot spot for sturgeon fishing. Part of its reputation comes from the fact that the largest sturgeon ever landed from a pier, a 190-pound giant, was caught off it. The Vallejo Pier, under the old Highway 37 bridge, where this fish was caught, was declared unsafe and torn down. Now fishing is from the public wharves by the Ferry Terminal.

Fishing: Anglers fishing from this wharf have a realistic chance to catch a sturgeon. Most may be less than legal size but once in a while a real behemoth is landed. An outgoing tide in the winter when the water is muddy from a storm is the best time—live grass, mud or ghost shrimp are the favored baits. A striped bass may be landed while fishing with the same bait as well as with sculpin or cut threadfin shad. Jacksmelt, rays, skates and flounder may be landed but it is the large sturgeon and striped bass that get anglers' adrenaline flowing.

Facilities and Contact: The Vallejo wharf is operated by the city of Vallejo Recreation Department. It has restrooms and a bait shop nearby. Several bait shops including Norm's bait and tackle near the launching ramp south of the wharf have bait and tackle.

Cost: Entry and parking   Entry and parking is free.

Directions to Vallejo Pier: Take Highway 37 west from Interstate 80 in Vallejo. Turn off at Wilson Avenue just before you start up the incline of the bridge. Go south until this street joins the Avenue of the Flags. Continue south to the Ferry Terminal for free parking and fishing access. From the south take Interstate 80 to the Sonoma Avenue exit (Highway 29). Go west and turn north (right) on the Avenue of the Flags to the wharf.

4. Point Pinole Pier:

Sturgeon	5
Striped Bass	5
Salmon	3
Surfperch	3
Other Fish	6

About Point Pinole Pier: Point Pinole on the east shore of the San Pablo Bay north of Richmond is an old explosives manufacturing plant—Atlas Powder Company made dynamite and gunpowder here until the 1950's. It is now one of the EBRPD parks. It has a variety of wildlife and a 1250 foot long fishing pier.

Fishing: This pier is well situated extending into the deep water of San Pablo Bay. Thousands of large sturgeon go through this area every year and anglers have a realistic chance to catch one. Use live grass shrimp, mud shrimp or ghost shrimp for serious sturgeon fishing. Striped bass are caught from this pier all year but fall and early winter is the best time to catch them. The shrimp baits used for sturgeon, or small bait fish like live shiner perch or sculpin often called a bullhead are excellent baits.

Anglers may also catch salmon here as they migrate up the Sacramento River in August through October.

While anglers may come here dreaming of a big sturgeon and some are caught, other fish are usually the ones that end up in their bags. Surfperch are caught in the winter using pileworms or live grass shrimp. Shark, rays, kingfish, and flounder are common all year.

Facilities and Contact: This is part of Point Pinole Regional Shoreline, an East Bay Regional Park. It has restrooms, hiking trails and parking. The fishing pier is a mile and one-half from the parking area but a shuttle bus takes you to the pier for a nominal fee. Contact EBRPD at 510-531-9300 for information.

Cost: Entry and parking $5.00 per vehicle.
Bus to fishing pier $1.50 per person

Directions to Point Pinole Pier: From the south take Interstate 80 north through Richmond and turn west on Hilltop Avenue. Turn right on San Pablo Avenue then left on Atlas Road and follow the signs to the park.

5. China Camp Pier:

Sturgeon	5
Striped Bass	3
Surfperch	2
Other fish	4

About China Camp Pier: China Camp is where Chinese immigrants fish for grass shrimp and other seafood. This is an area where grass shrimp have been plentiful and a fishing village sprang up here at the turn of the century to catch them. The village has been partially restored and a state park and camping are part of the complex. It has a wooden pier and a lot of history—fishing is tolerated but not emphasized.

Fishing: The grass shrimp in the area draw sturgeon and occasionally one is landed from this pier. A few striped bass are also caught. Anglers catch surfperch in the winter and into the spring. Kingfish, jacksmelt, flounder and sculpin may be caught. Pileworms or shrimp are good, all-purpose baits.

Facilities and Contact: This is a part of the China Camp State Park. It has 30 walk-in campsites, a historic village and a fishing pier but fishing facilities are minimal. Call the park at 415-456-0766 for information.

Cost: Entry and parking $5 per vehicle
Camping $15 per night

Camps here are at walk-in campsites. You must carry all your gear 50 to 300 yards from the parking lot.

Directions to China Camp Pier: Go north on Highway 101 through San Rafael and take North San Pedro Road east five miles to this park. The pier is in the park.

6. McNear Beach Pier:

Sturgeon	6
Striped Bass	5
Surfperch	2
Other fish	4

About McNear Beach Pier: The McNear Beach Pier a half mile south of China Camp is a 500 foot long first-class fishing pier with fish cleaning stations and good fishing. The pier is in a multi-purpose park operated by the Marin County Parks Department. The park has tennis courts, a fresh-water swimming pool, a lot of sandy beaches on the bay, a snack bar and group picnic areas.

This park and pier are open Wednesday through Sunday from 8:00

The China Camp Pier north of San Rafael is an old wooden fishing pier.

AM to 8:00 PM in the summer and 8:00 AM to 5:00 PM in the winter.
Fishing: Anglers have some expectation of catching sturgeon from this pier in the winter. The best time to catch these fish according to sturgeon guru, Keith Fraser, is during the bottom half of a moderate outgoing tide. Fraser usually fishes from a boat but the same recommendation applies to pier fishing.

Striped bass take over as the premium fish in the summer and fall. Anglers catch surfperch here in the winter and into the spring. Kingfish, jacksmelt, flounder, and sculpin are caught all year. Pile worms or live grass shrimp, mud shrimp or ghost shrimp are the best baits.
Facilities and Contact: This 500 foot long pier is a first class fishing pier with fish cleaning stations with running water on the pier, restrooms and a snack bar nearby. It is operated by the Marin County Department of Parks. Call 415-499-6387 for information.
Cost: Entry and Parking $7.00 per vehicle weekends
                                  $5.00 weekdays
Directions to McNear Beach Pier: Go north on Highway 101 to the central San Rafael exit. Go east on 2nd street to 3rd street and continue on Point San Pedro Road. Continue about four miles and turn right onto Cantera Way into McNear's Beach County Park.

7. Point Benicia Pier:

Striped Bass	6
Sturgeon	5
Salmon	2
Other fish	4

About Point Benicia Pier: Benica, on the north shore of the Carquinez Strait has three public piers but the primary fishing pier is the Point Benicia Pier on the channel a short distance from where the largest sturgeon ever recorded was caught. You would think this would be a great sturgeon fishing area but it is out of the main route of sturgeon and striped bass are the primary premium fish caught here.
Fishing: Sturgeon are caught infrequently. Striped bass are caught more regularly. Anglers have a chance to catch salmon and even steelhead here as they migrate up the Sacramento River but most salmon and steelhead migrate through here quickly and few are caught. Flounder and a variety of small fish are landed.
Facilities and Contact: This pier is operated by the city of Benicia. For information call the Benicia Marina at 707-745-2628.
Cost: Entry and Parking are free.
Directions to Point Benicia Pier: Take the East 2nd Street exit off Interstate 780 and go south. Turn right on Military Highway then left on 1st Street to the pier.

8. Martinez Pier:

Striped Bass	6
Sturgeon	5
Salmon	4
Other Fish	4

About Martinez Pier: This pier is off the marina area of the city of Martinez north of the train depot and the main part of town. The marina has a well stocked bait shop, a party boat in the winter and a launching ramp.
Fishing: The Martinez Pier is good for striped bass and sturgeon during the winter months. In the fall anglers have some chance to catch salmon here as they migrate up the Sacramento River. The best salmon runs are in August and September. Anglers may catch flounder, sculpin and a variety of small fish all year.
Facilities and Contact: This pier is part of the Martinez Regional Shoreline Park operated by the city of Martinez. A bait shop with good fresh bait is located at the marina and restrooms are found close to the pier. For information, call the Martinez Marina Bait shop at 510-229-9420.
Cost: Parking is free at this pier.

McNear Pier on the San Pablo Bay east of San Rafael is a modern pier with fish cleaning and nearby restrooms.

Directions to Martinez Pier: Take the Marina Vista exit off Interstate 680 (just south of the Benicia Bridge). Go west to downtown Martinez and turn right on Ferry Street. Turn right on Joe DiMaggio Drive then left on North Court Street.

9. Pittsburg Pier:

Striped Bass	6
Sturgeon	5
Salmon	3
Other fish	4

About Pittsburg Pier: Pittsburg has a fully developed municipal marina with a fishing pier at the south end of the marina.
Fishing: Anglers catch a few salmon here as they migrate up the Sacramento River—the best salmon catches are in September and October. Striped bass and occasionally sturgeon are caught from this pier primarily in late fall and winter. Small fish like flounder and pesky bullheads are caught all year. Freshwater fish particularly catfish begin to show up in the catch
Facilities and Contact: This pier in Riverview Park is a new pier with fish cleaning facilities, restrooms and a baitshop nearby. Contact King's Bait & Tackle at 925-432-8466 for information.
License: A valid fishing license is required to fish from this pier. Only ocean and bay piers are exempt from license requirements.
Cost: Fishing and parking are free.
Directions to Pittsburg Pier: Take Highway 4 east to Pittsburg and exit at the Railroad Avenue off ramp. Go north on Railroad Avenue and turn left on East 3d Street. Make another left on Marina Boulevard. Follow this street as it turns right and becomes Bay Side Drive. The pier is in Riverview Park.

10. Antioch Fishing Pier:

Striped Bass	5
Sturgeon	3
Salmon	3
Other Fish	4

About Antioch Pier: Antioch has three fishing piers, one at the marina, a fishing pier and one at the base of the Antioch Bridge (this is the next pier discussed). This section will specifically discuss the fishing pier which has better facilities but fishing from the marina pier is similar.
Fishing: Striped bass are caught from this pier late fall and early winter and are its number one catch. Anglers have a realistic chance to catch salmon here as they migrate up the Sacramento River in September through November.

A real prize here is a keeper sturgeon. A few sturgeon are caught but most are short of legal size. Freshwater fish including black bass, catfish and crappie are caught.

Facilities and Contact: Restrooms are near the pier. For bait and information call King's Bait & Tackle in Pittsburg at 925-432-8466.

License: A valid fishing license is required to fish from these piers. Only ocean and bay piers below the Martinez Bridge are exempt from license requirements.

Cost: Fishing and parking are free.

Directions to Antioch Pier: Take Highway 4 east from Interstate 680 south of Martinez and take the Minta/G Street exit in Antioch. Take G Street north to its end and turn left one block to H Street then right to the pier at the end of this street.

11. Antioch Bridge Pier:

Striped Bass	5
Sturgeon	3
Salmon	2
Other Fish	4

About Antioch Bridge Pier: When the new high-rise Antioch Bridge was built over the San Joaquin River, the south end of the old bridge was converted to a 500 foot long pier. This pier on the east side of the new bridge is managed by the EBRPD.

Fishing: Striped bass are caught from this pier late fall and early winter and are its number one catch. The majority of the bass are below the 18 inch minimum length but a few are legal size. Anglers have some chance to catch salmon here as they migrate up the Sacramento River in late summer but the Antioch Marina Pier seems to produce better. Keeper size sturgeon, though rarely caught, are real prizes. Smaller fish including flounder, black bass and catfish are also caught.

Facilities and Contact: The Antioch Regional Shoreline Park including this pier is part of the EBRPD; restrooms are near the pier. For information call EBRPD at 510-531-9300.

License: A valid fishing license is required to fish from this pier. Only ocean and bay piers below the Martinez Bridge are exempt from license requirements.

Cost: Entry and Parking $5.00 per car

Directions to Antioch Bridge Pier: Take Highway 4 east from Concord through Antioch to Wilbur Avenue, the last exit before the Antioch Bridge. Turn right on Wilbur then left on Bridgehead Road and continue to the park and the pier.

12. Berkeley Pier:

Striped Bass	6
Surfperch	7
Halibut	6
Other Fish	5

About Berkeley Pier: This 3000 foot long pier at the Berkeley Marina was originally a Ferry Pier before the Bay Bridge was built. Railroad tracks running the length of the pier carried cargo and passengers to the ferry. Long since abandoned to that use, its main function now is fishing. The outer part of it is broken up and barricaded but the shoreward section is reinforced and makes a great fishing structure. It is well maintained and has consistently good fishing.

Fishing: A variety of fish are landed including halibut, striped bass, shark, surfperch and a number of small fish.

Facilities and Contact: This is just beyond the Berkeley Marina Bait Shop (510-644-6376)—a good place for bait and information.

Cost: Entry and parking is free.

Directions to Berkeley Pier: The Berkeley Fishing Pier is at the end of University Avenue. Take Highway 80 to University Avenue and go west to the end of this street. The off ramp from the south does not permit a left turn so you must go east then turn around to get to the pier.

13. Emeryville Pier:

Striped Bass	4
Halibut	2
Surfperch	3
Other Fish	4

About Emeryville Pier: Emeryville has two piers, one at the marina at the end of Powell and the other, Carlos Murphy's Pier, is off the freeway frontage road about a half mile north of Powell Street. The Marina Pier is a better fishing pier and is the one described but this description generally applies to both piers.

Fishing: Striped bass and halibut are the number one and two quality fish caught from this pier. Halibut are caught from April through July and most of the striped bass are landed from June through October.

Surfperch are a prized catch, at least in the winter months when anglers may catch a bucketful of fish from these piers. They are scrappy fish on light tackle and a delicious food fish. Anglers may also catch kingfish, rays, skates, other small fish and an occasional shark.

Facilities and Contact: For information, contact the Emeryville Sportfishing Center at 510-654-6040.

Cost: Entry and Parking is free.

Directions to Emeryville Pier: Take the Powell Street exit off Interstate 80 and follow it past the sport fishing center to the end to the pier at the marina. For the Carlos Murphy Pier, take the Powell exit then turn north on the frontage road west of Interstate 80. This pier is about one-half mile north of Powell.

14. Paradise Beach Pier:

Sturgeon	5
Surfperch	4
Striped Bass	3
Other Fish	5

About Paradise Beach Pier: This pier in Paradise Beach County Park on the east side of the Tiburon Peninsula is more noted as a pleasant, picturesque park protected from the winds than for fishing. It has loyal anglers that occasionally catch a sturgeon or striped bass but a few kingfish, surfperch or an occasional flounder is the more usual catch.

Fishing: This pier sees its peak during the herring spawn when sturgeon come to the area to dine on this delicacy (at least a delicacy to a sturgeon). The last half of March is the best fishing time—it is illegal to catch sturgeon from this pier during the peak of the herring spawn from January 1 until March 15. Herring roe or even fillets or chunks of herring are good bait. Striped bass are also caught during the winter and an occasional halibut is landed.

Ken Jones reports in his book, *Pier Fishing in California*, that this is a good place for striped bass anglers to come to catch bullheads (staghorn sculpin) which are a favorite bait for striped bass. You can use them here to fish for stripers but a better plan is to take them to San Pablo Bay or the Delta in the late fall and winter months to fish for striped bass.

Facilities and Contact: This pier managed by the Marin County Parks Department has a fish cleaning station and restrooms are nearby. Call 415-499-6387 for information.

Cost: Entry and Parking $7.00 per vehicle weekends
                                $5.00 weekdays

Directions to Paradise Beach Pier: Take Highway 101 to the Tiburon exit (Highway 131). Turn east on Tiburon and continue on Trestle Glen Boulevard. When this boulevard ends, turn right onto Paradise Drive and continue to Paradise Beach County Park. It is on your left.

15. Elephant Rock Pier:

Sturgeon	5
Surfperch	6
Striped Bass	4
Other Fish	5

About Elephant Rock Pier: This pier on the west side of the Tiburon at the east end of Shoreline Park is strictly for children—to fish here you must be younger than 16 years old. It is a short pier with its end built around a large rock, Elephant Rock, protruding into the center of the pier. It has minimal facilities but is in a good fishing location on the north shore of Raccoon Strait.

Fishing: This pier sees its peak during the herring spawn when sturgeon come to the area to dine on this delicacy. It is illegal to catch sturgeon here from January 1 to March 15 so the best fishing is after March 15. Herring roe or even fillets or chunks of herring are good bait. Striped bass are caught during the summer and kingfish and a variety of surfperch, rockfish, rays and shark are caught most of the year.

Facilities and Contact: This pier has minimal facilities but is in a good fishing location on the north shore of Racoon Strait. Parking is very limited—it is really for local children to walk to the pier and fish.

Cost: Entry and Parking No fee

Directions to Elephant Rock Pier: Take Highway 101 to the Tiburon exit (Highway 131). Turn east on Tiburon Boulevard and follow this boulevard to the right at the junction with Trestle Glenn Boulevard. Look for Shoreline Park on the right. This pier is at the east end of this park.

16. Fort Baker Pier:

Surfperch	7
Salmon	5
Striped Bass	4
Sturgeon	5
Other Fish	5

About Fort Baker Pier: Fort Point on the south side of the Golden Gate channel and Fort Baker on the north side protected San Francisco Bay from invading armadas. That need ended many years ago; their armaments are all gone and they are both part of the Golden Gate Recreation Area and are tourist attractions.

This pier at Fort Baker at the northern end of the Golden Gate Bridge is ideally located to intercept fish and is one of the better fishing piers in the Bay Area. Even if you don't catch fish, the view is worth the trip as you look out on San Francisco and the Golden Gate Bridge in their full glory.

Fishing: The Fort Baker Pier ranks very high for fishing for surfperch, salmon and striped bass. It is also very good for sturgeon when the season for these fish reopens March 15—fish here when the pier reopens and your odds of catching a sturgeon from a pier is about as good as it gets.

Facilities and Contact: This is part of the Golden Gate Recreation Area. Contact Fort Baker at 415-331-1540 for information.

Cost: Entry and Parking $5.00 per vehicle.

Directions to Fort Baker Pier: From the south, cross the Golden Gate Bridge and take Alexander (the 1st exit after the bridge). Turn south on Fort Baker Road down to this fort. The pier is northeast of the north tower of the Golden Gate Bridge. From the north on Highway 101, take Alexander (the 2nd Sausalito exit) and follow the brown signs to the recreation area.

17. Fort Point Pier:

Surfperch	7
Striped Bass	5
Salmon	3
Other Fish	6

About Fort Point Pier: Fort Point is the fortress that protected the San Francisco Bay located below the south side of the Golden Gate Bridge. Fort Point is the best fishing pier off the San Francisco Bay. Other piers jutting out from the San Francisco shoreline east of the Golden Gate Bridge, all part of the Golden Gate Recreation Area, have fishing.

One of the best striped bass fishing holes in the bay is at the south side of the south tower of the Golden Gate Bridge and in the channel between the bridge and shore. This area is full of rocks but there are striped bass there to catch when the tide is moving. An outgoing tide is best.

Hundreds of thousands of salmon migrate through this channel each year. Only a small fraction are close enough to shore for pier anglers to reach and your odds aren't high but you can dream and sometimes dreams come true.

Fishing: While this is one of the best fishing piers in the area, your odds of catching the premium fish of sturgeon, striped bass, salmon, lingcod and halibut from a pier is never high but you may be the one to catch the occasional fish. Primarily the catch is surfperch, sanddabs, jacksmelt, kingfish and maybe rockfish.

During the winter season, surfperch catches, particularly barred surfperch, can be very good. Bits of pileworm or grass shrimp are excellent bait for these fish. A moderate incoming tide (3 to 5-feet) is the best time to catch them.

Sanddabs can be caught by the dozen in winter and early spring. Rays, shark, kingfish, jacksmelt, rockfish and an occasional lingcod are landed.

Facilities and Contact: Hi's Tackle Box at 3141 Clement Street in San Franciso have very knowledgeable employees who can help you find good fishing of all kinds including the San Francisco area piers. Visit or call them at 415-221-3825 for information.

Cost: Entry and Parking Metered parking.

Directions to Fort Point Pier: Travel north on Highway 101 through San Francisco and exit at the Fort Point Presidio exit. Go north on Lincoln Boulevard. Turn left on Long Avenue which turns into Marine Drive. The pier is at the end of Marine Drive.

18. Municipal Pier:

Surfperch	5
Striped Bass	4
Other Fish	4

About Municipal Pier: A series of piers and wharves are found all around San Francisco. Two piers close to the Golden Gate are Fort Mason, and the 1850 foot long curved Municipal Pier. To the east is Fisherman's Wharf and Pier 39 then south is the Ferry Building, Oakland Bay Bridge and south past San Francisco to Brisbane and neighboring cities. Some are excellent fishing piers; others aren't very good. The Municipal Pier with a great view of the Golden Gate Bridge is one of the most scenic locations in the world but it is only rated as fair as a fishing pier. If you don't catch fish, you may not even care.

Fishing: Surfperch and other small fish are the top catch here. Anglers have some chance to catch salmon here as they migrate toward the Sacramento River in August or September. Striped bass are caught from this pier all summer and halibut are landed in the spring and summer; there aren't many of these premium fish but they are usually legal size and can be large.

Facilities and Contact: This pier has restrooms close-by. Restaurants and other services aren't far. The National Park Service administers both Fort Mason and the Municipal Pier.

Cost: Some parking is free and some is metered but both are very limited. Arrive early to find a spot.

Directions to Municipal Pier: This pier is at the north end of Van Ness Street and is a couple blocks west of Fisherman's Wharf. Take Van Ness north to the bay and look for parking.

19. Pier 7:

Halibut	3
Striped Bass	2
Surfperch	6
Other Fish	4

About Pier 7: This pier located in San Francisco north of the Ferry Building and north of the Oakland Bay Bridge is one of the longer fishing piers in San Francisco. Fishing is considered good for the area. A steady stream of boats and ferries, the Oakland Bay Bridge, the pyramid-shaped Transamerican Building, Coit Tower and the downtown area puts this pier in the center of a scenic area. You won't be bored but you may spend more time watching boats than catching fish.

Fishing: Surfperch are the top catch from this pier. Striped bass and halibut may be caught but it takes some luck.

Facilities and Contact: This pier rebuilt in 1991 has running water, a fish cleaning station and benches.

Cost: Entry and Parking Metered parking—parking is very limited.

Directions to Pier 7: This pier is two blocks north of the Ferry Building off Embarcadero Street, the street that runs along the San Francisco Wharves. You can drive north on Embaradero or ride BART to the Embarcadero station in San Francisco and walk to the pier.

20. Agua Vista Park Pier:

Surfperch	6
Striped Bass	3
Sturgeon	2
Other Fish	5

About Agua Vista Park Pier: This pier and the one a little north at Mission Rock are in the working wharf area of San Francisco. Other piers from the Oakland Bay Bridge to the southern border of the city have similar fishing.

Fishing: The primary catch here is surfperch or small rockfish. Live grass shrimp or bits of pile worm are good bait for small fish. If you want to try for striped bass, a shiner surfperch fished beneath a bobber is a good way to attract one. Sturgeon are a long shot—you have much better odds of catching shark or rays.

Facilities and Contact: This pier is a part of Agua Vista Park.

Cost: Entry and Parking Free parking is available.

Directions to Agua Vista Park Pier: Go north on Interstate 280 toward San Francisco and exit onto Mariposa Street. Go east to the end of the street and turn left onto China Basin Street. The park is on the right.

21. Candlestick Point Pier:

Surfperch	7
Striped Bass	4
Sturgeon	2
Other Fish	5

About Candlestick Point Pier: This is actually two piers operated by the California Department of Parks and Recreation as a State Recreation Area. They are at Candlestick Point beyond Candlestick Park where the 49ers play and the Giants baseball team plays until their new downtown stadium is finished. (The official name is 3Com park but everyone knows it is really Candlestick Park.) The first pier is off the street but the second and better one is a half mile from the parking lot—why do you always have to pay a price to get to the best fishing?

Fishing: This pier is an excellent place to catch surfperch when they are around in the winter and spring. This is one pier where anglers have a decent chance to catch striped bass in the summer and some chance to catch a large sturgeon in the winter and spring. Shark, jacksmelt, kingfish, flounder, rays and skates may also be landed here.

Tips From the Experts: "This is the best fishing pier in this area," says Ken Jones, fishing pier guru and author of the book *Pier Fishing in California.*

Facilities and Contact: The area has restrooms but no bait or tackle. Contact the Candlestick Point SRA at 415-671-0145 for information.

Cost: Entry and Park $5.00 per vehicle.

Directions to Candlestick Point Pier: Take Highway 101 south from San Francisco and take the 3Com park exit. Go east on Haney Way then

make a right turn on Jamestown Avenue to the Candlestick Point State Recreation Area.

22. Brisbane Fishing Pier:

Surfperch	5
Striped Bass	2
Sturgeon	2
Other Fish	4

About Brisbane Fishing Pier: The Brisbane Fishing Pier is out of the town of Brisbane on the north side of Sierra Point.

Fishing: The prime catch here is surfperch in the winter and spring. Jacksmelt and kingfish, sharks and rays are caught most of the year. Fishing can be good for surfperch and occasionally sturgeon and striped bass are landed.

Facilities and Contact: This pier managed by the city of Brisbane has a fish cleaning station but it has no restroom.

Cost: Parking is Free

Directions to Brisbane Fishing Pier: Take Highway 101 south from San Francisco to the Sierra Point Parkway. Travel east on this road to its end and turn left onto Marina Boulevard to the parking lot.

23. Oyster Point Pier:

Striped Bass	3
Surfperch	3
Sturgeon	1
Other Fish	3

About Oyster Point Pier: Oyster Point is just south of Brisbane.

Fishing: Fishing for striped bass is the top attraction here though anglers catch more shark and rays. Surfperch fishing is okay in the winter months and halibut may be landed in the spring and summer. Sturgeon are a very long shot. Kingfish and a variety of small fish are the normal catch.

Facilities and Contact: This pier has a restroom nearby and a marina where anglers can buy some tackle and snacks.

Cost: Free parking is close-by and entry is free.

Directions to Oyster Point Pier: Take Highway 101 to Oyster Point Boulevard. Go left on this road and make a right onto Marina Boulevard to the pier at the end of this street.

24. San Mateo Bridge Pier:

Sturgeon	4
Striped Bass	3
Surfperch	3
Other Fish	3

About San Mateo Bridge Pier: This pier is the west end of the old San Mateo Bridge that was replaced about 20 years ago by the current bridge.

Fishing: Sturgeon and striped bass are the most desired catch here and they are caught occasionally but shark, rays (fishing for these primitive fish is rated as good) and a variety of small fish including surfperch in the winter and spring are what most anglers catch.

Facilities and Contact: This pier is operated by San Mateo County. Contact the Coyote Point Marina in San Mateo at 415-573-2594 for information.

Cost: Entry and Parking   Free parking is found near the entrance to the pier.

Directions to San Mateo Pier: Take Highway 92 east from Highway 101 in San Mateo and take the Foster City Boulevard exit to the right. Make a left turn onto East Hillsdale Boulevard to the pier. From the east, cross the San Mateo Bridge, take the Foster City Boulevard exit, cross over the freeway and follow the above directions.

25. Ravenswood Pier:

Sturgeon   5
Surfperch   3
Other Fish   4

About Ravenswood Pier: When the Dumbarton Bridge was replaced about 15 years ago, both ends of the old bridge were wisely left in place as fishing piers. This pier is the west end of the old Dumbarton Bridge.

Fishing: The south end of the San Francisco Bay is a good place to catch sturgeon during the winter and spring months. You won't catch one very often but you have some chance for a super trophy. You can also catch a variety of surfperch, jacksmelt and small fish as well as shark and a ray.

Facilities and Contact: This pier has restrooms and a fish cleaning station.

Cost: Parking and Entry $5.00 per vehicle

Directions to Ravenswood Pier: This pier is at the west end of the Dumbarton Bridge in East Palo Alto. Take the Willow Road (Highway 84) east from Highway 101 in Palo Alto and turn right to the Ravenswood Open Space Reserve.

26. Dumbarton Pier East:

Sturgeon   5
Surfperch   3
Other Fish   4

About Dumbarton Pier East: This pier is the east end of the old Dumbarton Bridge that was replaced about 15 years ago by the current bridge.

Fishing: Just as its mirror image pier on the west side of this bridge, fishing for sturgeon is good and it is fair for surfperch. Rays and shark are often caught. Both Dumbarton piers are similar but I would give the nod by a small margin to this East Bay pier.

Facilities and Contact: This pier has restrooms and a fish cleaning station.

Cost: Entry and Parking is free

Directions to Dumbarton Pier: This pier is at the east end of the Dumbarton Bridge in Newark. Take the Thornton Avenue exit off Highway 84 east of the toll plaza. Go south almost a mile and make a right turn onto Marshlands Road. Follow this road to the pier—don't give up; it is about three and one-half miles to the pier. .

27. Alameda Channel Piers:

Striped Bass   5
Surfperch   4
Halibut   2
Other Fish   4

About Alameda Channel Piers: A channel between the island town of Alameda and the Oakland waterfront has fishing piers scattered from end to end and the quality of fishing varies largely. The Fruitvale Bridge Fishing Piers (one on the Oakland side and one on the Alameda Island side) have consistently good catches and these are the piers I will describe. FDR Pier just north of Jack London Square at the Oakland Waterfront is another noted fishing pier but its parking is limited and expensive. If you fish this area, search out these and other piers and learn how to fish them.

The pier at the town of Pacifica jets out into the ocean and is the location for major sports fish catches including many salmon and striped bass.

Anglers crowd onto Pacifica Pier when fishing is good.

Fishing: In the San Francisco Bay outside Alameda Island is good fishing for some of the larger fish including sturgeon, halibut and striped bass. Good fishing carries over onto the piers in this channel. The Fruitvale Bridge Fishing Piers provide a reasonable chance at a striped bass and some chance for a halibut, surfperch or small fish which are usually on the bite.

Shiner perch are frequently caught from these piers and they make excellent bait for striped bass. Keep them alive in a bucket of water and fish one under a float to try for a striped bass.

Facilities: The Fruitvale Piers both have some free parking but no restrooms or bait shops.

Directions to Fruitvale Bridge Fishing Piers: Take the Fruitvale exit off Interstate 580 in Oakland and turn west (actually southwest) to the bridge to Alameda Island. Take the Alameda Avenue left off this street before the bridge to the fishing pier. For the pier in Alameda, cross over the bridge and work your way back to Marina Drive.

28. San Leandro Fishing Pier:

Surfperch   4
Striped Bass   2
Sturgeon   2
Other Fish   4

About San Leandro Fishing Pier: The San Leandro Pier is at the San Leandro Marina south of the Oakland airport.

Fishing: This is not one of the best fishing piers in the bay. Expect to catch surfperch, kingfish, flounder and other small fish. You always have a long shot at a striped bass and a longer shot at a sturgeon.

Facilities and Contact: This pier is part of the San Leandro Marina that has services. For information, contact the San Leandro Marina at 510-357-7447.

Cost: Parking and Entry is free.

Directions to San Leandro Fishing Pier: From the north or south take Interstate 880 to Marina Boulevard in San Leandro. Take Marina Boulevard west to the San Leandro Marina and the fishing pier.

29. Pacifica Pier:

Salmon   8
Surfperch   8
Striped Bass   6
Other Fish   7

About Pacifica Pier: Pacifica Pier, a 1000 foot long pier in the open ocean a few miles south of San Francisco, is the mother of all fishing piers in the Bay Area. At most piers, salmon and striped bass are a rarity; here they are almost routine. Anglers catch them regularly and catch many smaller fish.

This is not a secret fishing spot. When fishing is good most of the pier is lined with people and the biggest challenge may not be hooking fish but to get the fish past all of the other lines without tangling lines. It is festive and people are generally having a good time. Unfortunately there can be a seedy side to this pier. Some people seem to be trouble makers, maybe influenced by too much to drink. Laws aren't always obeyed. Some groups may catch their two salmon each when fishing is red hot, barbeque the smallest ones for lunch, dispose of the bones and catch more salmon to replace them. If you can overlook this element that may or not be there on a given day, it is a great place to catch fish.

Fishing: Some days anglers may land more than 100 salmon and other days they may land several tens of striped bass. These are unusual but be there at the right time and you have a good chance at a salmon or two. Striped bass anglers have better success casting pencil poppers or other lures from the beach a mile north of the pier or south near Pedro Point.

A favorite method to attract large fish is to catch bait fish—anchovies are about the best—and keep them alive or at least fresh in a bucket of water. Then hook the bait fish on an eight foot long leader with a snap swivel and a bobber rig that slides on one end of the leader opposite the hook end.

To deploy the rig, first cast your main line with a heavy eight-ounce weight then snap the leader to the line and let it slide down to the water. When the bobber starts dancing, the baitfish is being threatened by a larger fish. When it goes under and stays under, quickly reel in until the weight at the end of the line contacts the slider and land the fish. This method works surprisingly well.

This is as good a fishing spot as you will find for surfperch but it is the salmon and striped bass that draw anglers. A variety of small fish and an occasional halibut and shark are landed.

Tips from the Experts: "We will have a few days over the year where anglers will catch as many as 100 striped bass and have had days when anglers catch as many as 1000 salmon from this pier," says Joe Jimno who operates the bait shop at the entrance to the Pacifica Pier. "The premium fish are usually caught on anchovies. Anglers use fresh or frozen anchovies, prawns and grass shrimp. They fish the bait about eight feet under a bobber then wait until a fish cruises by and takes the bait fish."

Facilities and Contact: Jimno manages a bait shop at the entrance to the pier. Call him at 415-355-0690.

Cost: Fishing is free but you may need to pay metered parking.

Directions to Pacifica Pier: Take Highway 1 south from San Francisco to Pacifica. Take the Francisco/Palomar exit; turn right on Palomar then left on Beach Road to Santa Rosa Avenue. Park along the street or in public parking.

30. Pillar Point Harbor Pier:
    Surfperch 5
    Other fish 4

About Pillar Point Harbor Pier: This harbor is a hub of fishing activities. Almost a dozen charter boats originate here; commercial anglers work from this port and fishing is permitted from the main pier. This pier has the look, the feel and the smell of a busy fishing port and is a fun place to watch the boating and marine activities. Nearby restaurants including the Shore Bird serve fresh, excellent seafood meals.

One morning when I went on a charter boat one angler fishing from the pier had already caught half a bucket full of surfperch by the time our boat left and was catching one after the other. Anglers drop crab traps then fish to catch a combination for their meals.

Fishing: While not rated high for fishing, at the right time anglers catch surfperch. It all depends on the season—winter is the best time to catch these fish. Small fish like jacksmelt and anchovies are caught often. This is a fair place to catch crab dropping crab traps right off the pier. Anglers cleaning fish at the nearby fish cleaning table will donate fish heads for bait.

Facilities and Contact: Two bait shops are at this pier; restrooms are conveniently located at the entrance to the pier and you can purchase meals at the pier or in nearby Pillar Point. Call Huck Finn Sportfishing at

Anglers relax on benches on the Santa Cruz Pier waiting for a bite.

415-726-7133 for information.

Cost: Entry and Parking is free.

Directions to Pillar Point: From the north, take Highway 1 south to Capistrano Road in El Granada (there is a traffic light at this corner), make a right turn then a left turn into the marina. From the east take Highway 92 to Half Moon Bay then go north on Highway 1 to Capistrano Road and make two left turns.

31. Santa Cruz Wharf:
    Surfperch 4
    Salmon 2
    Other Fish 3

About Santa Cruz Wharf: The 2750 foot long Santa Cruz Wharf is the largest fishing pier in the area. It has two lanes of auto traffic onto the pier and has several hundred parking places. It is a fully developed wharf with many shops, fish markets and restaurants. The beach adjacent to the wharf has a historic and popular boardwalk with many rides and attractions including the Big Dipper, one of a few remaining wooden roller coasters.

Fishing: Surfperch are the number one catch off this wharf—plentiful in the winter and excellent eating. Anglers also catch jacksmelt, mackerel, small rockfish, sardines, rock crab and have a very long shot at a salmon or striped bass. The most successful anglers are the sea lions that lounge on the platforms below the pier.

Facilities and Contact: This wharf is highly commercialized with boat rentals, party boats (Stagnaros) and has parking for a few hundred cars. Call the Santa Cruz Chamber County Conference and Visitor Bureau at 800-833-3494 for general information. Call Santa Cruz Boat Rental at 408-423-1739 for rental boats.

Cost: Entry and Parking You take a ticket going onto the wharf and pay for parking when you exit.

Directions to Santa Cruz Wharf: From the Bay Area, take Highway 17 south to Santa Cruz. Continue into Santa Cruz on Ocean Street. Turn right onto Water Street then turn left onto Front Street. When Front Street ends, make a left onto Washington Street and continue onto the wharf (drive onto the wharf and find parking).

32. Capitola Wharf:
    Surfperch 6
    Halibut 1
    Other Fish 5

About Capitola Wharf: This 500 foot long pier is more famous for its beauty than its fishing. Set in a picturesque cusp in the ocean east of Santa Cruz, it is one if the prettiest piers off the California coast.

Fishing is permitted from Capitola Wharf and it is a fair fish pier but more serious anglers can rent wooden boats with outboard engines. Get a free fishing map and motor to places nearby where you have a better chance to catch quality rockfish, maybe lingcod and even salmon.

Fishing: Surfperch are what most anglers fishing from the wharf hope to catch in the fall, winter and spring months. Shark, rays and skates are a possibility. Sardine, jacksmelt, mackerel and other small fish are the normal catch from the pier. An occasional rockfish and rarely a lingcod is caught.

Your odds of catching a salmon are not good. Still, you never know when one may cruise by and decide it likes your bait—stranger things have happened. Halibut and striped bass are also long shots.

Facilities and Contact: This pier has a bait shop that rents boats. Call Capitola Boat and Bait at 408-462-2208 for information and to reserve a boat.

Cost: Entry and Parking   Find metered parking—it is very scarce.

Directions to Capitola Wharf: This wharf is in the city of Capitola by the Sea east of Santa Cruz. Go south from San Jose on Highway 17. Then take Highway 1 south (you are actually going east on 1) to the city of Soquel and turn right on Bay Avenue. Make another right onto Capitola Avenue and right again on Stockton. This street becomes Cliff Drive. Turn left on Wharf Road and you are at the pier.

33. Seacliff Pier (concrete ship):

Surfperch	6
Salmon	1
Striped Bass	2
Other Fish	5

About Seacliff Pier: Seacliff Pier is the most unusual pier in our area. It is a concrete ship with a history—well a rather short history as a ship. Built during World War I in Oakland, it wasn't quite finished at the end of the war and sat at the dock where it was built until 1929. It was towed to Seacliff Beach south of Santa Cruz and beached in shallow water just off the shore. A pier was built to connect her with shore; a restaurant, dance hall, a large heated swimming pool and carnival booths were built in and on the ship. The sponsoring organization went broke in two years and a heavy storm cracked the ship in 1932.

Damage has accumulated and more and more of the ship was fenced off. Now it is mostly off-limits but still serves as a fishing platform for local

and visiting anglers catching resident fish using the broken-up ship's interior as a home.

Fishing: Small fish like surfperch are the primary catch. Fall and winter months are the best times to catch these fish. They are an excellent food fish so catch enough and you can have a great fish-fry. You may catch other small fish including jacksmelt, sardines, mackerel, kingfish, anchovies and maybe an occasional shark and rock crab.

Salmon, halibut and striped bass aren't on the list of fish regularly caught from this pier but they are caught occasionally. You may be the one to catch one of these premium fish.

Facilities and Contact: Seacliff Beach is a California State Beach with camping right on the beach. The pier has a fish cleaning station and restrooms in the park are near the pier. For information and camping reservations call 408-429-2850.

Cost: Entry and Parking $5.00 per car
Camping $16.00 per night

Directions to Seacliff Pier: Take Highway 17 south from the South Bay Area to Highway 1 at Santa Cruz. Turn on Highway 1 south (you are actually traveling east here) and take a right turn at Aptos on State Park Highway to the park. The signs indicate Seacliff State Beach.

34. Monterey Wharves:

Surfperch	5
Striped Bass	1
Other Fish	4

About Monterey Wharves: Wharf Number One (also called Fisherman's Wharf) in Monterey harbor is a center of tourism with a profusion of seafood restaurants, open air fish markets, souvenir and commemorative clothing shops and candy shops. You can buy fresh fish to take home, a fresh seafood lunch or dinner or a seafood cocktail that comes in a paper cup (a plastic fork is included) with maybe a slice of sourdough bread. You can also buy a different kind of food—not to eat but to feed to begging sea lions.

This wharf is the place to board party boats to catch rockfish and lingcod all year or salmon and albacore in season or to take a whale watching trip. But Wharf Number Two to the east and the Coast Guard Pier to the west are better piers for fishing.

Fishing: Occasionally fishing is good when a school of sardines or other fish gets trapped in this semi-enclosed harbor. During winter months surfperch are landed from these wharves. Jacksmelt, mackerel, sardines, rockfish and an occasional striped bass or halibut may be caught here.

This harbor has a profusion of sea lions. Small fish are easy pickings for these mammals that are always anxious for a seafood meal and they, not anglers, make the best catches.

Facilities and Contact: Wharf Number Two has a fish cleaning station and has restrooms nearby in the parking lot. Monterey is noted for its wharf but its primary attraction is its world famous aquarium that shows the varied life of Monterey Bay in natural and beautiful displays. No visit here is complete without a trip to this facility. The area has a great variety of hotels, motels and restaurants for all budgets. For information, contact the Chamber of Commerce at 408-649-3207 or the aquarium at 408-648-4860.

Cost: Entry and Parking   Parking is metered—
bring lots of quarters.

Directions to Monterey Wharves: To reach both Monterey Wharves, take the Del Monte exit in Monterey to the right off Highway 1. Turn right into the wharf parking lot at the marked signs at Washington Street.

The Capitola Pier in the city of the same name is in a picturesque setting but parking is very limited.

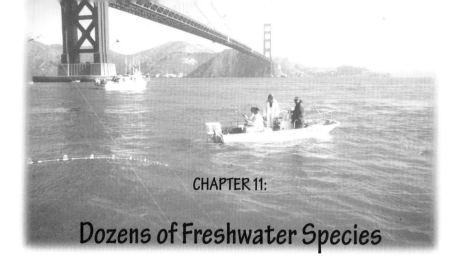

CHAPTER 11:

Dozens of Freshwater Species

The San Francisco Bay Area has many different freshwater and saltwater fish. This chapter describes each of the major freshwater sports fish caught in the Bay Area; chapter 12 describes the Bay Area's saltwater fish. Popular game fish are covered but bait fish and non-game fish are not included.

Anadromous fish (they live much of their lives in saltwater but return to freshwater to spawn) including salmon, striped bass and sturgeon may be caught in both saltwater and freshwater. Each species is listed where it is usually caught. Many salmon are caught in freshwater but most are caught far upstream, near their spawning sites away from the Bay Area. Few are caught in freshwater in the Bay Area so they are described only in the saltwater section. Sturgeon caught in the Bay Area are mostly caught in saltwater bays so they are described in the saltwater section. The anadromous American Shad is in the freshwater section because almost 100 percent of the shad catch is made in freshwater.

Striped bass are major game fish caught in saltwater in the bays and ocean beaches and also in freshwater in the Delta and as landlocked fish in lakes. So stripers are described in both the freshwater and in the saltwater chapters.

Trout

Trout are by far the most popular freshwater fish in the Bay Area. Stocked rainbow trout are the mainstay of fishing at most lakes in this area. When trout are in lakes in the fall, winter and spring, anglers flock to the lakes. When the lakes are too hot for trout, other fish like catfish are stocked and the number of anglers falls off sharply. Anglers have good success catching trout from shore, trolling or anchoring and fishing with bait from their own boats or from rented boats. Many five to 15-pound trout are caught; some are even larger.

If we had to rely on the number of trout naturally spawned, it would be a very different story because very few trout spawn here. The secret is trout farms and tanker trucks. Hundreds of thousands of trout are spawned and reared to large size to make them exciting to catch. Most are reared by the California Department of Fish & Game, Mt. Lassen Trout Farm and other suppliers.

Trucks with cool, oxygen rich water keep these fish healthy for their trip to the lakes and streams in the Bay Area. During the cool months, half a dozen or more truckloads of trout are spread among the lakes and streams each week; the waters are filled with trout and anglers can usually make a good catch. Anglers pay a daily fishing fee at many lakes, usually $3.00, and that money pays to stock fish. Almost all are rainbow trout. Occasionally the manager of some lake will make a special purchase of brown trout or brook trout but that is unusual.

Species: Rainbow Trout: *Salmo gairdneri*
Description: Rainbow trout are the favorite fish of many anglers across the United States. They are found in every state and dominate freshwater fishing in cool regions. In California they are found through all but the hottest regions of the state albeit planted trout available primarily in the

cool months in the warmer part of the state. Rainbow trout favor a cool water temperature of 54 degrees Fahrenheit.

Most trout are freshwater fish but a few are steelhead, an anadromous species spawning and growing as juveniles in freshwater then going to the ocean for most of their life. Unlike Pacific salmon that die once they have spawned, steelhead may go to sea and return to spawn several times during their adult life. Steelhead have recently been listed as threatened or endangered in most rivers and streams. They have always been a limited resource in the Bay Area but now anglers can not fish for them and must release any that are accidentally caught in many rivers. Even when you can keep steelhead, release them to help rebuild populations for your children and grandchildren.

Range: Rainbow trout are found in almost every state from Alaska to Florida. They are the most popular and most plentiful freshwater fish in the Bay Area. Each year several hundred thousand are stocked in lakes and rivers in this area. Lake Chabot, Lake Berryessa, San Pablo Reservoir, Lake Del Valle, Lake Merced, Contra Loma, Lafayette, Loch Lomond Reservoirs, Coyote Lake, the Lexington Reservoir, San Justo Lake, Marin County lakes and Putah Creek are some of the top lakes in the area.

Size: DFG stocked trout are usually about ten inches long and weigh about one-third of a pound. Privately stocked fish are usually a one-pound average but fish up to 10 to 15-pounds and occasionally larger are stocked. In the wild, trout grow to over 30-pounds in freshwater and over 40-pounds when they migrate to the ocean.

Records: Largest: 42-pounds 2-ounces caught in Alaska
Largest in California: 27-pound 4-ounce steelhead
Largest in the Bay Area: 17 to 18-pound stocked trout from several lakes

Where they live: These fish roam lakes freely and their depth is determined largely by the water temperature. In the fall, winter and spring when the surface water is cool, they will usually be found in the top 10 to 15 feet of water. In the summer they follow the cool water down and may be 15 to 50 or 60 feet deep.

What they eat: Trout in nature eat aquatic insects, small fish, worms and other food that is washed into their river or lake. Put-and-take trout grew up on fish pellets but quickly revert to eating their natural foods where they are stocked.

Best Fishing Area: Near shore, off points and in coves are particularly productive fishing areas in lakes. In rivers and streams, these fish are found in riffles or in deep holes: the largest fish are usually in holes.

How to Catch Trout: Trout are a perfect fish for fly fishing. Flies that imitate their natural food are very effective. Anglers using spinning outfits have good success catching rainbow trout from shore using prepared bait like Power Bait, worms, salmon eggs or flavored cheese. Anglers in boats may anchor and fish with these same baits or may troll lures, bait or a combination of the two like flashers followed by a night crawler. In rivers, casting a lightly weighted bait or fly into the water above a deep hole or pool and letting it drift into the deep hole will often draw a strike.

Regulations: The daily limit and possession limit for all species of trout in most lakes is five fish with no size limit. These fish are fragile and may die if released so catch-and-release is not encouraged. A daily fishing fee is charged in many public waters, usually $3.00 and anglers must have a valid California fishing license. Private lakes like Parkway Lake don't require a fishing license but the fishing fee is much higher.

Black Bass

Black bass including largemouth, smallmouth and spotted bass have a group of devoted anglers who become almost fanatical in their quest to catch bass. Many pay big dollars for the latest, fastest bass boat filled with equipment, have half a dozen or more expensive rods rigged and ready to cast and several tackle boxes filled with soft plastic lures and artificial lures.

Northern largemouth bass normally grow to about 10 pounds maximum. The largest substrain of largemouth bass, Florida Bass, were planted in Northern California in 1969. They have grown to as large as 18-pounds and add a new dimension to big bass in our area. The largest one in the Bay Area was a 17-pound 7-ounce bass found floating dead on Lake Chabot. The largest one caught by an angler was 17-pound 3-ounces caught from San Pablo Reservoir.

Largemouth bass are found in most lakes in the area. Smallmouth bass and largemouth are found in the Delta. Smallmouth fishing is good in the Russian River near Jenner and in Lake Berryessa. Some are caught from Putah Creek above Lake Berryessa. Spotted bass are popular outside the Bay Area. Lake Berryessa has many spotted bass and a few may show up at other lakes in this area.

Bass can be caught every month and every day of the year. Fishing begins to get really good when the water begins to warm in the spring and they began to feed to get ready to spawn. Catches are excellent as fish spawn and males guard their nests. They will strike anything that aggravates them and this is when you can sight-fish wearing Polaroid glasses to see fish under water and dropping a bait or lure right on the fish.

After spawning the male guards the fry from predators for some time. Put a lure that looks and acts like a predator near these small fish and the adult guard will take it. When catching fish off a nest or guarding fry, put the fish right back where you caught it so it can resume its guard duties. Fishing is best as the water warms in March and continues good through June or July.

Bass are challenging fish and usually require good casting skills. While some are caught on bait or trolling, most are caught by anglers using a trolling motor to slowly move around a body of water casting to likely looking fishing spots. To be successful anglers must know exactly where to find bass, to make near perfect casts time after time, to outguess other anglers as to where the bass will be hanging out and what lure and presentation will entice them to strike.

Many people can't tell one species of bass from another and really don't care. The fishing methods are the same and whether the bass you just caught is a largemouth, smallmouth or spotted bass may be unimportant to you. If you really want to know, study the pictures and the description of each fish and you can identify each species. Florida strain largemouth bass and northern largemouth bass are so identical, only an expert can tell the difference and even they may need to make a blood test to be sure. But there is no confusion about the really big fish. Any bass weighing more than 10-pounds is almost surely a Florida bass.

Black bass fishing has its own vocabulary. You need to know that a crank bait is not a bait at all in the concept of something like a minnow, worm, cricket or crawfish. Instead it is a plastic or wooden lure with two or three treble hooks hanging from it. You might guess that a lure with a concave front surface that makes a popping noise when you jerk it along the surface of the water is called a popper. You probably won't guess that a thin minnow shaped lure is called a jerk bait or that a plastic tube with a split skirt that is stretched over a molded lead head on a hook is called a gitzit. You may not know walking-the-dog has nothing to do with your pet.

Don't worry, you can't mistake plastic worms or plastic grubs. A stick bait really does look much like a stick but that doesn't help in knowing how to use it. Popular colors like black, purple, motor oil, or pumpkinseed are fairly obvious; a green weenie really does look a lot like an elongated hot dog and a salt and pepper color is light with a black fleck as you would expect. You will quickly pick up as much terminology as you need to start catching bass.

Species: Largemouth Bass: *Micropterus salmoides*

Description: Largemouth bass are a warm water species favoring water temperatures of 65 to 75 degrees Fahrenheit. Two subspecies are found in the Bay Area; the northern largemouth bass that normally grows to about 10-pounds maximum and Florida Largemouth Bass that are topped by the world record 22-pound 4-ounce bass.

Range: Largemouth bass, one of the most widely distributed freshwater fish, are caught in all of the Western States except Alaska and most of the Midwest and Eastern states. For large bass in the Bay Area, fish Lake Chabot or San Pablo Reservoir; the best bass fishing is in the Delta; anglers can catch many fish though most weigh less then 5-pounds and few exceed 10-pounds. Lake Berryessa in the North Bay and Anderson and Calero Reservoirs in the South Bay are excellent bass lakes.

Size: With the introduction of Florida Largemouth Bass in Northern California in 1969, the maximum size of this species slowly increased to an 18-pound largemouth caught from Hidden Valley Reservoir near Clear Lake by Kevin Hall. Today many of the largest Florida strain bass up to almost 22-pounds have been caught from Southern California lakes. The largest largemouth bass caught in the Bay Area was a 17-pounds 3-ounce

fish caught from San Pablo Reservoir. Lake Chabot has had fish almost the same size caught with a 17-pound 2-ounce fish landed. An even larger 17-pound 7-ounce bass was found dead floating on this lake and is mounted and displayed in the lake's bait shop.

A fish caught from Spring Lake in Santa Rosa in 1997 within my definition of the Bay Area reportedly weighed 24-pounds, a new world record. The weight was made on a bathroom scale and the fish was released. While I would love to report that the largest bass ever caught came from the greater Bay Area, measurements of the fish in comparison with the angler's hand suggest the fish is smaller than reported.

Records: Largest largemouth bass: 22-pounds 4-ounces caught in Georgia in 1932

Largest California largemouth bass: 21-pounds 12-ounces

Largest Northern California largemouth bass: 18-pounds

Largest Bay Area largemouth bass: 17-pounds 3-ounces

Where they live: Largemouth bass are a relatively shallow water fish found in stained water (muddy water) barely deep enough to cover their backs to depths of several tens of feet. They move into shallow water to spawn in the spring. Florida bass are planted as small fish and grow large. They spawn but cross with the smaller northern bass cousins and soon lose their super large size. Northern bass are naturally spawned.

What they eat: These fish eat crayfish, worms, other fish, frogs, insect larvae: even snakes, baby ducks and rodents swimming on the surface.

Best Fishing Area: Largemouth bass like areas that have both cover, like tulles, a fallen tree or docks and a deep water escape route nearby. Find an area like this and you will almost surely find bass.

How to Catch: Plastic baits including worms, grubs, crayfish and baitfish imitations fished along the bottom slowly is the number one method to catch bass. They are also caught on diving or surface lures including a variety of crank baits and spinner baits. Surface lures like Pop-Rs and Zara spooks are good early morning lures. Poppers are good flies for fly fishers. Weedless surface lures like soft plastic snag proof frogs cast into open spots in the middle of tulles or weeds present lures in areas not normally fished and may draw explosive strikes.

Lures are normally cast and retrieved. Precise casts to the side of docks, to a submerged bush or to inlets in tulles have the best chance to entice a bass. A foot pedal operated trolling motor is ideal to put you into good casting positions leaving both hands free to cast but a conventional trolling motor will suffice. Trolling for bass is also a good fishing technique.

Regulations: The daily limit for black bass of all species is usually five fish with a minimum size of 12 inches total length. Most bass anglers release their fish to maintain a good fishery.

Species: Smallmouth Bass: *Micropterus dolomieui*

Description: Smallmouth bass are solid bronze color compared with a brown coloration with dark markings along the side of a largemouth. When a smallmouth's mouth is closed, the back of the mouth does not come back as far as the fish's eye: the mouth of a largemouth protrudes back behind its eye. Smallmouth prefer cooler (65 to 68 degrees) and are usually found in clear water.

Range: Smallmouth bass are found in almost all of the lower 48 states. They are concentrated in cooler, northern states and few are found in southern warm water states. They are found in Lake Berryessa, Lake Del Valle, the Delta—particularly the northern part of the Delta—and other lakes and rivers in the area.

Size: Smallmouth bass don't get as large as largemouth. A three-pound smallmouth is a good fish and anything over five-pounds gets into trophy status.

Records: Largest Smallmouth Bass 10-pounds 14-ounces caught in Tennesse

Largest California Smallmouth Bass: 9-pounds 1-ounce

Largest Bay Area Smallmouth Bass: Not recorded

Where they live: Both smallmouth and largemouth bass live in rivers and both live in lakes. They often share the same body of water but smallmouth bass prefer cooler water ranging from 65 to 68 degrees Fahrenheit whereas largemouth are comfortable in water temperatures up to 75 degrees. Consequently smallmouth are found more in cooler rivers and lakes and in the cooler parts of lakes. Ideal habitat for these fish is a shale or rocky bank but stumps or fallen trees often hold these fish.

What they eat: These fish eat other fish like minnows or threadfin shad and crawfish. They also eat worms and may take an occasional insect or rodent from the surface of the water.

Best Fishing Area: Fish shale or rocky banks in lakes and flowing water in rivers. Don't pass up any structure such as underwater ledges or fallen trees or submerged stumps. A classic smallmouth area is a sloping rocky underwater bank.

How to Catch: Fish bait or lures like those for largemouth bass. Fishing a plastic worm slowly along a rocky bank is a good fishing method. Top water poppers or crank baits are good in the morning or evening hours or along banks of rivers. Floating a river and casting to the shoreline is a classical way to fish for smallmouth bass.

Regulations: Same as largemouth bass.

Species: Spotted Bass: *Micropterus punctulatus*

Description: Alabama Spotted Bass (usually shortened to just spotted bass) are a warmer water fish favoring a temperature of 75 degrees. They were introduced into lakes in California because largemouth bass spawn very shallow. When lakes are drawn down in the spring, the largemouth eggs may be left high and dry. Spotted bass spawn deeper; their eggs remain submerged and usually hatch. This makes them ideal for lakes that draw down water during the spring spawning. They are very aggressive bass, relatively easy to catch and provide great sport. The mouth of a spotted bass is between the largemouth and smallmouth bass in size going back as far as the back of its eye. Like a smallmouth bass the first and second dorsal fins are connected: the first and second dorsal fins are separated on a largemouth bass.

Range: Spotted bass are found in most states in the Continental United States but are abundant in the southern states that have the warm water these fish prefer. Lake Berryessa is the class of the spotted bass lakes in the Bay Area.

Size: Spotted bass are smaller than largemouth bass: a typical fish weighs a pound or two and any fish over five-pounds is a trophy fish.

Records: Largest Spotted Bass: 9-pounds 9-ounces caught at Pine Flat Lake, California

Largest California Spotted Bass: Same as Above

Largest Bay Area Spotted Bass: Not recorded

Where they live: The number one spotted bass lake in the Bay Area is Lake Berryessa. They are found around docks, in tulles, and off points.

What they eat: Like other bass, spotted bass eat other fish, worms, frogs, insects and almost anything that swims in or on the surface of the water.

Best Fishing Area: Spotted bass are caught around any structure that would hold largemouth bass. They are also found free swimming in lakes so look for water temperatures that are comfortable. Submerged high spots often hold these fish.

How to Catch: Spotted bass are aggressive. They will take a slow moving worm or a fluke (a soft plastic baitfish imitation) fished with short jerks that simulate a wounded bait fish. They will also attack a fast moving spinner, a buzz bait, a crank bait or a surface lure fished in the morning and evening.

Regulations: Same as largemouth bass.

Catfish

Catfish are one of the most widely distributed fish in the United States; every state in the lower 48 has catfish. The first fish I ever caught was a catfish. They range from small species called bullheads to large blue catfish that can weigh more than 100-pounds. Catfish are identified by the barbels (feelers) around their mouth; freshwater catfish have eight feelers.

Catfish are said to sting you with their whiskers but that isn't the case: their whiskers are soft and pliable. Their dorsal fin and pectoral fins have stiff sharp spines that will inflict a painful puncture wound. Avoid these fins and you can handle them without injury.

Catfish caught in clear water have a mild flesh and are an excellent food fish. When the water contains certain kinds of algae, their flesh takes on the taste of the algae and has a strong unpleasant flavor.

Species: Channel Catfish: *Ictalurus punctatus*

Description: Channel catfish are warm water fish favoring water of 82 to 85 degrees Fahrenheit. They have spots on their white sides when they are young and have a deeply forked tail. After a couple of years, the spots disappear and these fish have a dark back and sides and a light underside.

Range: Catfish are found in most lakes and rivers thoughout the Bay Area. They are abundant in the Delta. Catfish are stocked in most Bay Area lakes during the warm summer months when water is too warm for trout. They are very tough, adapt to almost any water, become resident and grow to very large size.

Size: Catfish stocked in lakes normally weigh one to three-pounds. They grow to much larger size and some trophy catfish are stocked. Catfish up to 35-pounds have been caught from San Pablo Reservoir and Lake Chabot and 25 to 35-pound catfish have been caught from many lakes in the area. Specimens up to 20 plus pounds are caught occasionally from the Delta.

Records: Largest Channel Catfish: 58-pounds caught in South Carolina
Largest California Channel Catfish: 52-pounds 10-ounces
Largest Bay Area Channel Catfish: 35-pounds

Where they live: Channel catfish prefer clean, flowing water though they are very successfully stocked in still water lakes. These fish live on the bottom looking for bait fish to come to them or for food to be washed to them by moving water. In the Delta where water is flowing as the tides go in and out, they are found behind pilings of old docks and in deep holes along tulles. In lakes they are around structure or weeds, in coves or along ridges on the bottom.

What they eat: Catfish, particularly large ones, are generally night feeders using their barbels to find food. Crawfish, small fish, and clams are mainstays in their diet.

Best Fishing Area: Cast your bait into structure such as pilings or downed trees or into deep holes when fishing in the Delta. Lakes have little visible structure so fish off points, in coves or areas where you have had success before. Ask at the bait shop at the lake to find the best areas and observe other anglers to see where they are catching fish.

How to Catch: Many catfish are caught fishing from shore but a boat gives anglers the advantage of fishing more areas. Favorite baits include meat stripped out of small clams, mackerel, chicken liver, anchovies or prepared baits. Catfish are primarily night feeders so evenings, mornings and nights are the best time to catch these fish.

Regulations: Catfish may be caught all year and have no size limit and no bag limit in the Delta and other natural areas. Where they are planted, the limit is usually five or 10. San Pablo and Lafayette Reservoirs have a limit of 10 catfish. Most other Bay Area lakes have a bag limit of five catfish.

Species: White Catfish: *Ictalurus catus*

Description: White catfish have a light underside with a darker beige or blue back. As with a channel catfish, both their dorsal fin and pectoral fins have sharp rays that can inflict a painful puncture wound. One of these fish looks much like an adult channel catfish but they have 19 to 23 rays in the anal fin compared with 24 to 30 rays in that fin of a channel catfish.

Range: White catfish are scattered across much of the United States and are abundant in Northern California including the Bay Area. These are the dominant catfish caught in the Delta comprising more than 90 % of Delta catfish.

Size: White catfish are generally small fish weighing up to three-pounds. Any over six-pounds are trophy size.

Records: Largest White Catfish: 22-pounds caught from a
California pond
Largest California White Catfish: 22-pounds
Largest Bay Area White Catfish: Not recorded

Where they live: These fish are found in fresh or brackish water preferring still water or a slow current.

What they eat: White catfish eat a wide variety of food including worms, clams, insects, small fish, frogs and crawfish.

Best Fishing Area: The Delta is the primary area to catch these fish. They are found in deep holes or around structure like old pilings, sunken stumps or at the edges of tulles.

How to Catch: Bait with a lot of natural or artificial flavor attract catfish. The meat of freshwater clams, liver, mackerel and anchovies are favorite baits. Small fish are caught all day but the largest fish are usually caught at night.

Regulations: Same as for channel catfish.

Panfish

Crappie, both black and white varieties, redear and bluegill are the most abundant panfish in the Bay Area. Found in the Delta and many tributaries to the Delta as well as many lakes, these panfish are an often overlooked resource. I've had days when I have caught as many as 80 to 100 crappie in San Pablo Reservoir but I only keep enough for one or two meals. Similar numbers can be landed from Lake Berryessa and areas in the Delta. Their flesh is a delicate sweet white meat that makes it my favorite freshwater fish. Bluegill and other sunfish are a great fish for youngsters to find quick action when fishing and are found in the Delta and many area lakes.

Species: Black Crappie: *Pomoxis nigromaculatus*

Description: Black crappie are very narrow bodied, light colored fish with black spots scattered all around their bodies and on their fins. They can be distinguished from white crappie by the different patterns of their

spots and blacks have seven or eight hard rays in their dorsal fin while white crappie have only six. Counting the hard rays in their dorsal fin is the sure way to identify these fish. Their favorite temperature is 70 degrees.

Range: Black crappie are found in most states. The more abundant of the two types of crappie in the Bay Area, they are plentiful in Lake Berryessa, San Pablo Reservoir and the Delta and are found in several other lakes and rivers in the Bay Area.

Size: Typical crappie weigh about half a pound or less and any weighing more than a couple of pounds are exceptional.

Records: Largest black crappie: 4-pounds 8-ounces caught in Virginia
            Largest California black crappie: 4-pounds 1-ounce
            Largest Bay Area black crappie: Not recorded

Where they live: Crappie are small and are eaten by many other fish. They don't survive in open water but live in protected areas like submerged brush, under docks and at drop offs in lakes and rivers.

What they eat: Crappie eat small fish like minnows, worms and insects.

Best Fishing Area: Find brush or docks and you will likely find crappie. Anything that floats on the water is also likely to draw fish. These are school fish and any time you find one crappie, you will likely find several more.

How to Catch: A minnow fished under a bobber is a good bait for these fish. Worms and artificial crappie jigs also fished under a bobber are also good. Crappie have a tender mouth and must be played gently.

Regulations: Crappie fishing is permitted all year; they have no minimum size and the daily bag limit is 25.

Species: White Crappie: *Pomoxis annularis* 61 degrees

Description: White crappie are a very narrow, deep bodied fish like black crappie but they have spots in a number of vertical bands along their bodies. They are found in cooler water than black crappie favoring water temperatures of about 61 degrees. To really distinguish between the two

species, count the number of spines in the dorsal fin. A black crappie has 7 or 8 dorsal spines and a white crappie has only 6 spines in its dorsal fin.

Range: White crappie are native to the Midwest, the South and the Southeast. They have been introduced into California and in the Bay Area are found in the Delta, in Lake Berryessa and a few other lakes.

Their habitat, food, fishing methods and regulations are the same as for black crappie.

Size: A typical size is about half a pound and any over two-pounds are trophy class fish.

Records: Largest white crappie: 5-pounds 3-ounces caught in Mississippi
            Largest California white crappie: 4-pounds 8-ounces
            Largest Bay Area white crappie: Not recorded

Species: Bluegill: *Lepomis macrochirus*

Description: Bluegill are one of the most abundant panfish. They have deep flat bodies like a crappie. Their bodies are typically dark blue though the color has a great variation from almost yellow to a light blue. They have six dark vertical bands along their bodies and a bright blue to a dark blue tab at the back of their gill plates. They are small, rarely growing to more than 9 inches long but are voracious fighters. When I catch one I am always amazed at how hard they can pull for their size. Find water ranging from 60 to 70 degrees Fahrenheit and you will likely find hungry bluegill.

Range: These fish were originally found in the midwest and south but have been widely introduced and are found in every state in the contiguous United States. In the Bay Area they are found in the Delta and most warm water lakes.

Size: A typical bluegill weighs less than a pound. Even a half pound bluegill is a good fish.

Records: Largest Bluegill: 4-pounds 12-ounces caught in Alabama
            Largest California Bluegill: 3-pounds 8-ounces
            Largest Bay Area Bluegill: Not recorded

Where they live: These fish live in warm water around aquatic vegetation or structure.

What they eat: Bluegill eat worms and insects.

Best Fishing Area: Fish near shore near brush or weeds or in shallow regions of a lake or Delta. These fish become very active at sunset or near sunrise. You can catch them on small artificial lures particularly surface lures though they are caught on bait all day. They are great fish to catch on small surface flies like poppers.

How to Catch: Many young anglers have had their first fishing success catching these fish on a bit of worm fished under a bobber. Fly anglers find they are great little fish taking dry flies or small poppers and putting up a good fight on a light rod.

Regulations: All small sunfish including bluegill may be caught all year and there is no limit: you can catch as many as you are willing to clean.

Anadromous Fish Caught in Freshwater

Species: Several important species in the Bay Area migrate to sea but are caught in freshwater as they return to spawn. Salmon are such a species and while they are caught in this area, most are caught farther upstream near Oroville and Red Bluff. Steelhead are also anadromous but only a few are caught in the Bay Area. Northern California coastal rivers and streams are great sources for these fish. In the case of steelhead, new regulations classify them as endangered or threatened and will give them added protection. Sturgeon are also caught in freshwater but most are caught in the saltwater bays and channels so they are covered in the saltwater section.

However, two anadromous species have very important catches in freshwater. Striped bass are caught both in freshwater and saltwater and are a major species in each so are included in both the freshwater and saltwater sections. American Shad (usually simply called shad) are caught almost totally in freshwater so are included in this section.

Species: Striped bass: *Morone saxatilis*

Description: Striped bass are not related to black bass and their physical appearance is very different. They are shaped more like a salmon though chunkier and are a bright white or silvery fish identified by seven black lines running most of the length on each side of their bodies. The ideal water temperature for striped bass is 60 to 70 degrees.

These are naturally anadromous fish and their natural life cycle is between freshwater to spawn and live part of the year and saltwater. However, they have been put in situations where they have no route to the sea and have survived and thrived. Striped bass have been stocked in lakes but in the Bay Area they have become landlocked by exporting water from the Delta. The larvae are very small and can not be screened from the water and make a one way trip to all lakes that get Delta water.

Range: Striped bass are a native East Coast fish that were introduced into California in 1879. They were a huge success and are now one of our most important gamefish. They are found from the Delta up the Sacramento and San Joaquin Rivers to above Sacramento and Modesto, and in many lakes, particularly ones that get water from the Delta including San Luis Reservoir and O'Neill Forebay, Contra Costa Lake, Lake Del Valle and will surely be found in El Vaquero Reservoir south of Brentwood when it starts to fill with water from the Delta.

Size: Striped bass typically weigh seven to ten-pounds but many in the 15 to 20-pound range are caught. Occasionally a 40-pound or larger one is landed.

Records: Largest landlocked Striped Bass: 67-pounds 8-ounces caught in O'Neill Forebay

Largest California Striped Bass: Same as above

Largest Bay Area Striped Bass: Same as above

Where they live: Stripers are found in many lakes and in the Delta. Large adults are the supreme predator so need not seek cover to avoid being eaten. They go to where they have a ready food supply

What they eat: Adult striped bass feed primarily on other fish. In lakes that have planted trout, stripers thrive on them.

Best Fishing Area: Striped bass herd hatchery trout into shallow areas of a lake and can often be seen breaking the surface chasing trout. Find a shallow area near the bank where stripers can drive and corner their prey and you will likely find striped bass.

Stripers are found in deep channels in the Delta and in cuts through berms where water flows and brings food during changing tides.

How to Catch: Bait like butterfly-cut (a way of preparing the bait)

threadfin shad is the number one bait in the Delta. Mudsuckers and bullheads (actually a sculpin) are also good bait. The bait is fished on the bottom and the striper is allowed to run before setting the hook. In lakes, large lures that imitate rainbow trout are favorite lures. Top water lures and diving lures are both effective. Casting the lure is more successful than trolling. Fly anglers catch these fish using large flies that imitate bait fish.

Regulations: Striped bass may be caught all year. The limit is two and the minimum size is 18 inches except in San Luis Reservoir, O'Neill Forebay and all canals in the state or the federal water project south of highways 132 and 580. In these waters the limit is 10 and there is no size limit.

Species: American Shad: *Alosa sapidissima*

Description: Shad are anadromous fish that enter freshwater rivers to spawn. They prefer water temperatures of about 66 degrees for spawning. They are a silver, oval bodied fish that are hard fighters and a great sport fish but are too bony to be a favored food fish. Some are prepared cutting out most of the bones in a complicated process and others are smoked.

Range: Shad are an East Coast fish that were introduced into the Sacramento River in 1871. They are found in the Sacramento/San Joaquin River system migrating as far north as the Red Bluff diversion dam and south to about Modesto and are also found in the Russian River.

Size: A typical shad weighs three to five-pounds but occasionally one about twice that size is landed.

Records: Largest American Shad: 11-pounds 4-ounces caught in Massachusetts

Largest California American Shad: 7-pounds 5-ounces

Largest Bay Area American Shad: Not recorded

Where they live: Shad spend most of their lives in saltwater but enter the Sacramento/San Joaquin River in mid-May or later. Essentially all the catch is made from late May through June or into July after they have entered rivers.

What they eat: Shad eat small plankton dominated by possum shrimp when they are in the Sacramento River.

Best Fishing Area: Most shad in the area covered by this book are caught from the Sacramento River at Freeport south of Sacramento, the American River and the Russian River. They are caught north all the way to the Red Bluff diversion dam.

How to Catch: Shad eat only very small organisms and anglers can't duplicate their food. However, they are attracted by flashy lures and flies. Shad darts that are a leadhead lure with the head painted bright colors like red and white or green and white and sparse beadhead flies attract these fish. Spin casting or fly fishing are good ways to catch them. Some anglers fish from boats but many have good success from shore or wading.

Regulations: American shad may be caught all year. They have no minimum size and the limit is 25.

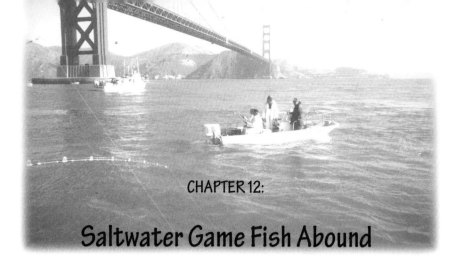

CHAPTER 12:

Saltwater Game Fish Abound

Saltwater species found in the ocean and San Francisco and San Pablo Bays provide a variety of large game fish in the Bay Area. The most popular (salmon) to the most abundant (rockfish and surfperch) and the largest (white sturgeon) combine to form an unparalleled combination of quality fish.

A good way to get an overview of these fish and to understand their habitat is to visit the Monterey Bay Aquarium. The great variety of sea life in the Bay Area is on display in this facility. You will learn about the different sea-life, the history of the area, and see the beauty of the species on display.

Only the most popular and the most abundant saltwater game fish are described. More than 50 rockfish species are found off our coast and only the most common ones are included. Bait fish including anchovies, mackerel, and sardines are critical to the food chain in the ocean but they are not game fish and are not described. A whole range of fish from eels to many rockfish and several members of the sole or flounder family that are caught occasionally have not been included.

The fearsome white shark has a major breeding area off San Francisco and Bodega Bay and have a large presence at the Farallon Islands. Most divers avoid their area. These shark are protected so anglers cannot pursue them. Other shark include thresher shark and mako shark that are caught occasionally and many smaller species are abundant. Only the largest or most abundant species are included.

Warm water fish aren't normally found off our coast but when El Nino brings warm water to our shores, many of these species will visit and are caught including a profusion of albacore tuna, a few bluefin tuna, white sea bass, bonito, and occasionally a marlin or a Dorado. The greatest El Nino ever recorded hit in 1997 and 1998 and our sports fishing was turned upside down: warm water species were everywhere. Each El Nino year has a similar effect usually bringing good albacore fishing but I don't ever expect to see another period that had as many warm water fish for so long as 1997 and 1998.

Striped Bass

Striped bass were transplanted to the West Coast from the East Coast in 1879 when a few were brought cross-country by train. One hundred thirty-two survived and were released near Martinez. In 1882 an additional 300 were transported cross-country and released. They flourished far beyond anyone's wildest dreams. The population was estimated at three million adult fish from the 1940s to the 1960s.

Huge quantities of water are exported from the Delta; industrial, municipal and agricultural runoff has polluted the water and the striper population has dropped to one quarter that level. Striper eggs, larvae and juvenile fish are carried with the water so any body of water that gets Delta water also gets striped bass. They thrive and good striper catches are made in lakes that get Delta water.

Species: Striped Bass: *Morone saxatilis*
Description: Striped bass are anadromous fish living much of their life in

saltwater in the San Francisco and San Pablo Bays and off ocean beaches. They may live 40 years or more spawning tens of times during their life cycle. Their ideal water temperature is 60 to 70 degrees Fahrenheit.

Range: Striped bass range from Oregon to Southern California. Young fish are very small and are included in water taken from the Delta. Any lake that gets water from the Delta and that includes many Bay Area, Central and Southern California lakes also gets striped bass. Often these fish do very well particularly in San Luis Reservoir and adjacent O'Neil Forebay where a world record landlocked striper was taken.

Size: A typical striped bass caught in the ocean and bays weighs 5 to 10-pounds. The minimum size limit for these fish is 18 inches total length; stripers below this limit are rarely caught in saltwater. Historically many have been taken in the 30 to 50-pound range with an occasional larger fish. Today these very large fish are rare.

Records: Largest Striped Bass: 78-pounds 8-ounces caught off New Jersey
Largest land locked: 67-pounds 8-ounces caught in O'Neil Forebay
Largest in California: Same as above
Largest in Bay Area: Same as above

Where they live: Striped bass live in the Bays, Delta, Sacramento and San Joaquin Rivers, the ocean and lakes. Often they are free swimming fish, waiting in protected water for the tides to bring a meal to them.

What they eat: Adult stripers primarily eat other fish like anchovies, small surfperch, herring, small stripers and also shrimp.

Best Fishing Area: The best fishing for these fish is in the San Francisco Bay and off the beaches of the Pacific Ocean in the summer and in San Pablo Bay in the fall. Anglers on sport fishing boats use live bait to catch stripers at the south tower of the Golden Gate Bridge, off Alcatraz Island, at Harding Rock, Shag Rock, Raccoon Strait and the Pacifica Beach. Watch for diving birds that probably indicate striped bass are chasing baitfish to the surface and birds are dining on the bait.

How to Catch: Striped bass are primarily caught with live bait when they are in the ocean or bays but they are also caught casting jigs, lures and trolling. Trolling or casting crank baits is effective in the bays. Fly fishermen take these fish casting baitfish imitations like Dan Blanton's Whistler series flies.

Regulations: The daily and possession limit for striped bass in saltwater is two fish and the minimum length is 18 inches. The Department of Fish & Game warns people to limit consumption of striped bass and other fish caught from the bays.

Salmon

The Bay Area is the place to fish for salmon in the lower 48 states. In recent years about seven out of 10 sports caught salmon from the ocean off our West Coast have been caught from the greater San Francisco Bay Area, from Monterey to Bodega Bay. The remaining 30 percent were caught off Northern and Southern California, Washington and Oregon. With this kind of catch, the great fight and potentially large size of salmon and their super food value, it is no surprise that salmon are the favorite saltwater fish for Bay Area anglers. A fleet of sport fishing boats go for salmon from every major port from Monterey to Bodega Bay and from inside the San Francisco Bay. Often salmon are caught close to port and several launching ramps provide access to anglers in private boats.

Chinook salmon, also called king salmon, completely dominate this species in the Bay Area. Coho or silver salmon have been a secondary species and now are almost non-existent in the Bay Area. They are a threatened species and must be released if they are caught. Chums, pinks and sockeye have been reported in the Sacramento River but they are either no longer in the system or are very rare.

Species: Chinook salmon: *Oncorhynchus tshawytscha*
Description: Chinook salmon, also called king salmon, are the largest of the five species of Pacific salmon weighing up to 100-pounds and more. These anadromous fish make epic spawning runs of up to 2000 miles up rivers. As with all Pacific salmon, they spawn once, then die. Most Chinook spawn three or four years from when they hatch although there is some variation within each population. Chinook rival sockeye salmon as the best food fish.

Range: Chinook salmon are found all along our West Coast from Alaska to Central California and make forays into Southern California in the spring. By far the largest concentration of these fish in the lower 48 states spawn in the Sacramento River and are caught out of San Francisco.

Size: A typical chinook salmon weighs six to 12-pounds but many weigh 15 to 20-pounds and occasionally one of these salmon weighs more than 40-pounds.

Records: Largest king salmon: 97-pound 4-ounces caught in Alaska
Largest in California: 88-pounds caught in the Sacramento River
Largest in California (saltwater): 52.2-pounds caught off Duxbury in 1997
Largest from the Bay Area: same as above

Where they live: Chinook salmon are spawned in rivers but travel to the ocean and live most of their adult life in the ocean. They make a big circuit in the ocean returning to their river of origin to spawn when they are three to five years old.

What they eat: Adult chinook salmon feed on baitfish, notably anchovies and herring. They also eat krill, a shrimp like planktonic crustacean.

Best Fishing Area: Monterey Bay has the best fishing for salmon early in the year and good fishing continues into July. The San Francisco Area has good salmon fishing throughout the season with peak fishing in June or July but fishing is often very good from opening day until August. The number in the catch usually falls off after August but the largest fish are caught near the end of the season, typically in October. Bodega Bay usually has very good salmon fishing in the summer with July the best month. Catches are less predictable at other times in the season. Salmon are caught in the San Francisco Bay particularly near California City and in the Sacramento River and its tributaries. The American River in Sacramento often has good salmon fishing but most other river fishing is outside the area included in this book and won't be covered.

How to Catch: Salmon are caught using two fishing methods. Until recently anglers trolled with heavy weights, diving plans or down riggers and that is still a good method for anglers fishing from private boats (though lighter weights are used). Now almost all sport fishing boat anglers and many anglers in private boats drift mooch with frozen anchovies or herring. Bait dominates both trolling and mooching but artificial lures can be used successfully in both cases.

Regulations: The season for salmon in the ocean is from the end of March through October north of Pigeon Point (between Santa Cruz and Half Moon Bay) and mid- March through August south of this point. The limit is two salmon. The minimum length and hook restriction has gone through a lot of fluctuation and continues to change as scientists try to find the best way to minimize mortality of threatened and endangered subspecies. The two most popular limits are "keep-your-first-two-salmon" or a 24 inch minimum length. Barbless circle hooks are required when using bait but lures fished without bait can have conventional barbless hooks. Usually anglers must release fish less than 24 inches but they must keep their first two salmon outside the San Francisco Bay in July, August and early September. While these regulations are current as this goes to press, check the latest state fishing regulations to determine seasons, size limits and gear restrictions.

Species: Coho salmon: *Oncorhynchus kisutch*
Description: It is important to be able to identify coho or silver salmon. Off the Bay Area and all of California they must be released. The primary identification is that silver salmon have white gums around their teeth: chinook salmon have black gums. Cohos have small round spots on their backs; chinook have large uneven spots on their backs. The tail fin rays on a silver are ribbed; they are smooth on a chinook. A coho has a few spots on its upper tail lobe; a chinook has spots on both tail lobes.

Coho are the most acrobatic salmon so if you catch one that jumps look extra carefully to see if it is a coho.

Range: Coho salmon were the most prevalent salmon off Oregon and Washington outnumbering chinook by a factor of three or more. Now many of these runs are threatened or endangered and the catch is nil. Coho catches off California have always been small compared with chinook but now they are almost non-existent.

Size: Coho salmon on average weigh less than chinook salmon. A 10-pound coho off California is above average and a 15-pound fish is getting into a trophy class.

Records: Largest: 33-pounds 4 ounce caught off New York
Largest in California: 33 pounds 8 ounces*
Largest from the Bay Area: not recorded
* The California record is not recognized by the International Gamefish Association.

Where they live: Coho live in the ocean but spawn in small coastal streams. These waters have been decimated with loss of habitat due to logging and some dumping into the rivers.

How to Catch: Coho salmon are rarely caught but fishing methods that take these fish are much the same as for chinook salmon. However, cohos are generally shallower than chinook and like a faster moving lure. Since they must be released, it is best to troll slowly or mooch to avoid these fish.

Regulations: All coho salmon caught in the Bay Area must be released.

Halibut, Flounder, Sole

Flatfish that live on the bottom and have both eyes at one side of their heads are excellent food fish. The underside is white and the top side of this family is mottled brown or tan to blend in with the bottom. Halibut are an important saltwater fish in the Bay Area. Most are California Halibut but a few are huge Pacific Halibut. Flounder were once an almost sure thing in the lower Delta but now they are caught infrequently. Sanddabs are abundant in the ocean though most anglers catch them for bait—they are excellent bait for large lingcod—they are also an excellent food fish.

Species: California Halibut: *Paralichthys californicus*

Description: California Halibut have short fins on both sides of their bodies and their overall shape is oval. A Pacific Halibut has longer fins around the center of its body that gives it an overall diamond shape. It's eyes are usually on the left side of it's body. California Halibut dominate the catch of halibut from the San Francisco Bay. Pacific Halibut are caught occasionally particularly in the ocean.

Range: California Halibut are found from the San Francisco Bay Area south to most of Baja. They are abundant in Bay Area and south of San Diego.

Size: The common size for these fish is about 10-pounds but they do grow much larger.

Records: Largest California Halibut—53-pound 4-ounces caught off California

Largest in California: Same as above

Largest from the Bay Area: not recorded

Where they live: Halibut live on a sandy bottom.

What they eat: Adult halibut will eat almost anything but they primarily eat other fish, squid and octopus.

Best Fishing Area: This species is caught in saltwater throughout the Bay Area in bays and off beaches. It bites best when a moderate tide is flowing in either an ebb tide or a flood tide.

How to Catch: Most halibut are caught on live anchovies. A three way swivel is used with a 12 inch leader to a weight and a six foot leader to a size 1 to 1/0 live bait hook. A lively bait is chosen and lip hooked. The fishing method is to bounce the weight along a sandy bottom while drifting with the tide. On a take, feed out line with the reel in free spool for a slow count to five to give the fish time to take the bait. Engage the drag, wait for the line to come tight and set the hook. Trolling lures along the bottom is also an effective fishing method.

Regulations: The daily and possession limit for California Halibut in the Bay Area is three fish a minimum of 22 inches long.

Species: Pacific Halibut: *Hippoglossus stenolepis*

Description: Pacific Halibut are the largest saltwater fish commonly caught off our West Coast and off Alaska. Fins on each side of their bodies are longer at the center giving them a diamond shape. Their eyes are usually on the right side of their body. These prized and delicious food fish are found infrequently off our coast and off shore fish are more likely to be this species.

Range: Pacific Halibut are found from the Farallon Islands to the Aleutian Islands. They are rare in the Bay Area with increasing abundance in their northern range.

Size: These are among the largest saltwater fish. They probably can weigh more than 500 pounds.

Records: Largest Pacific Halibut: 459-pound caught off Alaska

Largest in California: 53-pounds 8-ounces

Largest from the Bay Area: not recorded

Where they live: These fish live on a sandy bottom in depths of a few tens of feet to more than 1000 feet.

What they eat: Pacific Halibut eat almost anything including fish, squid and octopus.

Best Fishing Area: Most Pacific Halibut are caught while fishing for other species like rockfish, lingcod or California Halibut. The open ocean in relatively deep water is a good fishing location. Not many of this species of halibut are caught out of the Bay Area.

How to Catch: Fish with live baitfish, squid, octopus or chunks of fish.

Regulations: These fish may be caught from May 1 through September 30. The limit is one fish 32 inches total length or longer.

Sturgeon

White Sturgeon are the largest fish ever caught in the Continental United States. While the largest sport caught fish on record is a 468-pound fish caught by Joey Pallotta in Carquinez Strait in 1983, apparently much larger ones with reported weights of 1200 or more pounds were caught from the Columbia River early in this century. These were not landed within the definition of sportfishing so even if they had good verification (which they don't) they would not qualify for a sport fishing record. The white sturgeon is a common fish but another species, green sturgeon, are caught occasionally in the bays and Delta.

Species: White sturgeon: *Acipenser transmontanus*

Description: White sturgeon are the predominant fish of this species in Northern California making up more than 90 % of this class fish. They are

most easily distinguished from green sturgeon (the other local species) by a round, more blunt nose compared with a pointed nose for green sturgeon. They are a slow growing fish and the very large ones are more than 100 years old. They have a very high value as a food fish and are commercially grown for sale as a premium seafood. Their eggs are cured as caviar, an expensive delicacy.

Range: These fish range all the way up and down our West Coast but are rarely found south of Monterey. The Bay Area has by far the largest population of these fish in California with almost all of them spawning in the Sacramento/San Joaquin River systems. A few have been found in the Russian River.

Size: White sturgeon are the largest fish found in fresh water in North America. Very large fish have been reported and sturgeon weighing up to about 1200-pounds caught commercially in gill nets from the Columbia River in the early 1900's are believable.

Records: The largest fresh water fish on record is a 468-pound sturgeon caught by Joey Pallotta in the Carquinez Strait between Vallejo and Martinez. Since then regulations have changed and any sturgeon over 72 inches (about 100-pounds) must be released unharmed. That record will stand unless some state relaxes the laws to permit take of super sized fish.

Records: Largest white sturgeon: 468-pounds caught in Carquinez Strait

Largest white sturgeon in California: Same as above

Largest white sturgeon from the Bay Area: Same as above

Where they live: Little is known about sturgeon but white sturgeon are anadromous living in the ocean and spawning in fresh water. They live in the bays and Delta feeding on the bottom.

What they eat: Sturgeon have a proboscis type mouth that acts like a vacuum cleaner taking food from the bottom. They eat all types of shrimp, small fish and clams.

Best Fishing Area: The San Pablo Bay is the number one fishing area for sturgeon followed by Carquinez Strait, the San Francisco Bay and the lower Delta. Some are caught in the Delta and the Sacramento River as far north as the Feather River.

How to Catch: The best bait for sturgeon is mud shrimp, ghost shrimp and grass shrimp. Herring roe and even a filet of a herring are good bait when herring are spawning in the bay. Small live bait fish like mudsuckers are also good bait. Fishing in the bays is best after a storm when water is flowing fast and muddy. They are caught on incoming or outgoing tides with the last half of the outgoing tide best. Winter is the best time to catch them in the bays and spring is better in the rivers as they move farther inland to spawn.

Regulations: The daily and possession limit is one sturgeon between 46 and 72 inches. Sturgeon either smaller than the minimum or larger than the maximum must be released. The season is open all year but parts of the bay from the Oakland Bay Bridge to the Golden Gate Bridge to Richmond are closed to sturgeon fishing January 1 to March 15. See the Sport Fishing Regulations for the exact boundary.

Species: Green sturgeon: *Acipenser medirostris*

Description: The green sturgeon is a minor player compared with white sturgeon making up less than 10 % of the population of this class fish. They are smaller and have a more pointed snout that white sturgeon. Their food value is lower and they are not an important sports fish.

Range: These fish are mostly found in the San Pablo Bay with some in the San Francisco Bay. Some are in the larger rivers north of the Bay Area including the Klamath and the Smith as well as farther north in the Columbia and Fraser Rivers.

Where they live: Little is known about sturgeon but green sturgeon are anadromous living in the ocean and spawning in fresh water. Most of them have been caught in the San Pablo Bay so this is apparently where to find the greatest concentration of these fish.

What they eat: Sturgeon have a proboscis type mouth that acts like a vacuum cleaner taking food from the bottom. They eat all types of shrimp, small fish and clams.

Best Fishing Area: The San Pablo Bay is the primary area where these fish are caught.

How to Catch: These fish are caught as an incidental catch by anglers fishing for white sturgeon. Mud shrimp, grass shrimp and ghost shrimp are the primary baits that attract these fish.

Size: Smaller than white sturgeon, these fish are said to reach 350-pounds but most that are caught weigh less than 50-pounds.

Records: The IFGA does not have a separate record for green sturgeon and California recognizes sturgeon as a class and that is dominated by white sturgeon.

Regulations: Regulations group all sturgeon in one class so the restrictions for white sturgeon also apply to green sturgeon. Only those fish measuring 46 to 72 inches total length may be kept. The Jan 1 to March 15 closure in the San Francisco Bay applies to these fish as well as white sturgeon.

Lingcod and Cabezon

The Pacific Ocean off California has more than 50 bottom dwelling fish. Most of these are in the rockfish family but the largest, the lingcod, isn't a member of that family. Lingcod may weigh more than 50-pounds and are the king of the bottom fish. Anglers measure their success not by how many fish they catch but the number and size of lingcod they land.

Species: Lingcod: *Ophiodon elongatus*

Description: Lingcod are long, rather slender fish with fins all along their backs. They sit on the bottom on their large, strong pectoral fins, their

mottled coloration blending in with the bottom waiting for prey to swim past. With a stoke of its powerful tail, one overtakes its prey, opens its mouth and inhales its meal.

Lingcod are sleek fish but their jaws are hinged in a way that their mouths spread and are greatly enlarged when they open their mouths. They have pointed, needle sharp canine teeth that securely hold any fish they catch so they can hold and eat rather large fish.

Females may gain one-third of their weight in egg mass and lay up to 500,000 eggs or more. They will spawn year after year. After a female has spawned during the late fall and winter, the smaller male stays with the nest and guards the eggs voraciously. People can approach very close; you almost have to nudge them from their nests. These males are easy prey to spear fishermen but most divers know they doom the nest (small fish will eat the eggs) if they take the guard so pass by these fish.

Range: Lingcod range from Mexico to Alaska and are abundant all along this area. They are plentiful off Northern California but the largest ones come from farther north.

Size: Historically lingcod weighing more than 20 pounds have been common. Today they are depressed and most lings are much smaller than 20 pounds.

Records: Largest Lingcod: 69 pounds caught off British Columbia
Largest in California: 56-pounds
Largest from the Bay Area: not recorded

Where they live: Lingcod live on the bottom in rocks in depths of a few feet to as much as 1000 feet deep. They have no swim bladder to stabilize them at mid-depths so lay in wait on the bottom or must maintain a little motion to suspend off the bottom.

What they eat: Lingcod eat any form of marine life that swims by with fish, squid and octopus their primary food.

Best Fishing Area: The Farallon Islands, Fanny Shoals, Cordell Bank and Point Sur south of Monterey are the best lingcod fishing areas. Deep Reef, 14 miles southwest of Pillar Point was good ling fishing but has been fished heavily and catches have suffered. Lingcod are found all along our coast so some can be caught any place. Even shore anglers catch them occasionally.

How to Catch: Jigbars or live bait are superb lingcod catchers. Chrome plated diamond jigbars in weights from four to 12-ounces or blue and white or other colored bars like Tady jigs in the same weight range are the best lures. Jig the bar off the bottom to catch lings and other rockfish. A slight variation is to tie a drop loop about 18 inches above the jig and add a shrimp fly or plastic grub or shrimp imitation off that loop.

The best live bait is mackerel, sanddabs, octopus and anchovies. The bait should be on an 18 inch to two foot leader off the main line. Frozen whole squid and octopus are also good bait and may be used off a drop loop just above a weight attached to the bottom end of the leader.

Often a lingcod will attack a hooked rockfish and hold on until the prospective meal is played to the surface. If a companion stands by with a net or gaff and acts quickly as the fish comes to the surface, the lingcod, not even hooked, can often be landed.

Regulations: Twenty-five years ago anglers could legally catch 10 lingcod of any size off California. Anglers didn't usually catch that many but we often landed one or more 15 to 25-pound lingcod and occasionally one even larger. Since then they have become less common and a large fish weighing more than 20-pounds is very unusual. In the late 70's, the limit was dropped to five and the minimum size was 22 inches. In 1997 and again in 1999 that limit was dropped. The current limit is two lingcod and the minimum size is 24 inches.

Species: Cabezon: *Scorpaenichthys marmoratus*

Description: A cabezon is a large sculpin and has a large blunt head and very large rounded pectoral fins. With its fins extended, it looks much larger than it really is: a defense mechanism to scare off would-be predators. These fish have a reputation as having the best tasting flesh of the bottom fish but don't eat the roe: it is poisonous.

Range: Cabezon are found all along our coast from Alaska to Mexico. They are found over a wide range of depths from rocky crevasses near shore in shallow water to depths of several hundred feet deep. Usually they are in the rockiest environment where hooks get snagged and anglers lose a lot of tackle.

Size: These fish are reported to grow to 30 inches long and 25-pounds though the common catch is much smaller: 5 to 10-pounds is typical.

Records: Largest cabezon: 23 pounds caught off Washington State
Largest cabezon in California: 23-pounds 4-ounces*
Largest cabezon from the Bay Area: not recorded
*The IGFA does not recognize this California record.

Where they live: These fish live in the rockiest place they can find in all depths that are commonly fished.

What they eat: They eat small fish, shrimp, mussels, clams and sea worms.

Best Fishing Area: Fish from shore or from a boat to catch these fish. Anglers in boats have the best success because they can fish areas that haven't had as much fishing pressure. The shallows around the Farallon Islands are an excellent place to catch cabezon.

How to Catch: Fish right in the rocks with stout line using octopus, squid or a variety of baits. These fish will also take jig bars but the loss of terminal tackle is high and the cost of lost jigs adds up.

Regulations: Cabezon may be landed all year. The limit is 10 fish but a few of them are usually mixed in with other bottom fish where the cumulative limit is 15 fish.

Rockfish

More than 50 species of rockfish are found off our Pacific Coast. Many are caught but about a dozen form the bulk of the catch off San Francisco. Some of the largest are yelloweye rockfish, bocaccio, copper rockfish, cowcod (though most of these are caught farther south) and Vermilion. The most abundant are blue rockfish and yellowtail rockfish. Most rockfish are territorial bottom dwells. Anglers must get their lures right down in the rocks and reefs on the bottom; that is a formula for catching fish but it is also a formula for losing terminal tackle. But that is the price of catching these fish and lost tackle is all part of this kind of fishing. Blue rockfish and yellowtail rockfish are often found in schools off the bottom.

All of the species of rockfish are excellent food fish. They have a white flesh that is delicious deep fried, grilled, broiled, baked, poached, smoked, in chowder, choppino or as a base for almost any fish dish. Rockfish are a prime commercial catch and most are sold as Pacific Red Snapper. This name would imply they are a red fish but whether red, blue, brown or black, the fillets are white once the skin is removed and all can be sold as red snapper.

More than 50 members of this family are caught off California and most of those are caught off the San Francisco Bay Area. I have described eight that are the largest, most premium or most abundant of these species. I suppose you could go fishing for rockfish and catch a limit of 15 of them without catching a single one of the eight I have described but that would be very unusual. Some of the others are brown rockfish, green spotted rockfish, widdow rockfish, chilipeppers, flag rockfish (very colorful but also quite rare), canary rockfish, quillback rockfish and many more.

Species: Bocaccio: *Sebastes paucispinis*

Description: The word bocaccio means big mouth in both Spanish and Italian and these fish live up to this description. They are brown in color and are characterized by a large mouth that extends behind the eye of the fish. With that characteristic, they are like large mouth bass but these are a narrower bodied fish with a more pointed nose than a bass.

Range: Bocaccio are found all along our coast from Mexico to Canada and are abundant in the Bay Area. Historically they comprised 35 to 40 percent of the commercial rockfish catch though the population of these fish and the percentage in the sports catch has fallen dramatically over the years.

Size: A typical bocaccio weighs five-pounds but many weighing up to 10-pounds or more are landed. These are often the largest rockfish in an angler's daily catch.

Records: Largest Bocaccio: 21-pounds 4-ounces caught off Washington State
Largest California Bocaccio: 17-pounds 8-ounces
Largest Bay Area Bocaccio: Not recorded

Where they live: Juvenile bocaccio are pelagic fish. At the age of about two years bocaccio, like most rockfish, descend to the bottom becoming territorial fish living in rocks and reefs and may move no more than a few hundred yards from home base for the rest of their lives. Adults can be found in depths from 200 to 750 feet.

What they eat: Bocaccio eat other fish, squid, octopus and crabs.

Best Fishing Area: Almost any rocky bottom 200 to 750 feet deep hold adult bocaccio. Cordell Bank, the Farallon Islands, Deep Reef southwest of Pillar Point and Point Sur are some of the best places to catch these fish.

How to Catch: The standard fishing method for bocaccio is drift fishing bait or lures just off the bottom. Shrimp flies with a strip of squid or a piece of anchovy are good rigs. Live bait, anchovies, sardines, small mackerel, squid or octopi are probably the most effective bait. Bocaccio may also be caught on heavy metal jigs worked along the bottom.

Regulations: The daily limit and possession limit for all rockfish taken together is 15. In most cases, all may be the same species but in 1997 the daily bag limit of bocaccio was reduced to three fish.

Species: Yelloweye Rockfish: *Sebastes ruberrimus*

Description: Yelloweye rockfish, also called turkey cod, are bright red or orange and do indeed have a yelloweye. They are relatively short and stocky and are prized as a food.

Range: Yelloweye rockfish are found all along our coast from Mexico to Canada. They are not one of the most plentiful rockfish in the Bay Area but are such a premium fish, they are included here. They are more abundant as you go farther north and that is evident even from the southern part of this area out of Monterey where they are caught infrequently to the northern part at Bodega Bay and Cordell Bank where they are caught with some regularity.

Size: These fish are one of the largest members of the rockfish family. A typical yelloweye rockfish weighs about 5-pounds but some weigh 15-pounds or more.

Records: Largest yelloweye rockfish: 33-pounds 3-ounces caught off Alaska
Largest California yelloweye rockfish: 18-pounds 3-ounces
Largest Bay Area yelloweye rockfish: not recorded

Where they live: Young yelloweye rockfish are pelagic fish. At the age of about two years they, like most rockfish descend to the bottom becoming territorial fish living in rocks and reefs and may move no more than a few hundred yards from home base for the rest of their lives. They can be found in depths from 200 to 600 feet.

What they eat: Yelloweye rockfish eat other fish, squid, octopus and other sea life.

Best Fishing Area: Almost any deep rocky bottom holds adult yelloweye rockfish. Cordell Bank is the number one place to catch these fish in the Bay Area.

How to Catch: The standard fishing method for these fish is drift fishing bait or lures just off the bottom. Live bait, anchovies, sardines, small mackerel, squid or octopus are excellent bait.

Regulations: The daily bag limit and possession limit of rockfish is 15 in aggregate and all 15 may be the same species with additional restrictions for some species. Yelloweye rockfish are not so abundant that anglers should expect to catch more than a couple in a day.

Species: Vermilion Rockfish: *Sebastes miniatus*

Description: Vermilion are a highly prized red rockfish characterized by its bright vermilion color. Often called red snapper or Pacific red snapper, they are not related to the true red snapper, an East Coast fish. Their bright color makes them an especially attractive food fish when served whole.

Range: These fish are found all along our West Coast from Alaska to Mexico.

Size: A typical vermilion weighs about four-pounds and a 10-pound fish is a very large specimen. .

Records: Largest Vermilion: 12-pounds caught off Oregon
Largest California Vermilion: 14-pounds 9-ounces*
Largest Bay Area Vermilion: Not recorded
*The IGFA does not recognize this California record.

Where they live: Adult vermilion are territorial bottom dwellers living in and around rocks and reefs. They may move no more than a few hundred yards from their home throughout their adult lives.

What they eat: Vermilion eat small fish, squid and octopus.

Best Fishing Area: These are deep water fish and are commonly caught in depths of 200 to 500 feet of water. Any rocky bottom in that depth may hold these fish. They are caught more often from our southern ports and Monterey is the best area for these fish in the Bay Area.

How to Catch: The standard fishing method is drift fishing bait or lures just off the bottom. Live bait fish or squid, anchovies, shrimp flies with a strip of squid, sardines, small mackerel, octopus, or frozen squid are some of the most effective bait.

Regulations: The daily bag limit and possession limit on rockfish is 15 in aggregate and all 15 may be the same species with additional restrictions for some species. Vermilion are caught only occasionally and a catch of one or two is a good catch for a day.

Species: Yellowtail Rockfish: *Sebastes flavidus*

Description: Yellowtail rockfish and their almost identical cousin olive rockfish (*Sebastes serranoides*) are mid-depth fish that have made up a large percentage of the sports catch. They are often caught on every hook on an angler's rig. A recent decline in their numbers make them less available and a smaller part of the catch.

This species is identified by a dusty green body and yellow fins and tail as its name implies.

Range: These fish are common from Alaska to Mexico and have been a large part of the sports catch until their numbers radically declined in recent years.

Size: A typical yellowtail rockfish weighs a couple of pounds and a five-pound fish is a large specimen..

Records: Largest yellowtail rockfish: 5-pounds 8-ounces caught off Washington State
Largest California yellowtail rockfish: 5-pounds 8-ounces
Largest Bay Area yellowtail rockfish: Not recorded

Where they live: These fish are found in a variety of areas ranging from rocky or sandy bottoms to mid-depths above the bottom.

What they eat: Yellowtail rockfish eat small fish, squid, and octopus.

Best Fishing Area: These fish are caught off the bottom but they are also found in schools and may be caught at mid-depths.

How to Catch: A string of red and yellow shrimp flies tipped with a strip of squid or bare hooks baited with strips of squid are good rigs for these fish. When you catch fish, drop down to the same depth to catch more of them.

Regulations: The daily bag limit and possession limit on rockfish is 15 in aggregate and all 15 may be the same species with additional restrictions for some species. Yellowtail are caught much less frequently now and a catch of half a dozen is a good catch for a day.

Species: Blue Rockfish: *Sebastes mystinus*

Description: Blue rockfish have a small mouth like small mouth bass and its similar relative, a black rockfish (Sebastes melanops), has a large mouth that extends behind its eye like largemouth bass. Both are school fish that cover the full column of water from the bottom to the surface and are caught by conventional fishing as well as fly fishing.

Range: These fish are common from Alaska to Mexico and have been a large part of the sports catch until their numbers radically declined in recent years.

Size: A typical blue rockfish weighs one to two-pounds and they rarely weigh more than five or six-pounds.

Records: Largest blue rockfish: 8-pounds 6-ounces caught off Alaska
Largest California blue rockfish: 3-pounds 14-ounces
Largest Bay Area blue rockfish: Not recorded

Where they live: These are school fish found in a variety of areas ranging from rocky or sandy bottoms to mid-depths to the surface in water depths to 300 feet or more.

What they eat: Blue rockfish eat small fish, squid, and octopus.

Best Fishing Area: Fish for blue and black rockfish from the surface all the way to the bottom. When you catch one, try to get back to that depth to catch more.

How to Catch: One of the unique aspects of these fish is that they are often shallow and may be caught on flies. Most however are caught in the traditional method with shrimp flies and bait. The bare shrimpfly attracts these fish even after the bait is gone. They are often caught on every hook on an angler's rig.

Regulations: The daily bag limit and possession limit on rockfish is 15 in aggregate and all 15 may be blue or black rockfish.

Species: China Cod: *Sebastes nebulosus*

Description: China Cod are short, chunky rockfish with large, sharp spines in their dorsal fins. They are a mottled black, with a bright yellow stripe down their sides and white spots on their heads and bodies.
Range: They are found all along our West Coast.
Size: A typical China Cod weighs one or two-pounds and five-pound fish is a large one.

Records: Largest China Cod: 3-pounds 11-ounces caught off Washington
Largest California China Cod: 1-pound 12-ounces
Largest Bay Area China Cod: Not recorded
The California record isn't representative of the true size of these fish. While they are not large, I am certain I have seen many China Cod weighing more than the official California record.
Where they live: China Cod make their homes in rock and rubble on the bottom.
What they eat: These fish eat other fish, squid, octopus and crabs.
Best Fishing Area: Fish in rocks and reefs where you catch fish but you will also lose tackle.
How to Catch: Use bait or bait on flies to catch these fish.
Regulations: The daily bag limit and possession limit for rockfish is 15 in aggregate and all 15 may be China Cod. A catch of two to four in a limit of rockfish is a good catch.

Species: Copper Rockfish: *Sebastodes caurinus*

Description: Copper rockfish are tough customers. They seem particularly strong and I am always surprised that they aren't larger than they are when I catch one. They are deep bodied, chunky fish with large spines in their dorsal fins. They are light colored with copper colored markings on the head and body.
Range: They are found along our West Coast to as far south as Point Conception.
Size: A typical Copper rockfish weighs two to three-pounds. A five-pound specimen is a good fish.

Records: Largest Copper Rockfish: 6-pounds 1-ounce caught off Alaska
Largest California Copper Rockfish: 8-pounds 3-ounces*
Largest Bay Area Copper Rockfish: Same as above
*The IGFA does not recognize this California record.
Where they live: These fish live in moderate to shallow waters off our coast.
What they eat: Copper rockfish eat other fish, crabs, squid and octopus.
Best Fishing Area: Most of these fish are caught in shallow to moderate depths. I have caught several offshore at Bodega Bay.
How to Catch: Use bait like strips of squid or flies with bait fished on the bottom to catch these fish.
Regulations: The daily bag limit and possession limit on rockfish is 15 in aggregate and all 15 may be the same species with additional restrictions for some species. Copper rockfish are caught only occasionally and a catch of two to four is a good catch for a day.

Albacore

Species: Albacore: *Thunnus alalunga*

Description: When albacore tuna come to the Bay Area, they are the number one sports fish. They are fast, large, strong, tough, never-give-up fish. There is no limit on the number you can catch and, anglers may

catch one fish after another if they find a large school of them. They are found in numbers only when the water is unusually warm. That means El Nino years bring these fish to our area.

Anglers may land one to two albacore on a typical tuna trip but when they are abundant like they were in 1997, anglers may average 10 or more; most people wear out before the day is over and either stop fishing or just go through the motions and still may catch fish.
Range: Albacore make a large circuit around the Pacific Ocean swimming north along our shore then circling west to Japan and south of the Hawaiian Islands.
Size: A typical Albacore weighs ten to 15-pounds.

Records: Largest Albacore: 90-pounds caught off Santa Cruz (record is pending)
Largest California Albacore: Same as above
Largest Bay Area Albacore: Same as above
Where they live: These fish roam the oceans following schools of bait fish.
What they eat: Albacore eat anchovies, herring and other bait fish.
Best Fishing Area: These fish are far offshore on a typical year but may come within a few miles of shore on an El Nino year. Typically the season is from July or August to October but it can be longer in extreme El Nino years like 1997.
How to Catch: Fast troll feathered or plastic jigs to locate schools and fish with live bait or lures when schools have been found.
Regulations: There are no size restrictions, or limits to the numbers anglers can catch and they can be caught all year.

Shark

Species: Leopard Shark: *Triakis semifasciata*

Description: Leopard shark are a common shark found in the bay waters. They are easily distinguished by the leopard spots all along their bodies. At one time they were easy to catch but anglers have turned their attention to them and that, along with deteriorated water quality in the bays, have reduced their numbers until now they are caught far less frequently. They are considered one of the best food fish in the shark family and are particularly good smoked.
Range: Leopard shark are found all along our West Coast in shallow water and in bays.
Size: A typical leopard shark is three or four feet long and they may grow to a length of seven feet.

Records: Largest leopard shark: 40-pounds 10-ounces caught off California
Largest California leopard shark: Same as above
Largest Bay Area leopard shark: Not recorded

Where they live: These fish are found in the bay and in shallow ocean waters.

What they eat: Leopard shark eat anything they can catch primarily other fish, squid and octopus.

Best Fishing Area: The sandy areas of the San Francisco Bay are particularly good areas to catch leopard shark.

How to Catch: Live bait or cut bait fished from anchor has been the best way to catch these fish.

Regulations: Leopard shark can be caught all year.

Species: Blue Shark: *Prionace glauca*

Description: Blue shark are one of the most common offshore sharks throughout this entire region. They have a bright blue back and a white underside. They frequently show up at fishing boats and occasionally take a rockfish or a lingcod from the line. I've caught them trolling for salmon

using anchovies for bait. When salmon fishing is good, we break them off but on slow salmon days, we sometimes play them to the boat and release them.

I have seen reports that they are a good food fish but I have found they have a strong uric acid taste even when bled as soon as they are caught. A person marooned on an island with no meat would be thankful for one but people who have a variety of fish find other species far better food.

Range: Blue shark are found all along our West Coast from British Columbia to Mexico. They are plentiful offshore but are found frequently in the Monterey Bay.

Size: A typical blue shark weighs about 50-pounds and is seven feet long; they may grow to 12 feet or more.

Records: Largest blue shark: 454-pounds caught off Massachusetts
Largest California blue shark: 231-pounds
Largest Bay Area blue shark: Not recorded

Where they live: These fish roam the surface.

What they eat: Blue shark eat other fish and any sealife they find.

Best Fishing Area: The Monterey Bay is a particularly good area to fish for blue shark.

How to Catch: These fish are easily attracted to chum or blood from any animal. Casting or slow trolling bait or lures is a good way to catch them. They are an excellent fish to catch on a fly rod using any fly that resembles a bait fish.

Regulations: Blue shark can be caught all year. At one time we thought they were a predator to sport fish and killed any shark we caught. But they are not fast enough to catch a healthy sport fish and aren't a threat to our popular fish so now we release them.

Species: Sevengill Shark: *Notorynchus maculatus*

Sixgill Shark: *Hexanchus corinum*

Description: These two classes of cowshark are found in the deep parts of the bay where anglers target them and in offshore waters where they are rarely caught. As their names imply, they are identified by the six or seven gill openings on each side of their heads. Both of these fish are particularly good food fish.

Range: These shark are found all along our West Coast from Mexico to British Columbia. They are not an abundant shark but they are a special catch inside the San Francisco Bay.

Size: A typical sixgill shark is about 6 feet long but they grow to more than 15 feet long and may weigh more than 1000-pounds.

Records: Largest sixgill shark: 1069-pounds caught off the Azore Islands
Largest California sevengill shark: 276-pounds
Largest Bay Area cowshark: Not recorded

Where they live: These fish are found in deep water in the bay or in moderate depths in the ocean.

What they eat: Their diet includes other fish, crab, squid, and octopus.

Best Fishing Area: The deep holes in the San Francisco Bay are where most of these fish are caught.

How to Catch: Anglers catch small fish for bait, keep them alive, then use them to catch these fish or use large fish fillets to take them.

Regulations: Cow shark can be caught all year. They are not abundant so do consider releasing these fish.

Species: White shark: *Carcharodon carcharias*

Description: White shark can be huge and they conjure up an image of killer, vicious, man-eater. While their attacks on seals are quick, vicious and efficient, attacks on people are apparently cases of mistaken identity but that doesn't make them any less dangerous. They can be found all along our coast but their primary breeding area is around the Farallon Islands to Bodega Bay and Half Moon Bay none of which are places to swim or dive.

White shark grow up to 30 feet long and more. They have a dusty gray back, a white stomach and rows of huge, sharp teeth that take huge chunks of flesh from their prey.

Range: White shark are found all along our West Coast from British Columbia to Mexico.

Size: White shark grow to a length of 30 feet or more and weigh as much as a ton.

Records   Largest white shark: 2664-pounds caught off Australia
Largest California white shark: No catches recorded
Largest Bay Area white shark: No catches recorded

Where they live: These fish roam the surface

What they eat: White shark eat sea lions and fish.

Regulations: White shark are protected and may not be caught.

Surfperch and Seaperch

These two categories of fish are in the same family. The difference is surfperch are usually found in the surf in shallow water over sandy bottoms and the seaperch are generally found in deeper water around rocks or structure. Only two of about a dozen surfperch are listed but what is said about them is typical to the family.

These are small fish but their broad sides give them a lot of power in the water and they are scrappy, at least for a while, when they are hooked. They are an excellent tasting food fish but it may take two or three to make a meal for a person.

Some of the common members of this family and their distinguishing features are as follows: barred surfperch have brown or green vertical bars on their bodies; walleye surfperch, as you would guess, have big eyes; striped seaperch have colorful stripes running the length of their bodies and rubberlip surfperch have lips that are large and look like they are made of rubber.

One member not listed is the Shinerperch that is a small member of this family easily caught around pilings in the bays very important as a bait for other fish, particularly for striped bass and halibut.

Species: Silver surfperch: *Hyperprosopon ellipticus*
Description: This fish has a silver body. It can be distinguished from a walleye surfperch because it has a smaller eye.
Range: Silver surfperch are found all along the West Coast of the continental United States. It is caught inside the San Francisco and San Pablo Bays.
Size: A typical silver surfperch is about eight inches long and weighs less than a-pound.
Where they live: These fish seek protection around structure in the ocean and bays like pilings and piers.
What they eat: They eat sand crabs, clams, mussels, fish eggs, small fish, and worms.
Best Fishing Area: Fish around pilings and structure to catch these fish. Winter and spring is the primary season for them.
How to Catch: The best bait is live grass shrimp but sand crabs dug from the beach or artificial flies or plastic grubs will also catch them.
Regulations: Surfperch may be taken all year. There is no limit and no size limit on these fish.

Barred surfperch: *Amphistichus argenteus*
Description: Barred surfperch are identified by a series of vertical bars with spots between the dark bars. They are one of the largest and rank among the most frequently caught surfperch.
Range: These fish are found all along our West Coast. Most are caught along ocean beaches.
Size: Barred surfperch are one of the largest of these fish attaining a size of up to 18 inches and weigh up to four-pounds.

Records: Largest Barred surfperch: 4-pounds 8-ounces caught off
       California
       Largest California Barred surfperch: Same as above
       Largest Bay Area Barred surfperch: Not recorded
Where they live: These fish are usually found near the beach in saltwater.
What they eat: The dominant food for these fish is sandcrabs. A CDFG study found 90 percent of barred surfperch had sandcrabs in their stomachs and these crabs made up 90 percent of their diet.
Best Fishing Area: Fish the surf along the beaches to catch these fish. Fish dips in the floor of the ocean near the beach and don't overcast. They can be in quite shallow water.
How to Catch: The best bait for Barred surfperch is sandcrabs: you can look for blow holes in the sand after a receding wave and dig them from the sand. Flies are also good for these fish and fly fishers wading ankle to knee deep into the surf catch them on a variety of flies.
Regulations: Surfperch may be taken all year. There is no limit and no size limit on these fish.

Species: Other Saltwater Fish:

Many other species are caught in the bays and the ocean off the San Francisco Bay area. A brief list of some of the more plentiful fish include: Tommy Croaker (Kingfish): *Genyonemus lineatus* that are caught off the piers and from boats when drift mooching for salmon or for rockfish. They are typically less than 10 inches long and are good fighters for their size. They have a metallic taste when cooked and are not considered a good food fish.

Jack Smelt *Atherinopsis californiensis* and Top Smelt *Atherinops affinis* are two species often caught off piers in the San Francisco and San Pablo Bays. The jack smelt is a very large member of this family ranging up to 18 inches in length. Small bits of fish, or mussels or pileworms are good bait.

Pacific Sanddabs *Citharichthys sordidus*. These fish are a small bottom fish in the flounder family and are a sweet meated food fish. Their primary use for offshore anglers is as bait for lingcod. Some anglers like them so well as a food fish they are reluctant to use them for bait. They are caught on the bottom using small hooks like size 4 hooks and a small strip of squid. Use a lot of hooks so you can catch several at a time.

Starry Flounder *Platichthys stellatus*. These distinctively marked fish with alternate rays of dark and light in their fins and tails were once plentiful in the bays and in the shallows in the ocean. Few are found now but recent catches indicate they may be making a comeback. This fish as well as most of the founder and sole family have excellent eating, sweet tasting flesh.

Pacific Mackerel *Pneumatophorus japonicus*. This small, fast fish may be caught by the dozens from piers or from boats. Sometimes you can't get your bait or lures through them to catch the larger fish below the school of mackerel. Some are eaten but they are more valued by most anglers as live bait for lingcod and bottom fish or as cut bait for fresh and saltwater fish. Two species of mackerel are caught but the Pacific Mackerel is the most common.

Other fish like bonito and white sea bass, large premium food fish that are abundant in warmer waters, are caught occasionally. Rays, skates, eels, and all other manner of fish are caught.

Rock crab and the premium Dungeness Crab that many people say is the best, sweetest crab in the world are caught by anglers setting crab traps or crab pots.

Index of Experts

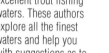